A HISTORY OF WEST AFRICA

MODERN REVIVALS IN AFRICAN STUDIES

Series Editor: Anthony Kirk-Greene

Geoffrey Kay (ed)
The Political Economy of Colonialism in Ghana: A Collection of Documents and Statistics, 1900 – 1960 (new introduction)
(0 7512 0079 4)

E A Brett
Colonialism and Underdevelopment in East Africa: The Politics of Economic Change, 1919 – 1939
(0 7512 0080 8)

Colin Newbury (ed)
British Policy Towards West Africa: Select Documents
Vol I: 1786 – 1874
Vol II: 1875 – 1914 (with Statistical Appendices 1800 – 1914)
Set (0 7512 0084 0)

Christopher Fyfe
A History of Sierra Leone (new introduction)
(0 7512 0086 7)

Christopher Fyfe
Africanus Horton: West African Scientist and Patriot (new introduction)
(0 7512 0085 9)

Martin S Kisch
Letters and Sketches from Northern Nigeria (new introduction)
(0 7512 0087 5)

J D Fage
A History of West Africa (new introduction)
(0 7512 0102 2)

A HISTORY OF WEST AFRICA

An Introductory Survey

J D Fage

Professor Emeritus of African History
University of Birmingham

Ashgate

Aldershot • Burlington USA • Singapore • Sydney

First published as 'An Introduction to the History of West Africa' 1955

Reprinted 1957
Second Edition 1959
Reprinted 1961
Third Edition 1962
Reprinted 1964, 1965
Fourth Edition, published as 'A History of West Africa: An Introductory Survey' 1969
Reprinted in 1969 by
the Syndics of the Cambridge University Press

Reprinted in 1992 by
Gregg Revivals
Gower House
Croft Road
Aldershot
Hants GU11 3HR
England

Reprinted in 2001 by
Ashgate Publishing Limited
Gower House
Aldershot
Hants GU11 3HR
England

Ashgate Publishing Company
131 Main Street
Burlington, VT 05401-5600 USA

Ashgate website: http://www.ashgate.com

A CIP catalogue record for this book is available
from the British Library

A CIP catalogue record for this book is available
from the US Library of Congress

ISBN 0 7512 0102 2

Printed and bound in Great Britain by Biddles Limited,
Guildford and King's Lynn.

Contents

Maps

Introduction to the *Gregg Revivals* Edition

In 1949 I went to teach history at the year old University College of the Gold Coast. Until, in 1961, this became the independent University of Ghana, its students worked for degrees of the University of London. However, under a scheme of 'special relationship' between London University and the young university colleges in the colonies, it was possible to secure considerable modification of London degree syllabuses to suit local needs and backgrounds – in our case, of course, those of African students living and working in an African country. It therefore fell to me to devise courses relating to the history of Africa, of West Africa in particular, and to persuade London University that, for students of the college in the Gold Coast, these might take the place of some of the British and European courses stipulated for its own history degree students.

The task of persuasion did not prove difficult. What most concerned London University's Board of Studies in History was to have it demonstrated that students taking our proposed African history courses should have adequate reading in depth available to them which might be thought broadly comparable to that available to university students of British or European history. In this respect it was possible to show that, from the sixteenth century onwards valuable materials relating to the African past had been printed in several hundred publications, and that sufficient of these were already available in our College Library or on order for it. But where there was a difficulty was that very few indeed of these works had been written specifically to meet the needs of students of African history. For the most part they were accounts of Africa, or of parts of it, written by people such as travellers, traders or missionaries, or – particularly in later times – such as colonial administrators or ethnographers and anthropologists. Within these works there could often be very valuable nuggets of information about the past, but to put these together to reconstruct a coherent view of change over time – history in the academic sense – was not easy for anyone who had not already received some training in the art of history, especially of history in an African context.

In short, there was a lack of African history textbooks. This was by no means absolute. In English, for instance, such a textbook had appeared as early as 1868, the *History of Sierra Leone* by A. B. C. Sibthorpe (himself a Sierra Leonian). If this was already a rare curiosity, tribute must be paid to men like W. E. F. Ward and C. R. Niven, who had written short histories for school use, of the Gold Coast and Nigeria respectively, that were published in the 1930s. Ward's more substantial *History of the Gold Coast* (first edition 1948) was one of the four books of West African history I was able to obtain in England before setting out for the Gold Coast, the others being Sir Alan Burns's generally comparable *History of Nigeria* (in its 1948 fourth edition, the first having appeared as long ago as 1929), Martin Wight's *The Gold Coast Legislative Council* (also 1948), and E. W. Bovill's *Caravans of the Old Sahara* (1933). These works were invaluable for our university courses but were of no use in West African schools. This may seem odd, bearing in mind that by the 1920s men like Ward (who, while teaching at Achimota, had collected oral traditions) and W. T. Balmer (headmaster at Mfantsipim) and their African contemporaries like E. J. P. Brown and J. W. de Graft Johnson – to name only Gold Coast examples – knew full well of the importance of African children being taught African history. But the fact of the matter was that the object of studying in English-speaking West African secondary schools was to gain the Cambridge School Certificate. The result was that only little boys and girls were taught any African history (often more or less at a level equivalent to 'King Alfred and the burnt cakes'); older children were drilled to pass examination papers dealing with Tudors and Stuarts, Napoleon and Bismarck and the like. (If in 1992 this now seems woefully eccentric, it should be remarked that their French-speaking African contemporaries learnt from textbooks which really did begin 'Nos ancêtres les Gaulois . . . '!)

So our university entrants reading history had virtually to start from scratch so far as African courses were concerned. While – despite the 'Nos ancêtres . . . ' of the French textbooks – there were quite a few introductory histories of Africa or of West Africa available for those who could read French (for example by Delafosse, Labouret and Hardy), the choice in English was very limited. I do not think that anyone had really essayed anything approaching a general history of Africa in English since Sir Harry Johnston, and his 1911 approach was too eurocentric even for 1949. Of the four books I had brought out with me, Wight's was too specialised for first year use, while those by Ward and Burns were limited to the bits of West Africa confined within their colonial boundaries and – as we came to see – were as much colonial history as they were African history. The imaginative title *Caravans of the Old Sahara* put me off reading Bovill until last, but I quickly appreciated that this alone had the wide sweep and the vision needed for first year students; it fully justified its more prosaic subtitle and was a marvellous 'Introduction to the history of the western Sudan'.

But Bovill's book had been out of print for some years; my copy had been given to me by my former Cambridge tutor when I told him that I was going to teach history in the Gold Coast. There were also a number of other out of print books which I thought might be useful for our students, so I tried to persuade their publishers to reprint them. My voice was one of those that eventually induced Bovill to write a new version of *Caravans* which he called *The Golden Trade of the Moors* (1958; second edition, with important revisions, 1968). Another book in which I had some interest was I. L. Evans's *The British in Tropical Africa*, and this brought me into contact with Charles Carrington, the Educational Secretary of the Cambridge University Press. He was well aware that there was going to be a very substantial market for textbooks in West Africa, but he maintained – correctly – that Evans's book, published in 1929, would need substantial rewriting before it could be presented to this new market, and that even then it would have a short 'shelf-life'. He therefore suggested that I myself might write a short history of West Africa that might be suitable for West African students, especially those in the teacher training colleges and in the schools, where there was now a relatively new School Certificate subject, 'The development of Tropical Africa', and which were shortly to establish sixth forms.

I accepted this challenge with some diffidence. I did not think that the time was ripe to attempt a substantive history of West Africa; I would not essay more than an *introduction* to the subject. So the book that was published in 1955 – in two editions, a cheap one for schools and a more expensive one for the 'general reader' – was entitled *An Introduction to the History of West Africa*. In the Forewords I explained that a 'would-be historian of West Africa' – unlike for example a historian of Europe – could not draw on any 'great accumulation of specialised studies by professional historical researchers'. Kenneth Onwuka Dike's *Trade and Politics in the Niger Delta* did not appear until the year after my book, and most of those in the great school of West

African historical writing of which he was a forerunner, scholars like Jacob Ajayi, E. J. Alagoa, Kwame Arhin, E. A. Ayandele, Boubacar Barry, Adu Boahen, Kwame Daaku, Joseph Ki-Zerbo and the like, if not still at school, were at best still studying for their first degrees – often at the new West African university institutions. When in 1952–53 *An Introduction* was being written, most of the sources available to me had necessarily been written by Europeans and as a consequence of European activities which had culminated in the colonisation of Africa, so that my Forewords also expressed the fear that the book gave 'too little attention to the specifically African aspects' of West African history and too much to 'its colonial side'.

Despite these manifest shortcomings, the book sold sufficently well to call for the appearance of second and third editions in 1959 and 1962 respectively. In these there were some corrections and additions, not only to bring it up to date with a rapidly changing political scene, but also to take note of the increasing wealth of the West African historical literature. In addition to the books flowing from scholars in Europe and America as well as the new university institutions in Africa, much important material was now appearing in periodicals: for example, the *Transactions of the Historical Society of Ghana* had commenced publication in 1952, the *Journal of the Historical Society of Nigeria* in 1956, and *The Journal of African History* (published from Cambridge) in 1960. By the mid-1960s, the volume – not to mention the quality – of this literature was such that I realised that the structure of the book I had written in the previous decade would not stand the strain of further tinkering. So, for the fourth edition, first published in 1969 and now the basis of this reprint, about half the book was entirely recast, and written at somewhat greater length, with the specific intention of reducing the earlier eurocentricity and making it more properly a work of African history.

To mark this ambition, a new title was adopted, *A History of West Africa; an Introductory Survey*. At first this did well enough; in all it sold some 130,000 copies to add to some 170,000 copies sold of the first three editions. But in the 1980s sales declined to only a few hundred a year. It became plain that, like all human creation, the book could not live for ever. It might perhaps be said that eventually what remained of the structure of my original creation of the 1950s had been swamped, sunk and drowned by the ever-rising tide of publication of original work on the history of West Africa. If it is now resurrected, it can only be because it has now itself become a small part of that history. Readers who now come upon it for the first time should be warned that it is very far from being the last work on its subject. I accordingly append a short list of what I consider to be some of the more important works bearing on the history of West Africa that have been published since the preparation of the bibliography that was provided in 1969.

J. D. Fage
July 1992

A Selection of Major Works on the History of West Africa published since the preparation of the 1969 Bibliography

Abitol, Michel	*Tombouctou et les Arma . . . , 1591 – 1833*, Paris, 1979
Abraham, Arthur	*Mende government and politics under colonial rule*, Freetown & London, 1979
Adamu, Mahdi	*The Hausa factor in West African history*, Zaria, 1978
Adeleye, Remi	*Power and diplomacy in northern Nigeria 1804 – 1906*, London, 1971
Ajayi, J. F. A., & Crowder, Michael (eds)	*History, of West Africa*, Harlow, 2 vols, 1971, 1974 (& later eds)
Akintoye, S. A.	*Revolution and power politics in Yorubaland . . . ,* London, 1971
Arhin, Kwame	*West African traders in Ghana in the nineteenth and twentieth centuries*, London, 1980
Asiwaju, A. I.	*Western Yorubaland under European rule, 1889 – 1945*, London, 1976
Baier, Stephen	*An economic history of central Niger*, Oxford, 1980
Barry, Boubacar	*Le Royaume du Waalo*, Paris, 1972
Bathily, Abdoulaye	*Les portes de l'or: Galam . . .* , Paris, 1989
Brenner, Louis	*The Shehus of Kukawa*, Oxford, 1973
Boulègue, Jean	*Les anciens Royaumes Wolof*, Paris, 1988
Connah, Graham	*Three thousand years in Africa; man and his environment in the Lake Chad region*, Cambridge, 1981
Crowder, Michael	*West Africa under colonial rule*, London, 1968
Curtin, Philip D.	*Economic change in precolonial Africa: Senegambia . . . ,* Madison, 1975
Daaku, K. Y.	*Trade and politics on the Gold Coast, 1600 – 1720*, Oxford, 1970
Gbadamosi, T. G. O.	*The growth of Islam among the Yoruba*, London 1979
Hargreaves, John	*West Africa partitioned*, 2 vols, London, 1974, 1985
Hopkins, A. G.	*An economic history of West Africa*, London, 1973
Hogendorn, Jan, & Johnson, Marion	*The shell money of the slave trade*, Cambridge, 1986
Igbafe, P. A.	*Benin under British administration*, London, 1979
Iliffe, John	*The African poor*, Cambridge, 1987
Kea, Ray A.	*Settlements, trade and politics in the seventeenth century Gold Coast*, Baltimore, 1982
Kiéthéga, J. - B.	*L'or de la Volta noire*, Paris, 1983
Ki-Zerbo, Joseph	*Histoire de l'Afrique Noire*, Paris, 1972
Lange, Dierk	*Le diwan des sultans de Kanem-Bornu*, Paris, 1977
Last, Murray	*The Sokoto Caliphate*, London, 1967
Law, Robin	*The Oyo empire, c. 1600 – c. 1836*, Oxford 1977

Bibliography

Law, Robin	*The Slave Coast of West Africa, 1550 – 1750*, Oxford, 1991
Levtzion, Nehemia	*Ancient Ghana and Mali*, London, 1973
Levtzion, Nehemia, & Hopkins, J. F. P.	*A corpus of early Arabic sources for West African history*, Cambridge, 1981
Lovejoy, Paul E.	*Caravans of Kola . . . , 1700 – 1900*, Zaria, 1980
Lovejoy, Paul E.	*Transformations in slavery; a history of slavery in Africa*, Cambridge, 1983
Lovejoy, Paul E.	*Salt of the desert sun . . .* , Cambridge, 1986
McIntosh, Susan Keech, & McIntosh, Roderick J.	*Prehistoric investigations in the region of Jenne*, Oxford, 1980
Manning, Patrick	*Slavery, colonialism and economic growth in Dahomey, 1640 – 1960*, Cambridge, 1982
Manning, Patrick	*Francophone sub-Saharan Africa, 1880 – 1985*, Cambridge, 1988
Martin, Susan N.	*Palm oil and protest . . . Ngwa . . . 1880 – 1985*, Cambridge, 1988
Mason, Michael	*The foundations of the Bida Kingdom*, Zaria, 1981
Norris, H. T.	*The Arab conquest of the western Sudan*, Harlow & Beirut, 1986
Northrup, David	*Trade without rulers . . . south-eastern Nigeria*, Oxford, 1978
Person, Yves	*Samori; une révolution dyula*, 3 vols, Paris, 1968, '70, '75
Priestley, Margaret	*West African trade and Coast society*, London, 1969
Rimmer, Douglas	*The economies of West Africa*, London, 1984
Rimmer, Douglas (editor)	*Africa 30 years on*, London, 1991
Robinson, David	*The holy war of Umar Tal*, Oxford, 1985
Rodney, Walter	*A history of the Upper Guinea Coast, 1545 – 1800*, Oxford, 1970
Ryder, A. F. C	*Benin and the Europeans*, London, 1969
Saad, Elias N.	*Social history of Timbuctu . . . , 1400 – 1900*, Cambridge, 1983
Sa'ad Abubakar	*The Lamibe of Fombina*, Zaria, 1977
Shaw, Thustan	*Igbo-Ukwu, an account of archaeological discoveries in eastern Nigeria*, London, 1970
Verger, Pierre	*Flux et reflux de la traite des Nègres . . .* , Paris, 1968
Wilks, Ivor	*Asante in the nineteenth century*, Cambridge, 1975

Mention might also be made of the appearance of two further important English language historical journals, in 1968 of *The International Journal of African Historical Studies* (Boston) and in 1974 of *History in Africa* (African Studies Association of the U.S.), and also of the publication of two large multi volume histories, *The Cambridge History of Africa*, complete in eight volumes published in 1975 – 86, and of UNESCO's *General History of Africa*, publication of which began in 1981 and of which seven out of eight volumes had appeared by 1992.

Foreword

When in 1949 I was lucky enough to become one of the first teachers of history in what is today the University of Ghana, it quickly became apparent to me that the students then entering this African university were by and large apt to be much better informed about the histories of Britain and of western Europe than they were about the history of Africa. I was eventually urged to try and do something to help redress this unnatural balance, and the result was *An Introduction to the History of West Africa*, written for the most part in 1952–3, and first published in 1955.

This little book must have served some purpose, since six reprints were called for in the next ten years. In some of these, it was possible to incorporate corrections, changes and additions. But a demand for yet another printing convinced me that it was no longer possible to continue redecorating the fabric of a book which was planned some sixteen years ago: redevelopment, demolition and reconstruction on a considerable scale, had become urgently necessary.

In the early 1950s when, except for Liberia, all West Africa was under European control, and only a percipient few had realised how quickly its colonial territories would become completely independent, it seemed permissible, advisable even, to make the growth of European influence in West Africa one of the principal themes of the book. In fact there was little real alternative, because so little serious research into indigenous West African history had been done or published. Dr Dike's *Trade and Politics in the Niger Delta* and Dr Biobaku's *The Egba and their Neighbours* were still at best only on their publisher's horizon; the young West African universities had not had time to fashion the schools of historical research which are among their most notable achievements; the teachers of history and the research students in the universities of Europe and America who were concerned with African history could be counted only in ones and two, instead of by the score, as they are today; no international conference on the history of Africa had yet been held, and there were no journals specifically devoted to its study and furtherance.

The last fifteen or sixteen years, however, have seen what can only be described as a revolution in the scale and scope of serious research into the history of Africa. It is true that very much more still needs to be done than has been done, and that as many or more questions have been asked than answers have been agreed, but the questions are being asked, and there are now the scholars and the sense of purpose to enable them to be answered. Enough has already been accomplished to make it possible and necessary to treat the history of West Africa with the same broad sense of internal continuity that historians take for granted when they write the history of most other parts of the world. Moreover, there are now plenty of students studying West African history at all levels who demand that this should be done.

It has therefore seemed essential that whole sections and chapters of the original *Introduction* should be scrapped, and new material added in which an attempt has been made to place the African side of the story in a proper perspective. The first three chapters of the present work are entirely new, replacing the first two of the original with an attempt to establish the main themes of West African historical development up to about the sixteenth century. The original chapter 5 has been replaced by two new chapters, 6 and 7, the first looking at the relationship between the Atlantic slave trade and economic change in West Africa, in part on the basis of new evidence, and the second examining contemporary political developments in lower Guinea. Chapter 10, dealing with some West African states in the nineteenth century, is also new, and has no real counterpart in the original book.

The remaining seven chapters bear the same or similar titles to chapters of the original book in its enlarged, 1962 edition. If these chapters have not been completely re-written, it is in part because of pressures of time, in part because in recent years the author has become less interested in the external and colonial history with which they are largely concerned, and so less confident that he can reshape them in the light of recent research. Nevertheless each has been looked at critically, all have had changes made in them, and in some cases the amount of re-writing or of new material is considerable—perhaps a quarter of each of chapters 4, 5 and 13, for example.

The result is a somewhat longer book, which I hope will be thought to be better balanced and more useful than the *Introduction*, and of which substantially more than half is new. To avoid confusion with the original from which it has been developed, it seems best to present it under a different title.

In conclusion, I would like to acknowledge my great debt to the many individuals with whom I have talked West African history over the years, and notably the new generation of African-born scholars I have been fortunate enough to meet with in universities in West Africa and elsewhere. Many of these people may recognise ideas of their own which I have taken up—I would hope without too much distortion. I owe especial debts of gratitude to Professor Philip D. Curtin, of the University of Wisconsin, for allowing me to make use of some of his work on the Atlantic slave trade before it has been published, and for personally guiding me through its statistical difficulties; to Dr Peter Mitchell and Mr John R. Willis, of my own University of Birmingham, who have done their best to correct the naivete of my approaches to some of the problems touched on in chapters 6 and 10 in which they are very much at home; and to Professor Roland Oliver, of the University of London, who was kind enough to spare time to read and comment on the proofs. Finally I would like to thank the University of Birmingham, which gave me a term's study leave; Miss L. M. P. Scarborough, who did most of the typing; and, by no means least, my wife, who has lived through the strains of composition.

J. D. F.

Centre of West African Studies
University of Birmingham

A NOTE CONCERNING MONETARY VALUES

From time to time in this book, monetary terms are used to express volumes of trade, government revenues, development programmes and the like. These are given in £ sterling. It is important to appreciate that the (real) value of these £s is not that ruling at the time the book was written, but those ruling *at the periods referred to* (e.g., on p. 59, the figure of £100,000 for the annual value of the Portuguese gold trade on the Gold Coast in the early sixteenth century represents *sixteenth century £s*, which of course were worth many times the £s of the 1960s). For the benefit of those readers who are not accustomed to the English £, equivalent values are also given in U.S. $. The conversions are made at rates appropriate to the periods referred to, a nominal $4.0 for all times previous to the twentieth century, and thereafter as follows: up to 1939, $4.8 to £1; 1940–49, $4.0 to £1; and 1950–68, $2.8 to £1.

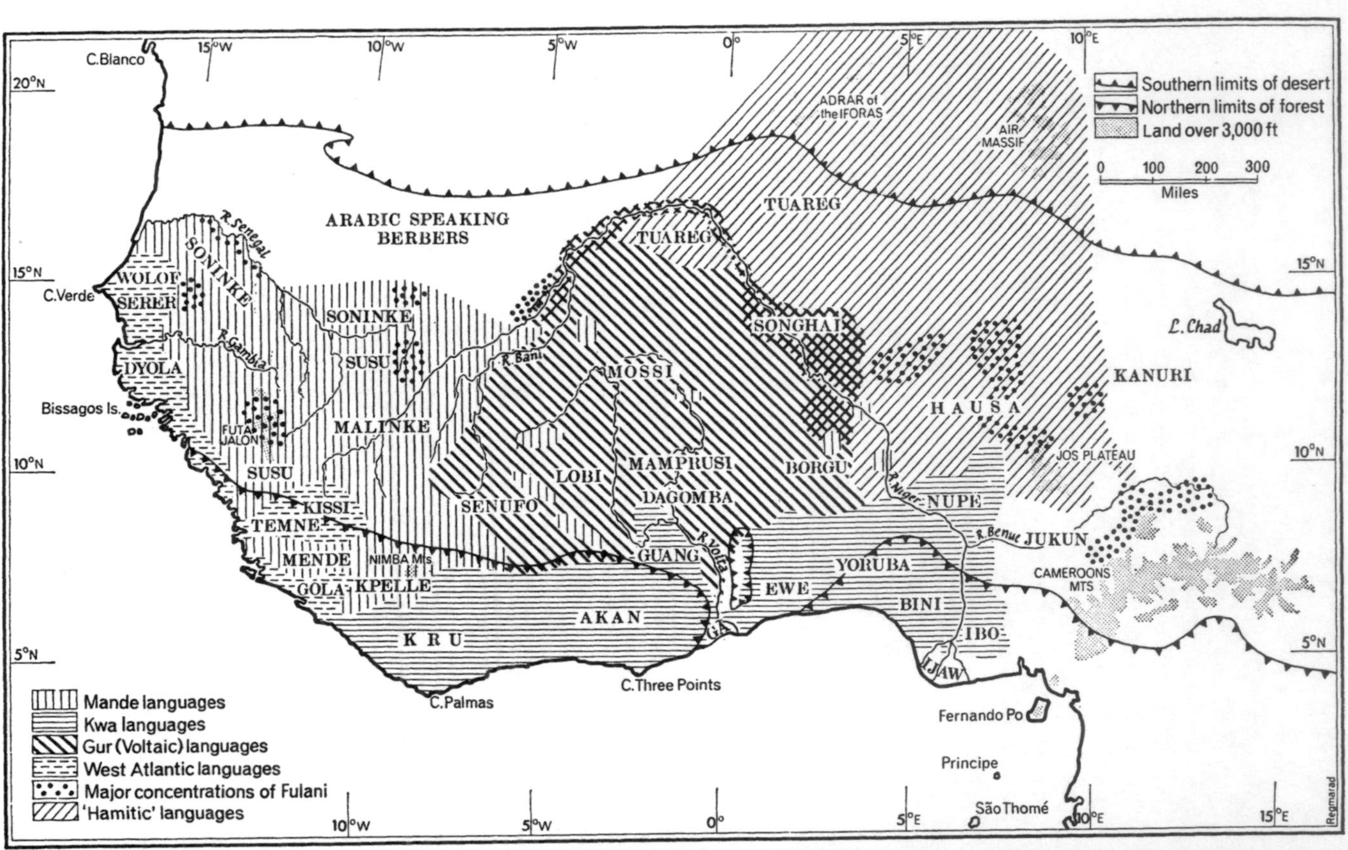

15°W
10°W
5°W
0°
5°E
10°E
15°E
20°N
15°N
10°N
5°N
C.Blanco
C.Verde
Bissagos Is.
C.Palmas
C.Three Points
Fernando Po
Principe
São Thomé
L. Chad
R. Senegal
R. Gambia
R. Bani
R. Niger
R. Volta
R. Benue
ARABIC SPEAKING BERBERS
TUAREG
TUAREG
ADRAR of the IFORAS
AIR MASSIF
SONINKE
SONINKE
WOLOF
SERER
DYOLA
SUSU
SUSU
FUTA JALON
MALINKE
KISSI
TEMNE
MENDE
NIMBA Mts
GOLA
KPELLE
KRU
AKAN
SENUFO
LOBI
MOSSI
MAMPRUSI
DAGOMBA
GUANG
GA
EWE
SONGHAI
BORGU
YORUBA
BINI
IJAW
IBO
NUPE
HAUSA
JOS PLATEAU
JUKUN
KANURI
CAMEROONS MTS
Southern limits of desert
Northern limits of forest
Land over 3,000 ft
0 100 200 300
Miles
Mande languages
Kwa languages
Gur (Voltaic) languages
West Atlantic languages
Major concentrations of Fulani
'Hamitic' languages
Regmarad

1

Beginnings

The first West African kingdoms

West Africa first comes unequivocally into the light of history in the eighth century of the Christian era. Writing in A.D. 773–4, shortly after the first Muslim conquest of North Africa, the Arabic author al-Fazari mentioned that across the Sahara from Morocco lay a country called Ghana, 'the land of gold'.

From this time onwards, references to that part of West Africa just south of the Sahara, which the Arabs called *Bilad al-Sudan*, 'the land of the black men', became increasingly more detailed and frequent in a growing stream of Arabic geographical and historical writings. In the ninth century, al-Yaqubi knew not only of Ghana, which had a powerful king under whom were other kings, and in all of whose territories gold was found, but also of the kingdoms of Kawkaw, Kanem and Mallel. It is difficult to be certain what al-Yaqubi meant by 'Mallel', though this is certainly a variant name for the Mande kingdom on the upper Niger usually known as Mali, which later supplanted Ghana as the major power of the western Sudan (see chapter 2). However, Kawkaw is usually accepted as a name for the capital of the Songhai kingdom whose seat was first at Kukyia, on an island in the middle Niger, about 120 miles upstream from the modern Tilabery, and later at Gao, on the Niger bend. Al-Yaqubi thought that Kawkaw was the greatest kingdom of the Sudan, with a large number of tributary states. Kanem, to the north and north-east of Lake Chad, was a kingdom inhabited by people called the Zaghawa, who seem to have been essentially nomadic, since al-Yaqubi said 'they have no use for towns' and that they constructed their dwellings from reeds.

By al-Yaqubi's time, Muslims from North Africa were operating well-established caravan routes of trade across the Sahara, and they were becoming increasingly familiar with the Sudanese kingdoms, especially with Ghana, a magnet for traders because of its exports of gold. In the tenth century, al-Mas'udi described how the merchants of Ghana obtained gold from communities living beyond the southern boundary of their state by 'the silent trade' or 'dumb barter', a process quite commonly met with in history where professional traders had to deal with less sophisticated peoples: 'When the merchants reach the frontier, they place their wares and cloth on it and then depart, and so the Negroes come, bearing gold, which they leave beside the merchandise, and then themselves depart. The owners of the merchandise then return, and if they are satisfied with what they have found, they take it. If not, they go away again, and the Negroes return and add to the price until the bargain is concluded.'

Ibn Hawqal, himself a merchant, tells us a fair amount about the trans-Saharan trade, and shows that it was of very considerable value, especially by the standards of the times in which he was writing (late tenth century). The caravans were conducted by the Sanhaja, desert nomads, Berbers akin to the inhabitants of Morocco, their main route running from Sijilmasa, in the oasis of Tafilelt in southern Morocco, to Awdaghost, just north of Ghana. These were both Sanhaja towns which served as collecting and distributing centres for the trans-Saharan trade, and both were rich and prosperous through this trade. On one occasion, Ibn Hawqal tells us, he saw a bill of exchange made out by a merchant of Awdaghost to a corresponding merchant in Sijilmasa for the sum of 40,000 dinars. This would be a large sum by any standards. The dinar was a small gold coin equivalent to the English half-sovereign; thus 40,000 dinars would be worth about £100,000 or $250,000 at the price of gold ruling in 1968. Because of its gold, Ghana was a very rich kingdom indeed.

Rather more than half a century after Ibn Hawqal, in 1067–8, the Spanish Muslim geographer, al-Bakri, put together a great deal of information concerning Ghana, thus providing us with our earliest detailed description of a West African state. From al-Bakri, and from the later *Tarikhs*, Arabic chronicles written by Sudanic Negroes themselves, it becomes apparent that Ghana was not the proper name either for the state or for its capital. Al-Bakri himself thought that Ghana was a title given to the king. This is doubtful, but what is certain is that the kingdom was situated in the area variously called Awkar, Baghena, or Hodh. This is a region, now desert, but, until the eleventh century at least, capable of providing pasture for cattle, whose southernmost limits are about 200 miles north-west of Segou on the upper Niger. According to a local sixteenth-century source, the capital was called Kumbi, and the dominant people in the state were the Soninke or Sarakole, northern members of the great block of Mande-speaking Negro peoples who inhabit so much of the western half of West Africa.

Al-Bakri's description of the capital city has to a considerable extent been confirmed by the work of modern archaeologists at the site now known as Kumbi Saleh. The city comprised two towns. One of these, apparently built of mud, contained the royal palace surrounded by its own wall, and was encircled by sacred groves in which the kings were buried and in which the Soninke priests practised their traditional animistic religious observances. Linked to this by a continuous built-up area was what al-Bakri called the 'Muslim' town, with twelve mosques, inhabited it would seem largely by Berber merchants from North Africa and the desert who had been attracted to settle in Ghana because of its trade; here the buildings were of stone and in the North African style. All around were wells, providing a supply of water adequate to permit of cultivation.

The king inherited his throne in the maternal line (the king of al-Bakri's time, Tankamanin, was the son of his predecessor's sister), and seems to have been an absolute monarch somewhat remote from his people. He and, to a lesser extent, his retainers, were very richly dressed, with many gold ornaments. He held court with great splendour, communicating with his subjects, who had to approach him on their knees, sprinkling their heads with dust, only through his ministers, some of whom were Muslims. When he died, he was buried in great state, together with food and drink and retainers for the after life, in a great earthen mound. Human sacrifices were made to dead kings on the great national festivals.

The wealth of the kingdom came from its trade, more especially from its export of gold dust (the possession of gold nuggets being a monopoly of the king), and from regular taxes on the imports which were exchanged for this gold. Al-Bakri tells us of fixed duties paid on each donkey-load of copper and of general merchandise, both of which we may presume to have originated in North Africa, and of salt. The latter, which came from salt deposits controlled by the Sanhaja and other tribes in the Sahara, was one of the Sudan's most valuable imports, because it is a necessity of life which is exceedingly scarce in the Sudan. Consequently, among the Sudanic Negroes it was as much valued as gold, often being used as currency, and sometimes, indeed, exchangeable for gold weight for weight. With the wealth from the gold trade, and from the taxes on imports, the king was enabled not only to maintain his large court but also to raise a large army (200,000 strong according to al-Bakri), with which he was able to gain yet more wealth by conquering and making tributary some of the surrounding peoples and states, including (about A.D. 990), the Sanhaja trading centre of Awdaghost.

The Arabic authors' accounts of other monarchies of the western and central Sudan in the tenth and eleventh centuries are less clear and detailed, presumably because, unlike Ghana, they had little or no gold, and so fewer North African merchants visited them. Nevertheless we are told of three, presumably small, kingdoms in the Senegal valley west of Ghana: Sanghana, Takrur and Silla. Sanghana was near the sea. Takrur achieved fame as the first West African Negro kingdom to convert to Islam, by the mid-eleventh century according to al-Bakri. Consequently it became an important centre for the diffusion of Islam elsewhere in West Africa. Silla was the western neighbour of Ghana, with whom it was at war when al-Bakri was writing. To the south of Ghana, in the upper Niger valley, we are told of the existence of the kingdoms of Mallel (Mali) and Daw. To the east was Kawkaw, whose king was said by now to be a Muslim, but whose people had dances and drumming which sound very pagan. Further east still, in the central Sudan, there was Kanem, which by the end of the tenth century may have been a more settled and stable state than it had been in al-Yaqubi's time a century earlier when, as we have seen, its Zaghawa people seem to have been essentially nomadic. At any rate it now had towns, and it possessed a monarchy which Muslim authors thought sufficiently strange to merit considerable comment. Thus *c.* 985, al-Muhallabi wrote that the Zaghawa exalted and worshipped their king as though he were God: 'They imagine that he does not eat, for his food is taken into his house secretly, and should one of his subjects happen to meet the camel carrying it, he is immediately killed. He has absolute power over his subjects . . . who spend their time cultivating and looking after their cattle. Their religion is the worship of their kings, for they believe that it is they who bring life and death, sickness and health.'

Eventually it is to be hoped that archaeology will fill out and confirm the somewhat slender picture given by Arabic authors of the West African Sudan in this earliest phase of its history, from the eighth to the eleventh century. Certainly only archaeologists can give us any idea of what was happening further south, beyond the Sudan grasslands, in the better-watered and more fertile woodlands and forest of the more southerly parts of West Africa beyond the ken of merchants and other visitors from North Africa, a region which collectively may most conveniently be called Guinea.[1] But the Arabic writers provide enough information for us to be certain that, by the tenth and eleventh centuries, some Africans of the western Sudan had acquired a considerable degree of civilisation, in that they possessed cities, organised monarchies and administrations, and sophisticated systems of trade and taxation. This complexity of political and economic organisation beyond the self-sufficient village of what might be called 'tribal' society—even if, as we may suppose, this still moulded the lives of the bulk of the people—is likely to have been the result of centuries of development. In the case of ancient Ghana, at least, the

[1] The name Guinea comes from a Moroccan Berber word meaning 'black', the phrase *Akal n-Iguinawen* having exactly the same significance as the Arabic *Bilad al-Sudan*, namely, 'the land of the black men'. It is applied to the southern half of West Africa because it was the name used by the Portuguese who explored the coastline by sea. Earlier Portuguese contacts with Africa having been almost entirely with Morocco (see chapter 4), they naturally took with them the Moroccan name for Negroland.

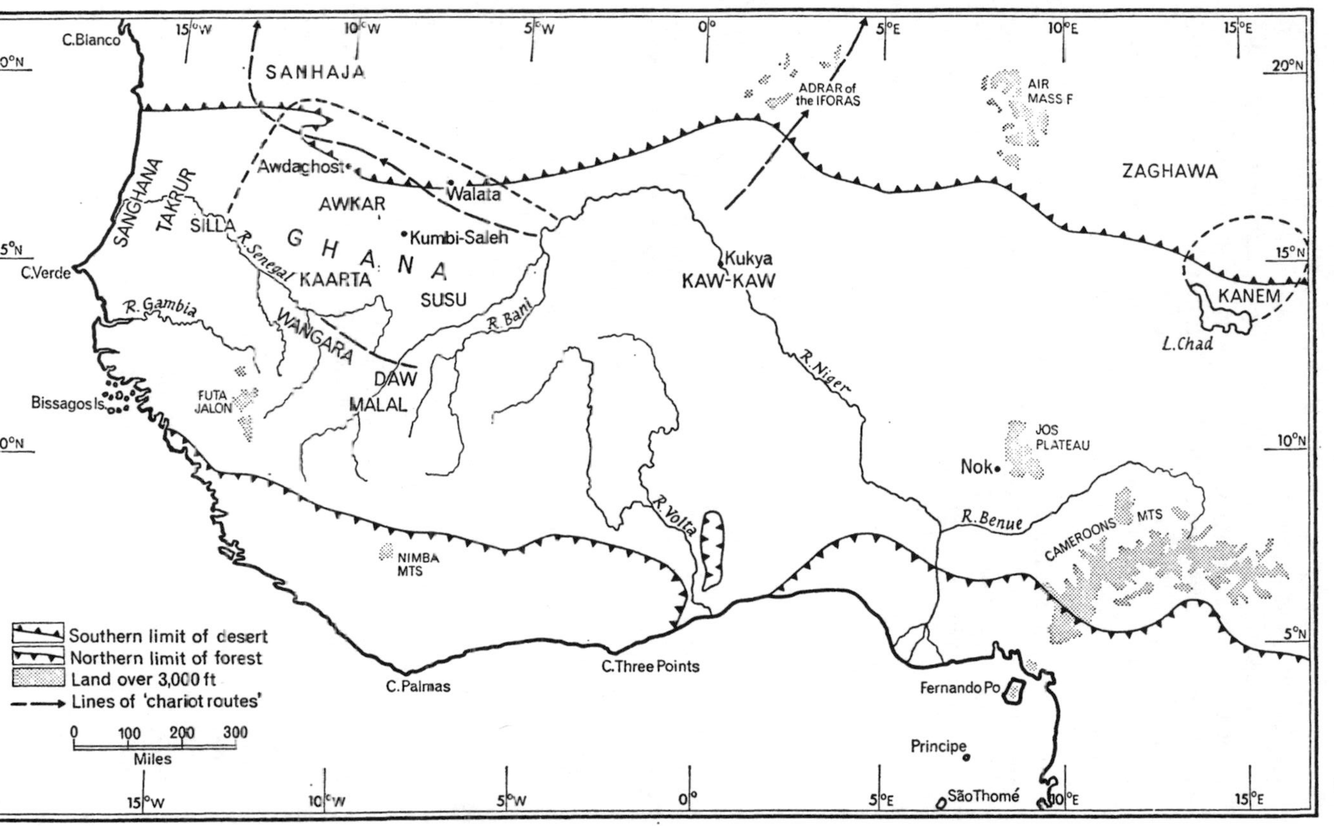

2 Major states known to have existed in West Africa in the eleventh century

literary evidence suggests that this development must stretch back to the eighth century and beyond.

In the light of present knowledge, we cannot be sure what sparked off this development. All we can do is to consider a number of possibilities. These are not mutually exclusive, and it seems likely that these may all have contributed, though doubtless in varying degrees, to the emergence of ancient Ghana, Kanem and the other early kingdoms which have been mentioned.

There would seem essentially to be three possible major explanations of the origins of these kingdoms and their associated economies:

(1) They were sparked off by political influences coming to the western and central Sudan from the outside, specifically from non-Negro lands to the north-east and north.

(2) They were the more or less natural consequence of the western and central Sudanic peoples' own 'Neolithic Revolution'.

(3) They were due to the fertilising influence of the growth of trans-Saharan trade.

Political influences originating from outside the Sudan, and the 'Hamitic hypothesis'

Of the three major possible explanations for the advance of the western and central Sudan towards civilisation, that of political influences from the outside is unlikely to have been the earliest in point of time. It is considered first here for two main reasons. It was an explanation which gained considerable currency as a result of the writings of the first investigators of the problem in modern times, namely the historians of the colonial period. Secondly, it is the explanation which would seem to be advanced by the earliest traditions of many of the peoples of the western and central Sudan themselves.

Most of those who, during the colonial period, sought to reconstruct the earliest history of Africa, were themselves outsiders, members of the colonising nations of western Europe. They came from a society which technologically and materially was vastly more powerful than was late nineteenth-century Africa, and which was therefore able to conquer, rule, dominate, and change Negro African societies in a most dramatic fashion. When these men began to discover the evidence for the earliest West African civilisations, they were therefore predisposed to think that these could not have been created by the Negro peoples they themselves had so easily conquered and come to rule. They believed, therefore, that they must have resulted from earlier invasions by alien conquerors comparable to themselves. The wished-for conquerors could be found near at hand in the non-Negro inhabitants of north-east and north Africa, who had indeed long been impinging on the Negroes of the Sudan.

There is no really satisfactory collective name for the non-Negro peoples of north and north-east Africa such as the Berbers and the ancient Egyptians. They are commonly called Hamites, but the terms 'Hamite' and 'Hamitic' can properly be applied not to the peoples, but only to the languages they speak (or which they spoke before the Arab and Muslim conquest), and in fact the modern view is that there is very little in these languages as a whole to distinguish them from the 'Semitic' languages of the peoples across the Red Sea (e.g. Arabic). The Hamitic-speaking peoples, who may well have also inhabited a large area of eastern Africa before it was occupied by its present population of Negroes speaking Bantu languages, are often quite dark-skinned. But in features and in physical type they are fairly easily distinguishable from the Negroes, and the European historians and anthropologists of the colonial period came to think of them as 'whites' like themselves. In fact, of course, many Europeans might be better described as 'pinks' rather than 'whites', and it is clear that considerable prejudice is attached to the classification of peoples by the colouring of their skins. By and large, nineteenth-century Europeans had convinced themselves that 'white'-skinned peoples represented a superior human type.

There thus developed an overall scheme for the interpretation of African history which may be termed 'the Hamitic hypothesis'. This assumed that the African 'Hamites' were 'whites' akin to the Europeans, and that they and their culture were inherently superior to the Negroes and their culture, so that wherever an apparently Negro people had made a striking advance, the explanation must be sought in 'Hamitic' influence or infiltration.

'The civilisations of Africa', the anthropologist C. G. Seligman wrote in 1930, 'are the civilisations of the Hamites; its history the record of these peoples and of their interactions with . . . other African stocks [such as] the Negro. . .' Seligman in fact leaves a general impression of wave after wave of incoming Hamitic pastoralists, 'better armed as well as quicker witted than the dark agricultural Negroes', imposing themselves on the Negroes, mixing with them, and galvanising them into political and economic advancement.

It is true that many of the African peoples who speak 'Hamitic' languages were pastoralists, and that the Negroes, especially in West Africa, were predominantly agriculturalists. But it is absurd to generalise that cattle-keepers are inherently 'quicker witted', superior to cultivators of the soil, the more so since agricultural cultures are usually accepted as being the more developed. In West Africa, as was most cogently pointed out by the American linguist, Joseph H. Greenberg, the stereotype of the all-conquering Hamitic pastoralist is peculiarly inaccurate. The only markedly pastoral West African people are the Fulani, who in the early nineteenth century did conquer the agricultural (and urban, commercial and industrial) Hausa. But it is the language of the Hausa which is 'Hamitic', while that of the Fulani is a West African Negro language.

Nevertheless, in at least two aspects, the Hamitic hypothesis was not altogether as absurd an interpretation of the African past as we may now be inclined to think. Agriculture was first developed in Africa in the lower Nile valley, and its people, the ancient Egyptians, spoke a 'Hamitic' language. On the basis of their agriculture, they went on, by about 3000 B.C., to develop one of the first great civilisations in world history. Among the major features of this civilisation was the concept of their king as supra-human, a god who could only marry his equally godly sister, and who was the absolute arbiter over the land and all human activities on it, especially perhaps of the times of sowing and harvesting. In these and in many other details, many Negro African kingdoms seem to have had so similar a type of kingship—usually referred to as 'divine kingship'—that it is tempting to conclude, as many good historians still do, that it must have spread throughout Africa from this Egyptian and 'Hamitic' source.

Secondly, it could be observed that where, in the savannas of the Sudan with between about 5 and 20 inches average rainfall per year, pastoralists coming out of the Sahara, such as the Tuareg tribes of the 'Hamitic'-speaking Berber peoples, competed for land and water with the Negro agriculturalists, the northerners did have certain qualities which permitted them to infiltrate and defeat the Negroes. These qualities were essentially military, for example the mobility afforded by their horses and camels, or the closely knit kinship discipline needed to enable their tribes to survive the hardships of desert life, and they do not permit of any assumption of inherent superiority, either racial or cultural, on the part of the conquerors. In fact the evidence usually suggests that culturally it was the Negroes who were the stronger, and that within a few generations the incomers had been absorbed by the Negroes and adopted their languages and culture in preference to their own.

The local West African traditions which attempt to explain the origins of the earliest kingdoms of the western and central Sudan, commonly do so in terms of the arrival of strangers from the north or north-east. In English or in French translation, the invaders are often referred to as 'white men', though the words which are translated as 'white' might often be better rendered as 'red'. This is perhaps less an indication of skin colour than of a concept of ethnic purity: the founding ancestors are viewed as 'red men' because they are thought of as the purest, truest ancestors of the present-day people. We are thus told that the first kings of Ghana, who were replaced by Negro Soninke kings only after a considerable number of generations, were not Negroes, but 'white men', who may have been Sanhaja Berbers. One Songhai explanation for the origin of the first dynasty of their kingdom is that it was founded by two brothers said to have come from the Yemen (south-west Arabia). Similarly the kings of Kanem, the Sefawa, thought of themselves as being descended from a family of Yemeni origin, and believed that they did not become wholly Negro until about A.D. 1200. These are not the only examples. The kings of the Hausa states, between Kanem and the Songhai kingdom, which may have come into being about the tenth century, were thought to be the descendants of immigrants from North Africa or the Near East, while the legend of the foundation of the Mossi and Dagomba kingdoms of the Upper Volta basin south of the Songhai also begins with the coming of a 'red ancestor' from the direction of Mecca.

Some commentators would dismiss stories of this kind as being simply inventions by West African Negro royal families and their supporters after their conversion to Islam (at various periods from the eleventh to the fourteenth century or later), when it was obviously advantageous for them to link their ancestry with the great historic centres of Muslim culture in the Middle East and North Africa. But such an explantion may be too simple. The terms in which the legends are expressed are obviously influenced by the spread and later dominance of Islam and its literate culture in the western and central Sudan, but it does seem that, although they must not be taken too literally, they do represent attempts to express essential historical truths. For one thing, stories of this kind are not limited to Muslim dynasties. There is, for example, the remarkable Kisra legend, widely spread, if not today very well remembered, among essentially pagan peoples along the Benue valley and up the Niger to Bussa and beyond. The story is of a Persian king, Kisra, who invaded Egypt but was later forced to flee to Nubia, i.e. the Nile valley above Egypt. Then, with some Nubian (and possibly Christian) followers, he is said to have gone westwards to what is now Nigeria, where he and his followers established the states from which the kingdoms of the Jukun (Kwararafa), Nupe, Idah, Borgu and Bussa, and also of some of the Hausa, and—far to the south-west—the Yoruba kingdoms were descended. It seems not improbable, too, that the legends of the foundation of the Songhai and the Mossi and Dagomba kingdoms should be linked up with the same basic story.

The early stages of the Kisra story do match with known historical events. An army of the Sassanid Persian king, Khusraw (Chosroes) II, did occupy Egypt in A.D. 616. When it was expelled by the Byzantines in A.D. 629, some of its soldiers may well have sheltered and been cut off in the Christian kingdoms which then existed in Nubia on the foundations of an earlier civilisation derived from ancient Egyptian colonisation among Sudanic peoples. These kingdoms, incidentally, had relations with the Yemen, in which Persian armies had also been active.

It is therefore not unreasonable to suppose that this situation, together with the even more momentous contemporary emergence in Arabia (A.D. 622–32) of the great new world religion of Islam, which quickly expanded into Egypt (A.D. 639–41) and then along the North African coastlands, could have set in motion a train of events which could bring important influences from the Nile valley (and, indirectly, from Arabia and even further afield) across the Sudan towards the Chad basin and West Africa. But if so, it would be unrealistic to think in terms of Egyptians, or Nubians, let alone Arabians or Persians, coming directly to West Africa. The connection with West Africa would be an indirect one, through the agency of the 'Hamitic' and other pastoral nomads of the Sahara, such as the Sanhaja in the west and the Zaghawa in the east, and the ancestors of the present day Tuareg in the centre. Ideas and influences from the great events in the Nile valley, in Arabia and in North Africa, would have been impressed on these people and, as they pressed southwards into agricultural lands in their search for grazing, would have been passed on to the Negro farmers.[1]

The Neolithic Revolution in West Africa

But it would be unreasonable to suppose that the corpus of great ideas stemming from ancient Egyptian civilisation and from the Near Eastern lands which gave birth to the great world religions of Judaism, Christianity, and Islam could have been brought to the West African Negroes in any very purposive form with the desert pastoralists as intermediaries. Culturally, the Negro farmers must have been more advanced than the infiltrating nomads, and capable, as has been suggested, of absorbing them and their ideas into their own society. Before the great events of the period round about the seventh century and afterwards, which may well have brought to West Africa new dynasties of kings and also have formed new political groupings, the West African Negroes had themselves embarked on the great adventures in human development which are usually termed the 'Neolithic Revolution'.

By the Neolithic Revolution is meant the great change by which men, instead of being dependent on the hunting of wild animals and the collection of wild fruits and roots for their sustenance, learnt to domesticate animals and to cultivate plants which they had specially selected as the most suitable sources of food, clothing and other necessities. Hitherto, men could only exist in small bands, roaming over, and competing with other animals for the resources of, large tracts of land. Now, as a result of

[1] This could well explain why some modern observers have thought that they could detect residual traits of Christianity, not only among the Tuareg, but even, for example, among the people of Nupe.

the Neolithic Revolution, they could be assured of regular, better and larger supplies of food from smaller areas. The human population could therefore greatly increase, and it could live in permanent villages on the best land and close by the best water supplies. Basketware and pottery were developed for food storage and transport, and weaving, building and thatching to provide clothing and houses; stone and bone tools for killing and skinning animals, for catching fish, for sewing, for carpentry, were improved,[1] and, ultimately, were gradually replaced by even better tools of metal, first of copper and bronze, and then of iron and steel.

Archaeologists have traced the earliest development of these momentous advances in the history of mankind in lands of the Near and Middle East from about 8000 B.C. or earlier.

By about 5000 B.C., the same process was well under way in Egypt. It is not known for certain when the Negroes of West Africa also began to experience the Neolithic Revolution, but the evidence available suggests that cultivation had been established in what is now the southern Sahara (then wetter than now) and the northern Sudan by about 2000 B.C. There is some argument as to whether the idea of cultivation occurred independently to the Negroes, or whether it was borrowed by them from the Nile valley. The latter is more probable, though it must be noted that the favoured cereal crops of Egypt and the Middle East, such as barley and wheat, were not suited to the conditions of the Sudan, and the Negro cultivators had to select local wild seed-bearing plants for cultivation and improvement, thus developing the African varieties of sorghum and millet (throughout the Sudan) and of rice (in the upper Niger valley).

Not much is yet known with certainty about the progress of the Neolithic Revolution through West Africa. It clearly began in the north, close to the edge of the Sahara desert, because the best environment for the cereal crops was the open savannas, especially when these had permanent supplies of water (which could also be used, through fishing, to supplement the food supply). Thus the Senegal and upper and middle Niger valleys, and the Lake Chad basin were probably important early centres. In and around the Bauchi plateau in what is now Northern Nigeria, archaeologists have demonstrated the existence of a completely developed neolithic culture, the Nok culture, beginning to turn to the use of iron and also producing fine sculptures, from about 800 B.C. to about A.D. 200. There is much ground for supposing that this culture and its peoples were directly ancestral to the kingdoms and peoples that we can discern in the Nigerian region from about the eleventh century onwards.

[1] 'Neolithic Age' means 'New Stone Age', since from the point of view of tools, polished stone tools came to replace stone tools made by chipping and flaking. The term 'Neolithic Revolution', with its very much wider implications, is due to the archaeologist Gordon Childe.

In its earlier stages, the Neolithic Revolution cannot have been effective in the woodlands and the forestlands south of the savannas, for its cereal crops were not well adapted to the woodlands, and could hardly be cultivated at all in the forest. Thus the spread of the Revolution—and of the dense populations that it made possible—south beyond the savannas must have been a slow and gradual process, for the most part along river valleys and gaps in the forest (such as that to the east of the lower Volta, from modern Ghana to Western Nigeria). In course of time, men learnt to cultivate rootcrops which were suitable for cultivation in the forest margins. But the number of African roots suited to development in this way seems to have been limited, and few were promising, other than the African varieties of yam (probably first cultivated in the region from modern Ghana to Western Nigeria). The agricultural exploitation on any scale of the forests and their margins had to await the introduction of new tropical crops from south-east Asia and America. The south-east Asian crops, including bananas and plantains, coconuts, and new varieties of rice and yams, are unlikely to have arrived, via East Africa, much before about A.D. 1000, and the American foodcrops, including maize and cassava, cannot have appeared until after *c.* 1500.

The upper Niger and the Senegal valleys and the Chad basin provided conditions for the Neolithic Revolution analogous to the lower Nile valley in Egypt. It is therefore not unreasonable to suppose that it may have led to not dissimilar consequences: a considerable growth of population, the beginnings of urbanisation and of organised government and administration, and, even perhaps, the flourishing of the idea of a king as a god-like being supreme over all his subjects, communicating on their behalf and for their well-being with the gods and their ancestors, and interpreting to them their will with regard to the possession and use of the land and its water supplies, and the sowing and harvesting of the crops. The concept of divine kingship may well have been as implicit in the Negro Neolithic Revolution as it was in that of ancient Egypt. The basic idea need not have been borrowed from Egypt through Nubia, the meeting-place for ancient Egyptian and Negro peoples and ideas. However, if some of the characteristic traits and practices of divine kings among the Negroes do so strongly resemble those of ancient Egypt that some connection is thought essential, it may well lie in the activities of the Saharan pastoralists from about the seventh century onwards. In touch both with Nubian and with Negro West African cultures, they could well have provided the agency by which traits and rituals of kingship as originally practised in ancient Egypt could have been grafted on to basically indigenous Negro concepts.

Something that very probably did pass into Negro Africa from Nubia was the knowledge and practice of making tools and weapons of iron.

Iron ore is a far less obvious and easy material from which to make metal than many other ores, for example, copper ore, though it is much more plentiful, and the implements which can be made from it are more efficient and durable, and also cheaper, than those made from copper and bronze, which were normally the metals first used for tool-making. Negro Africa is exceptional in this respect, since here men passed from the stone age into the iron age without a transition period of copper and bronze tool-making. Knowledge of iron-making first entered Africa from the Near East, where it had been discovered in the second millennium B.C., with the Assyrian conquest of Egypt in the seventh century. Egypt, however, possessed neither good supplies of iron ore nor of the timber needed to fire the furnaces to smelt it, and the first considerable iron-making industry in Africa was in ancient Nubia, which had both. It is doubtful, however, whether Nubia was the only dispersal point from which iron-making spread further into Africa. It seems more reasonable to suppose that, for the westernmost Sudan, knowledge of iron-working may have come in over the trans-Saharan trade routes from North Africa, where the Carthaginians were quickly aware of the value of the metal.

The developments associated with the Neolithic Revolution suggest that we should look for the earliest West African kingdoms of consequence in well-watered lands like the valleys of the Senegal and upper Niger, or the basin of Lake Chad. In fact the earliest kingdoms that are known to history, ancient Ghana and Kanem, for example, were situated not in the most favourable agricultural lands, but just to the north of them, in the zone where agriculture was giving way to desert pastoralism. It could well be, of course, that there were other, perhaps less extensive but as significant kingdoms to the south of Ghana and Kanem which we do not know about, because our main source of information for the early kingdoms comes from the Arabic writings of men who approached Negroland from the north and who did not penetrate far into it. Perhaps al-Yaqubi's mysteriously early 'Mallel' was one of these. Nevertheless, the fact that, of the early kingdoms, Ghana and Kanem were so far to the north does suggest the importance in early West African history of the third potentially state-forming influence that has been mentioned, namely trans-Saharan trade.

Trans-Saharan trade and its influence

Exactly when men began to travel to and fro, and to trade across the Sahara is not known, and may well never be known, because it probably derives from the period, corresponding to the last Ice Age in Europe, when the climate was appreciably wetter, and the Sahara was not desert but grassland on which both 'Hamites' and Negroes hunted game and, later, pastured their herds. As the Sahara began to dry up, noticeably by about 3000 B.C., the 'Hamites' seem to have withdrawn towards their main centres of population in the north and in the lower Nile valley, and the Negroes similarly towards the south. But contact would still be maintained through the practice, especially by the 'Hamitic' pastoralists, of transhumance. This (from the point of view of the northern edge of the Sahara) was the moving of their herds southwards with the winter rains, and northwards in the summer. The 'Hamitic' northerners in fact became the dominant pastoralists of the desert since they had direct access to supplies of, first, horses, and then camels—both, in their modern forms, introductions into Africa from Asia (the horse *c.* 1700 B.C., and the camel around the beginning of the Christian era). Neither animal, the horse especially, does well in West Africa, and stocks have to be renewed by periodical importations from across the desert. Thus the 'Hamites' had both increased mobility for themselves, and the ability to deny it to the Negroes.

Herodotus, writing about 450 B.C., speaks of the Garamantes, that is the people of the oasis of Djerma in the Fezzan (who in modern terms would be accounted Tuareg), raiding the 'Ethiopians', i.e. black-skinned peoples, across the Sahara in two-wheeled chariots each drawn by four horses. About 400 years later, another great early geographer, Strabo, says much the same of the Pharusii of the western Sahara, who may perhaps be equated with ancestors of the Sanhaja. There are other accounts from Herodotus and other ancient Greek and Roman sources of other journeys into or across the Sahara from North Africa, and there can be little doubt that its cities did receive, through the hands of the desert tribes like the Garamantes, exports from West Africa, including the mysterious precious stones called 'carbuncles', and almost certainly gold-dust and slaves. The Carthaginians, the great maritime trading people of Syrian origin who dominated the coastlands of North Africa for seven or more centuries until their conquest by Rome in 146 B.C., certainly seem to have traded for gold, through dumb barter, on the Atlantic coast south of Morocco, and this gold could only have come from West Africa.

In the story of Hanno's great expedition *c.* 420 B.C., we seem to have a record of a deliberate attempt to open up regular sea trade with West Africa, and to establish Carthaginian trading colonies as far south as possible. How far Hanno's ships actually went is a matter of considerable argument; he may very well have reached lands inhabited by Negroes, though it is perhaps unlikely that he was able to prospect as far as the Cameroons or even, indeed, as far as Sierra Leone (as some scholars would suppose). But however far he explored, it seems certain that his expedition could and did not succeed in opening up a regular sea trade with Negroland. The arid and waterless Sahara coastline, and the combination along it of northerly winds and currents would have made it

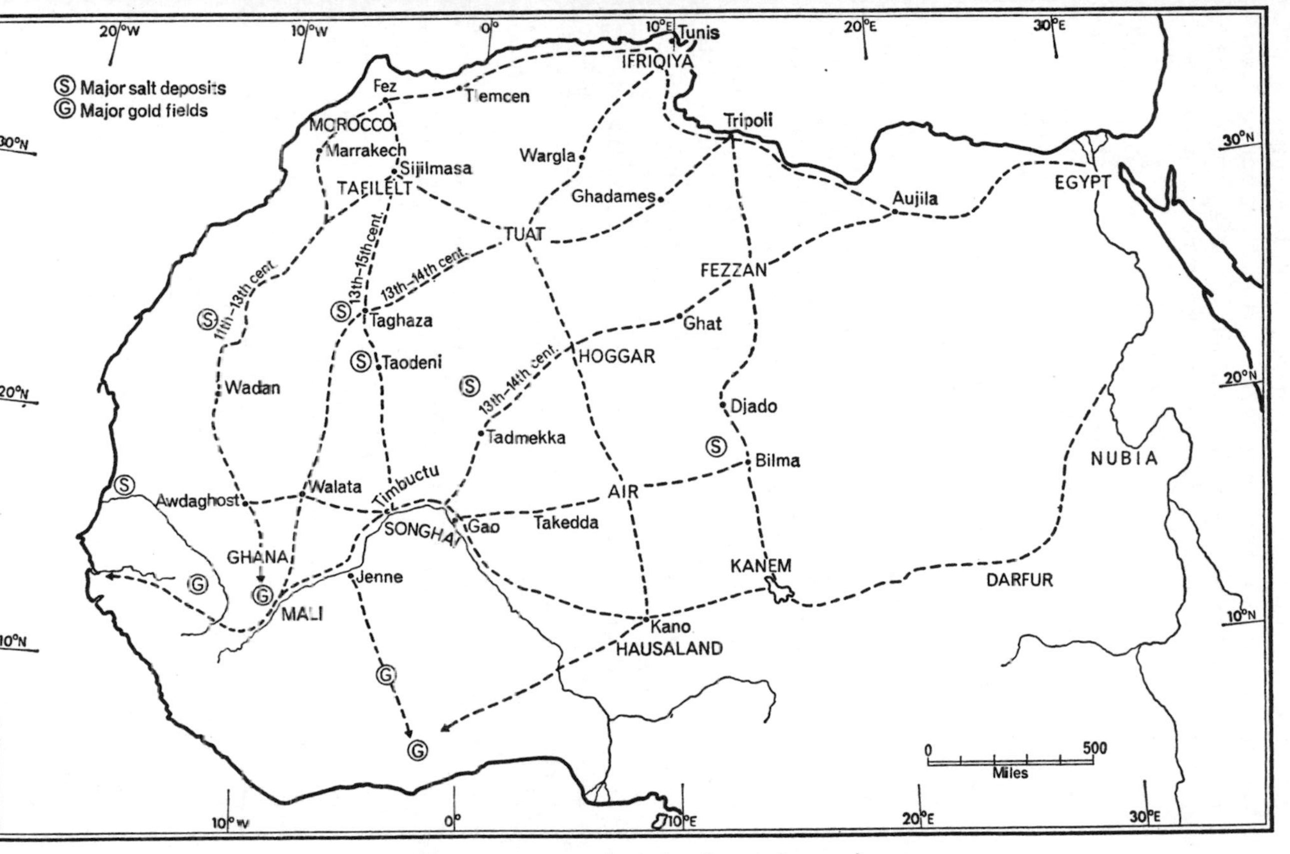

3 Major caravan routes, eleventh to fourteenth centuries

impossible for Carthaginian galleys, propelled mainly by the oars of their crew, who were accustomed to spending each night on land, to have established regular voyages to West Africa and back again. Certainly there is no evidence for Carthaginian trading colonies further south than southern Morocco.

The chariots of the Garamantes and Pharusii were very light fighting vehicles, unsuitable for carrying trade goods, but it is a point of considerable interest that Herodotus's and Strabo's accounts of their activities have been confirmed and given added point by the discovery on rocks in the Sahara of some hundreds of crude drawings or engravings of two-wheeled vehicles each drawn by four horses. The most significant aspect of these drawings is that they are almost all distributed along only two routes across the Sahara, a western one running from southern Morocco towards the upper Niger, and a central one running from the Fezzan to the eastern side of the Niger bend. The explanation of this must be two-fold. In the first place, these are routes which offer good hard-going to wheeled vehicles (later, of course, to horses alone[1] and to donkeys and camels—and, in modern times, to motor cars). Secondly, they either lead more or less directly towards the alluvial gold deposits of the upper Niger and Senegal valleys, a region which the Arabs came to call 'Wangara', or to the nearest point to North Africa on the River Niger, which affords a natural line of communication to these same gold resources.

The emergence of the important state of Ghana, astride the frontiers between Negroland and the desert just north of the agricultural and gold-bearing lands of the upper Niger and Senegal rivers, can thus be explained, at least in part, in terms of economic interest. North Africans and the desert pastoralists who conducted their trade for them wanted gold and agricultural products which the Negroes could offer, and in return they could provide metals and merchandise, and the all-important salt, which the Negroes needed. If a particular group of people—perhaps first a desert pastoral group, and then a Negro group (or some mixture of both)—could establish a strong political unit across the line of communication to the north, then they could influence the terms of trade to their advantage. The profits from the trade, from selling imports from the north to the Negro miners and farmers and from selling the latter's produce to the northern traders, and the taxes they could levy on the trade, would make them wealthier, and so more powerful, than all their neighbours, both to north and south, and so their state could grow and prosper at their expense. Equally, of course, the larger the states and the more effective their governments, the greater the security for traders, so that trade could further expand and prosper.

[1] It should be appreciated that men learnt to harness horses to vehicles before they learnt how to ride them.

Similarly, but less clearly perhaps, the emergence of Kanem, north of the agricultural lands around Lake Chad and seeking to expand northwards towards the caravan centres of the Fezzan, may have been another, albeit less spectacular, response to a comparable but weaker (because gold-less) commercial stimulus. Equally, the early importance of the Songhai kingdom on the eastern side of the Niger bend may be explained to some extent by the fact that this was where the trade route from the Fezzan towards the goldfields of Wangara first entered the Sudan of the Negroes.

2

The great states of the western and central Sudan

The decline and fall of ancient Ghana: the Almoravids

Whatever its origins, by the time (1067–8) that al-Bakri was writing, Ghana was a major Negro state, dependent for its prosperity and power on its control of West African exports, particularly of gold, to North Africa, and of the distribution in the western Sudan of the Saharan salt and the North African products brought in by the Sanhaja caravan traders. But already it had used its great power to take a step which was to lead to its decline and fall. This was its conquest, about eighty years earlier, of the southern Sanhaja trading depot of Awdaghost.

The basic interest of both the desert traders and the king and merchants of Ghana was the same: the maximum possible trade between the two of them. For one side to seek to dominate the other and to engross as much as possible of the profits of this trade to itself, was bound to cause trouble. This may explain why originally the Soninke Negroes of Ghana may well have freed themselves from Sanhaja kings. Now that the Soninke were using their independent power to try and dictate not only the terms on which they sold their gold but also, perhaps, the terms on which they would buy salt from the salt-deposits in Sanhaja territory, the Sanhaja were bound to want to redress the balance.

Initially, however, the Sanhaja were hampered in this aim because they were not a united nation. They were divided into a number of tribes, the most important of which were the Lemtuna and the Goddala, each with its own king and each jealous of its independence. Ghana's conquest of Awdaghost at first increased rather than diminished their divisions, leading to the break-up of a confederacy which had been achieved under a Lemtuna chief. However, the Sanhaja chiefs, and perhaps their people, were now at least nominally Muslims, even if they were still very much involved in the traditional animist rituals of their tribes. As a universal religion, Islam did provide a foundation on which a larger sense of common Sanhaja unity could be developed. When their prosperity, indeed their livelihood as traders, was being menaced not only by Ghana's control of Awdaghost, but also, as it happened, by simultaneous pressures from rival Berber groups on their northern trading depots in Tafilelt, the time was ripe for the exploitation of the sense of brotherhood conferred by Islam.

It was indeed exploited by a revivalist doctrine preached by a Muslim divine from southern Morocco, Ibn Yasin, who had been imported (*c.* 1040) by one of the Goddala chiefs who, having made the pilgrimage to Mecca, had become aware of the imperfections of his and his people's Islam.

Ibn Yasin was initially not very successful with his preaching of a strict adherence to the primitive principles of Islam, and he was forced to withdraw for a time to an island sanctuary situated, in all probability, close to the mouth of the River Senegal. Here he and a handful of converts, who, significantly, included two brothers, Yahia and Abu Bakr ibn 'Umar of the chiefly line of the Lemtuna, established a *ribat*, a combination of a religious seminary and a military training camp. Here a small, but well disciplined and fanatical army of followers, the Almoravids (from *al-murabitun*, 'the people of the *ribat*'), was built up. This eventually succeeded in conquering and uniting the Sanhaja tribesmen, who were then led on campaigns of conquest, conversion and plunder both south and north of the desert.

By and large conquests in Morocco and Spain, where a considerable Almoravid empire was eventually built up, proved more attractive and lucrative than campaigning to the south. But Awdaghost was soon recovered (*c.* 1054), and, ultimately, after a long war, a southern wing of the Almoravids led by Abu Bakr succeeded (*c.* 1076) in conquering Ghana and occupying its capital. The consequences of this were admirably and succinctly expressed by the great Arab Berber historian, Ibn Khaldoun, writing *c.* 1400: 'The kingdom of Ghana declined into utter weakness about the time that the empire of the Almoravids began to become powerful. [The Almoravids] extended their dominion over the Negroes, devastated their territory and pillaged their lands. Having subjected them to the *gizya*,[1] they exacted tribute from them and induced many of them to become converts to Islam. The authority of the kings of Ghana was destroyed, and [their southern neighbours] subjugated the country and reduced its inhabitants to slavery.'

The Almoravid mastery of Ghana lasted only a few years, in effect because, having now no common enemy and each group being anxious to secure as much of the spoils of victory as possible, the tribal sections among the Almoravids were soon quarrelling among themselves. About 1087, Abu Bakr was killed trying to suppress a revolt, and soon afterwards the old Soninke dynasty, though now apparently Muslim, was able to re-establish itself. But its power was greatly reduced. The Almoravid campaigns to north and south had thoroughly disrupted the western Saharan trade route to Tafilelt which was vital to Ghana's economic life. Their plundering and, even more, perhaps, the demands made by their

[1] The poll-tax levied by Muslims on non-Muslim subjects.

herds on the available grazing, had upset the delicate balance between man and nature on which agriculture depended in a region so close to the desert. Wells were neglected; the soil's essential cover of vegetation was denuded. The desert began to spread southwards until ultimately the lands in which Kumbi, the old capital, was situated could support neither towns nor, indeed, any sizeable number of people.

But before this had happened, the ancient kingdom began to break up. Its kings could no longer command the wealth necessary to maintain it, and because of the decline of the trade through it to the north, its subject peoples and its neighbours now had less need of it. About 1200, Sumanguru, the king of the Susu, a southerly Mande-speaking people who had achieved their independence of Ghana, was able to conquer and make tributary what was left of the old kingdom. One consequence of this was that the Muslim traders with North Africa who had previously lived there now withdrew, and established a new trading centre at Walata, about 150 miles north-north-east of Kumbi, where, presumably, they thought they would be freer from Negro interference.

It is possible, indeed, that by this time Kumbi was no longer either a commercial or a political centre of major importance. In the middle of the twelfth century, the famous geographer al-Idrisi wrote that, from about 1116, the capital of the Muslim king of Ghana was situated on the Niger, which was now a principal means of communication for the kingdom. It is uncertain whether this means that, following the conquest from the north and the devastation of their own lands by the Almoravids, the king and government of Ghana had withdrawn to the south, or whether their place as the major centre of political and commercial power in the western Sudan had already been usurped by more southerly Mande. There can be no doubt, however, that, by Sumanguru's time, there was intensive competition to assume the heritage of ancient Ghana among a number of the Mande clans of the upper Niger valley.

Sumanguru seems to have been the son of a Soninke soldier who was possibly an emigrant from Ghana, and he and his Susu followers were soon engaged in bitter fighting with a Mande clan called the Keita. The prize in this struggle was control of the upper Niger, which must now have become an important artery by which trade could bypass Ghana and Walata, and flow to and from North Africa via Timbuctu or Gao and the central trans-Saharan road to the Fezzan. After a long series of reverses, a Keita leader arose, Sundiata, who *c.* 1235 defeated Sumanguru, and, within a few years, had taken his place as the major authority over the Mandinka and Soninke, a sovereign to whom what was left of the old kingdom of Ghana paid tribute.

The empire of Mali

Thus was born the great empire commonly called Mali, though this name and its variants (e.g. *Mallel*, *Mel*, *Melit*) are really foreign forms (Berber and Fulani) of a word which for the southern Mande, the Mandinka of the Niger valley and further south, is *Manding*, and for the northern Mande (the Soninke) is simply *Mande*. It means no more than 'the place where the master, or king, (*mansa*) lives'; hence the centre of political power and, by extension, the lands ruled from it. There is evidence, both in the Arabic sources (as has been seen) and in local tradition, that the great state created by Sundiata and his successors was by no means the first Mande kingdom in the upper Niger valley, all of which can be called 'Mali' (or 'Mallel' etc.). What was new in this empire was its size, and the fact that it had consciously taken upon itself the role of successor to ancient Ghana as the major political and commercial power for the whole western Sudan. Sudanic historians composing *Tarikhs* (chronicles) in Timbuctu in the sixteenth and seventeenth centuries in fact make no distinction between Ghana and Mali; in their eyes, Ghana, like Mali, was a Mande empire (though controlled by northern Mande, Soninke, not by southern Mande, Mandinka), and Mali was simply an enlarged continuation of Ghana under a new dynasty.

This would seem to be good history. Sundiata and his successors took over ancient Ghana's role in developing and controlling the trade between the agricultural and gold-bearing lands of the Negroes and the tribes who controlled the caravan routes across the Sahara to and from North Africa, and in using the resultant wealth to provide a political and military power which could ensure peaceful conditions in which producers and traders could prosper over a wide area of the Sudan. They did this on a larger scale and more efficiently, and so they became richer and more powerful than the kings and government of Ghana. Their political capital may not always have been in the same place, but at the time of the apogee of their state it was almost certainly at Niani, on the River Sankarani, close by its junction with the Niger. This, and other possible later sites of the capital, such as Kangaba, were far from the desert and its potentially dangerous pastoral tribes. They were in the heart of Mande country, in good agricultural land, and adjacent to the alluvial gravels of the rivers of the upper Niger and Senegal—Wangara—which provided gold, and which, unlike the Ghana kings, they directly controlled. The River Niger itself, flowing to the east, gave them good access to the central trans-Saharan trade roads, which, following the Almoravid outburst, now afforded the best route of communication with North Africa, where Ifriqiya (Tunisia) and Egypt, rather than Morocco in the west, were now the most stable and prosperous states. The same river also gave them access to new sources of gold and other trade in more easterly parts of West Africa itself.

Not unnaturally then, although by about the end of the thirteenth century the Mali empire had been extended westwards towards the Atlantic down the Senegal and Gambia rivers, thus encompassing or making tributary Takrur and other western states, its main line of expansion was along the Niger to the east. By about 1300, its rulers had made their power effective as far as Gao, and thus had come to dominate the Songhai boatmen and fishermen who controlled activities on the Niger from just upstream of Timbuctu to as far downstream as Kebbi, on the borders of modern Nigeria. Timbuctu, founded *c.* 1100 as a Tuareg encampment, was developed as a major town for the trans-Saharan trade. Jenne, on the river Bani, emerged about the same time (late thirteenth or early fourteenth century) as the head of a new trade route developed by Mande merchants leading towards the south and south-east, towards the Lobi goldfields on the Black Volta and, beyond these, in what is now the south of the Republic of Ghana, valued supplies of kola-nuts and even richer sources of gold.

The Mali empire was at its peak about the middle of the fourteenth century, when its political power extended beyond Gao towards the borders of Hausaland, which was penetrated by Mande merchants and settlers about the mid-fourteenth century, and both north-east and north-west into the Sahara. Indeed the gates of the empire when approached from the north were the tributary towns of Walata and Takedda, both important Tuareg caravan centres, and the latter also, apparently, valued for its near-by copper mines. A good amount is known of Mali at this time. In 1324–5 *Mansa* Musa made a pilgrimage to Mecca via Cairo on such a magnificent scale as to excite considerable interest in Mali in the world of Islam, and a number of Arabic authors, such as al-Omari, used the opportunity to secure information about it from members of his retinue and other travellers. Then, in 1352–3, one of the greatest travellers of medieval times, Ibn Battuta, a native of Tangier, toured through the whole empire, visiting, among other places, Walata, Niani, Timbuctu, Gao and Takedda, returning home to dictate an entertaining account of what he had seen and learnt.

Clearly the Arab world was impressed by what it knew of Mali at this time. *Mansa* Musa was regarded as a very rich and powerful king. His fame was such that it very quickly extended to western Europe; Mali and a picture of its ruler appear, for example, on a map drawn by Jewish cartographers in Majorca in 1339. He travelled across the Sahara, so it is said, with at least 8,000 retainers, and taking with him so much gold that its value on the Cairo market is reported to have fallen by something like 12 per cent! He is said to have had an army of 100,000 men, including

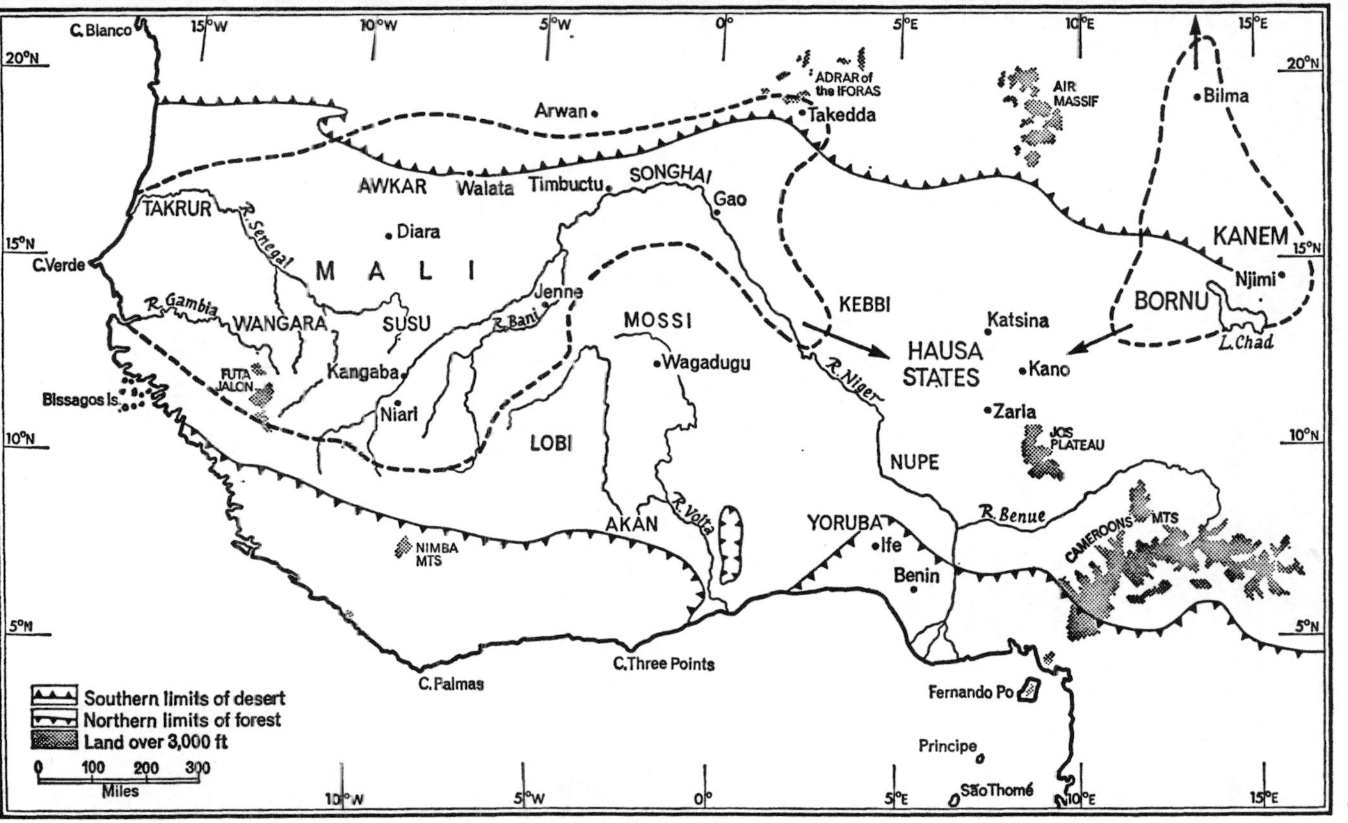

4 Major states in the fourteenth century

10,000 cavalry; he sent embassies to North African kings; there was even a hostel at Cairo for Sudanese students. The emperor, the principal administrators, and the merchants of the empire were all Muslims. (Musa seems not in fact to have been the first emperor to go on the pilgrimage; if his pilgrimage is better remembered, it is only because it was so splendidly and extravagantly conducted.)

Ibn Battuta, whose knowledge of the world was extensive (he had previously travelled throughout the Muslim world and even as far as China), has many good and few bad things to say of the country he saw at first hand. He was impressed by the justice and efficiency of its government, and by the good order it maintained: 'The Negroes are seldom unjust, and have a greater abhorrence of injustice than any other people. Their ruler shows no mercy to anyone who is guilty of the least act of it. There is complete security in their country. Neither traveller nor inhabitant in it has anything to fear from robbers or men of violence.'

Not only were the roads safe for travellers and merchants, but it was always easy for them to find good lodgings for the night without prior arrangement, and to buy food, in exchange for salt, spices or beads, from the many flourishing markets.

The general picture indeed is of a rich, prosperous, peaceful and well-ordered empire, in which effective government and organised communications and trade ran all the way from the Atlantic in the west to the borders of modern Nigeria in the east, and from the fringes of the forests in the south northwards into the desert. Nevertheless, the subsequent history of Mali was less happy. It would seem that its government never wholly solved a central political problem which was apt to perplex any major West African monarchy when it sought to extend its power beyond the central area inhabited by the people who owed a natural allegiance to kings who were descended from their own ancestral leaders.

Problems of West African kingdoms

This problem was, in essence, how to secure a continuity of power at the centre which would remain effective throughout the area, and over all the various peoples, that the monarchy sought to control.

By and large, West African systems of succession to office were not such as to produce only one possible heir to a chieftaincy or kingdom. There were usually a number of qualified heirs within the royal family, including brothers, sons and nephews of the reigning ruler, among whom a choice had to be made when the ruler died. This choice fell to a council of elders of the royal family, or of elders of the principal families within the community, or of ministers of the state, or perhaps to a senior woman of the royal family (a 'queen mother')—or to some combination of these. It was thus easy for there to be disagreement, and consequently civil dissension or strife, until one potential heir and his supporters emerged strong enough to overcome all the others.

So long as the political unit was a small one, the consequences were not too serious. The argument was a family matter, as it were, and ultimately the result would be accepted by the family as a whole or, if not, and the family remained divided on the issue, its different segments would still retain some larger sense of community, of belonging together. But when a particular people, such as the Mandinka of Mali, had created, by conquest and trade, a large kingdom or empire, encompassing many different groups who did not have a natural tradition of belonging together, then the consequences of a succession dispute could be very serious, and might lead to the break-up of the kingdom.

For one thing, the rewards of monarchy were so much greater, and so much more worth competing for in terms of wealth and power, that the rival heirs and their supporting factions might never compose their differences. Men who were totally outside the traditional ruling family and who, as army generals, for example, had some power and following of their own, might take advantage of the divisions in the ruling family to make a bid for the supreme power on their own account. Then too, a succession dispute within the royal family was no longer a purely local affair affecting only the people who owed a traditional allegiance to the king. Subject peoples, who had no such natural allegiance, might use the divisions at the centre to make a bid to regain their independence. Thus local traditional chiefs would cease to send the tributes on which the central monarchy had come to depend for much of its wealth and, therefor, its power. But even worse might happen if the central monarchy had sent its own men to rule its subject peoples. Such viceroys might well be members of the imperial royal family with legitimate claims to the central power, and they might have won enough local support, perhaps by marrying into the chiefly family of the people they had been sent to govern, to give them sufficient strength to rival and challenge the power of the capital.

In course of time, some West African kings learnt how to overcome at least some of these difficulties. They might nominate and train their heirs while they were still reigning. They might employ as their local viceroys, not kinsmen who could challenge for their throne, but commoners or slaves who owed all their power to themselves alone. They would try to curb the tendency of tributary peoples to re-assert their independence by keeping their kings in attendance in some capacity—in effect, as hostages—at their own courts. They might seek to establish administrative bureaucracies and military hierarchies which were entirely dependent on the monarchy, and not influenced in their allegiances by factions within the royal family. In this respect, they might try to make especial use of Islam, as a religion of literacy which demanded a universal allegiance of all believers irrespective of their family or tribal connections. But none of these schemes was successfully enough applied to maintain the integrity of the great empire of Mali. There seem to have been succession disputes even before the time of *Mansa* Musa. After his time (*c.* 1312–37), and especially after the time of his brother Suleiman (*c.* 1341–60), who was the *Mansa* during Ibn Battuta's visit, there were further and more damaging disputes. Two, if not three, of the *Mansas* of the thirteenth and fourteenth centuries are thought to have been usurpers from outside the immediate royal family, and one of these was from the provinces. The *Mansas* apparently were reluctant to use their Muslim religion as a new cement of empire because, as al-Omari (*c.* 1340) indicates, they thought that by so doing they might lose the traditional allegiance of the pagan gold-miners and farmers on whom the empire was dependent for its wealth. By the beginning of the fifteenth century, the central power was clearly weak and the empire was collapsing. The western provinces along the Senegal valley were lost; the Tuareg regained control of Walata and other desert towns, and even took Timbuctu; Mossi cavaliers began to raid from the south deep into the heart of the empire.

The Songhai empire of Gao

But the blow which proved fatal to the continued existence of the great Mali empire was the re-assertion of their independence by the Songhai of the Niger bend and middle Niger, for Mali was utterly dependent on the Songhai boatmen for its vital line of communication along the Niger beyond Jenne to the all-important trans-Saharan trade routes and to Hausaland.

The Songhai, with their long tradition of independent monarchy, seem always to be been restive under Mande hegemony. There is no real agreement as to exactly when they broke away and re-asserted their independence, probably because they did so, or tried to do so, whenever the central power in Mali was weak and divided. Eventually, however, a new Songhai royal family was established from the descendants of two brothers who had been employed at the Mali court, and about 1464 there succeeded to power a king, Sonni Ali, who was able to combine a knowledge of the Mande system of empire with the determined support of his largely animist Songhai people in a remarkably successful bid to destroy the remains of Mande power, and to establish in its place a Songhai empire.

Throughout his reign, Sonni Ali was almost continuously in the field, campaigning not only against the Mande, but also against all the other peoples who were seeking to profit from the disintegration of their empire, the Tuareg, the Mossi, the Fulani, indeed against any group that stood in his way. The result was that by the time of his death in 1492, the Mali emperors had been reduced to their original status of petty Mande kings in the upper Niger valley. Sonni Ali, having built up a large and invincible army largely from among the various groups he had defeated in battle, had gained firm control of the commercial heartland of the old empire, Songhai power being established in the three major cities of the trading network of the western Sudan, in Timbuctu and Jenne as well as in his own capital of Gao.

As a result of his ceaseless campaigning, the ruthless way in which he crushed all opposition to his ambition, and the animist Songhai basis of his power, Sonni Ali incurred the enmity—as well as the respect—of the important class of, largely Mande, merchants which had flourished under the Mali empire, and who formed wealthy, cultured and educated Muslim communities in the major cities. In the *Tarikhs* written by their scholars, Sonni Ali is depicted as a ruthless, power-hungry tyrant. In so doing, they stress the Songhai and animist element in his regime, and underestimate the extent to which in effect he was rebuilding the old decaying Mali empire under a new and more effective management. After his death, for a brief year, the new empire was ruled by Sonni Ali's Songhai son, Baro. But then the old tradition of a universal Mande order was reasserted by one of his generals, himself a Mande, indeed a Soninke, Muhammad Toure. In 1493 Muhammad used the largely non-Songhai army to defeat Baro, and to chase Sonni Ali's family down the Niger to Dendi, the Songhai homeland before their possession of Gao, establishing in its place a new dynasty, that of the Askias.

In both the military and geographical senses *Askia* Muhammad completed Sonni Ali's work by campaigns that caused the Mossi finally to withdraw into the upper Volta basin; re-established Negro power over the Tuareg of Takedda and Aïr in the desert, and ultimately took it to assert suzerainty even over the salt deposits of Taghaza which were so important to the Saharan traders; made tributary the western Hausa states; and extended the empire of Gao in the far west over the lands beyond Walata and north of the remnant Mali kingdom of Kangaba, though not as far as ancient Takrur and the Atlantic coastlands. But *Askia* Muhammad was successor not only to the military expansiveness of Sonni Ali, but also to that concept of a universal, peace-loving, Muslim, but Mande-centred empire, able to rank with any other Islamic state, that had been symbolised in *Mansa* Musa's great pilgrimage, a pilgrimage that he himself emulated in great and rival splendour in 1495–7. And when, in 1528, when he was old and blind, he was deposed by his sons, he left to them and their successors an uneasy inheritance.

In overthrowing Sonni Ali's son, Muhammad had encouraged the universally minded Muslim and Mande culture of the great western Sudanic trading cities to re-assert itself. Thereafter the directing hands of the Songhai empire—governors, administrators, generals, traders, divines, scholars, even the Askias themselves, were Mande or Mande-influenced people. Not unnaturally this built up a counter-reaction—perhaps first evident in Muhammad's own overthrow—among the animist Songhai who had first broken the old Mali empire and now, though still controlling the vital river route, felt cheated of the spoils of their victory. During the next sixty years, there were no less than eight occupants of the Askias' throne, and there was a continual series of succession crises, revolts and usurpations among Muhammad Toure's sons, nephews and grandsons. It is evident that in each crisis each candidate (or the contender for the throne on the one hand, and its occupant on the other) would seek the support of one of two sections into which the state was becoming increasingly divided: the party of the merchants and Muslims, mainly Mande but universal in its outlook, and widely spread throughout the cities and towns of the empire; and the ethnocentric party of the animist Songhai, who were concentrated in the country on either side of the great bend of the Niger in the heart of the empire.

The Moroccan invasion and its consequences

Which group might ultimately have gained the day in the Songhai state, it is impossible to say, because in 1591 its weakness and divisions were one of the factors which occasioned the sending against it across the Sahara of an expeditionary force of some 4,000 soldiers from Morocco. It was undoubtedly these weaknesses and divisions, more than the firearms and the discipline—learnt in Mediterranean wars with Turks and Spaniards—of this tiny army which enabled it to defeat many times its number of the Askia's cavalry and bowmen at the great battle at Tondibi (just north of Gao) which marked the effective end of the great Songhai empire.

The other, and more important, reason for the Moroccan invasion was, paradoxically, a consequence of the early strength of the Songhai empire, which had led it to extend its power to salt deposits across the Sahara at Taghaza and Taodeni, almost on the Moroccan frontier. This action, like Ghana's taking of Awdaghost five centuries earlier, had upset the commercial balance of the trans-Saharan trade in such a way as to make reprisals from the north practically inevitable. Both the Moroccan merchants and the Saharan tribes who conducted the trans-Saharan trade were bound to lose from a situation in which the Negro power which controlled the gold exports from West Africa also controlled the sources of supply of the salt so much needed in the Sudan. The Moroccan kingdom had made a

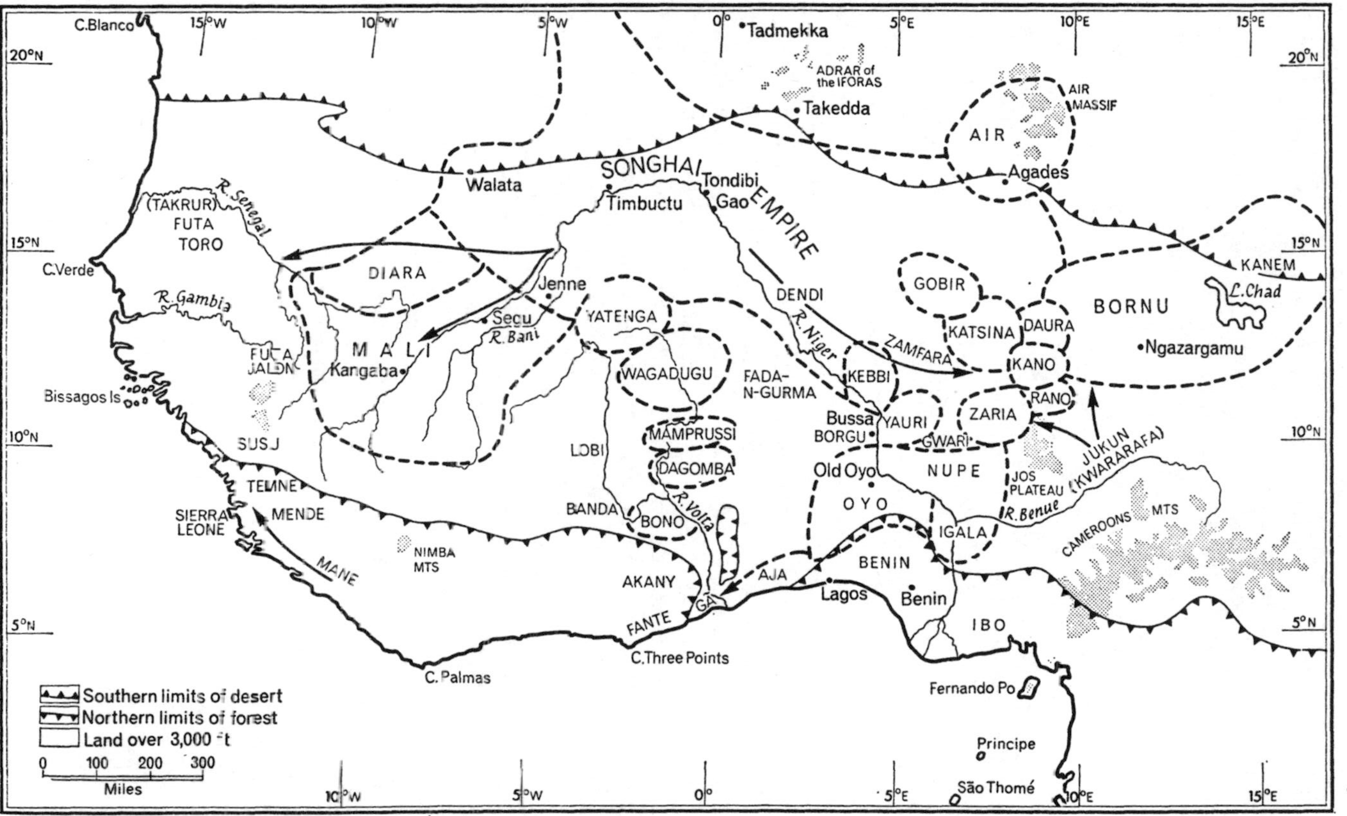

5 Major states in the sixteenth century

number of attempts to regain possession of Taghaza and Taodeni before finally, in 1590–1, launching its blow at the very centres of power and trade in the Songhai empire.

The king of Morocco's attempt to conquer the Songhai empire did not, however, meet with the approval of the merchants of his country, who could see that Moroccan possession of the trading cities of the western Sudan would be no more in the interests of their trans-Saharan trade than Songhai's possession of Taghaza or Ghana's possession of Awdaghost. They were right. The Moroccan expeditionary force, together with the reinforcements it received up to 1618, when the Moroccan government finally abandoned its adventure in the Sudan, proved strong enough to occupy Gao and Timbuctu and, ultimately, Jenne, the three principal commercial cities. But it was not strong enough to destroy the Songhai kings, who simply retreated into Dendi, the Songhai homeland, where, in more wooded country, they could ambush and beat back pursuing Moroccan forces. Nor, and more importantly, were the Moroccans strong or numerous enough to extend their power to the lands where the gold they sought was actually produced, nor to maintain and to police the trade roads which led to them through the territories of animist tribes. Thus though the Moroccan soldiers lingered on in the three cities and, through their marriages with local women, gave them a new ruling caste, the *Arma*, trade ceased to flow into Jenne, Timbuctu, and Gao in the old way, and the trans-Saharan trade from the two last which might have reached Morocco began to decay. Worse than this, the structures and habits of orderly government, which had been increasingly spread over the whole western Sudan from Ghana, Mali and Gao in turn, and which were so essential for the production and passage of trade goods, both within the Sudan itself, and to feed the more westerly trans-Saharan trade, were now broken up. Where formerly one government had dominated the whole scene, now there were several competing rivals: the *Arma* themselves, increasingly weak and divided; the remnant Songhai kingdom in Dendi; and the remnant Mande state on the upper Niger, which in the later seventeenth century began to revive and expand again as the Bambara[1] kingdom of Segu under kings of the Kululabi family. Segu, the most powerful of these states, was strong enough in the eighteenth century to seek to control Jenne and Timbuctu, but it had troubles of its own, which led to the formation of a rival Bambara kingdom, Kaarta, on its northern boundary. But none of the states was sufficiently strong and extensive to check incessant raiding into and through the Sudan from the Tuareg tribes of the Sahara, who often occupied or levied tribute on Timbuctu and Gao, or from Fulani spreading westwards through and from Macina.

[1] See chapter 10, p. 147, for the significance of this name.

The peaceful development of agriculture, industry and trade in the western Sudan thus suffered a considerable set-back from the Moroccan invasion and its consequences. The centres of economic and political power, which had already, with the rise of the Mali and the Songhai empires, moved eastwards from the area of ancient Ghana, shifted eastwards yet again, to the kingdoms of Kanem–Bornu and to Hausaland.

The kingdom of Kanem–Bornu and the Hausa states

The origins of the Sefawa kingdom, established first in Kanem, to the north of Lake Chad, and then in Bornu, to the south of it, and of the group of small monarchies of the Hausa, between Kanem–Bornu and the Niger, seem to lie, as suggested in chapter 1, in the infiltration of Saharan pastoralists into the lands occupied by Negro agriculturalists who were heirs to the Neolithic Revolution which had given rise to the Nok culture. The evidence of tradition suggests a number of waves of such infiltration, from the Zaghawa and similar peoples, extending over many centuries, but perhaps reaching a decisive peak between about the seventh and the ninth centuries. The consequences were somewhat different from those of the roughly contemporary interaction between Negroes and Saharan pastoralists further west.

In the first place, although the Hausa are today certainly regarded as a West African Negro people, the Hausa language is not a West African Negro language; it unquestionably belongs to the 'Hamitic' family of languages. This suggests that the degree of outside infiltration here must in some way have been much greater than further west, greater in length of time, greater numerically, or greater in cultural strength. In Kanem, the traditions of the Sefawa kings clearly recall a period of some centuries when, although they and their nobles were living among, and increasingly coming to dominate, local Negroes, they were retaining the purity of their royal line by choosing their wives from among the aristocracy of the Saharan nomads to the north of them. The first king to be regarded as a black man, Silim, did not reign until the early thirteenth century. Neither the ruling language of Kanem, Kanembu, nor the later dominant language of Bornu, Kanuri, is classed with the West African, Sudanic Negro languages. They are placed in a language family which Professor Greenberg calls 'Nilo-Saharan'. This is definitely not 'Hamitic', and, in so far as its speakers can be described in general ethnic and historical terms, they might be said to be the dark-skinned peoples who, inhabiting the Sahara and its fringes from north of Lake Chad to Nubia and the Nile valley, lived in lands where, for lack of rainfall, it was difficult to complete the Neolithic Revolution by developing agriculture, and where therefore pastoralism remained the dominant mode of life.

But like the 'Hamitic' pastoralists further west, the 'Nilo-Saharans' tended to drift south into lands where agriculture was possible, and to mix with their inhabitants. Around Lake Chad, the result was, first, the Kanembu of Kanem and, secondly, with a larger proportion of local people, the Kanuri of Bornu. This southwards movement was not restricted to the Chad region. It operated also in East Africa, with the Nilotic invasions of Bantu territory, and it had wider consequences also in West Africa, where the Songhai language is thought to belong to the 'Nilo-Saharan' family, and where too (as will be seen in chapter 3) there were repercussions almost throughout the area of modern Nigeria.

The picture for both Hausa and Kanem–Bornu seems to be of the pastoralists ('Hamites' in the Hausa case, 'Nilo-Saharans' for Kanem–Bornu) gradually settling down with small groups of Negro agriculturalists, whom they gradually converted into subjects, on the southern edges of the Sahara, close to Aïr and in northern Kanem. Here in the course of time, small territorial kingdoms developed which were larger than the political units, villages or walled towns, of the indigenous Negroes. As they became more firmly established, so these kingdoms themselves drifted southwards, so that their populations, and ultimately their rulers also, became more and more Negro, and more and more based on an agricultural and urban way of life. This was a process which by and large was carried further in Hausaland than in Kanem and Bornu which, as will be seen, seem to have been more subject to continuing incursions of pastoralists from the desert. In neither case were the economic motives encouraging imperial expansion as evident as they were further west, in ancient Ghana or Mali. The new kingdoms were on the small side, especially among the Hausa, who do not seem to have been much affected by trans-Saharan trade before about the fifteenth century. The Kanem–Bornu kingdom did to some extent feel the influence of the caravan route from the Fezzan and Ifriqiya, but its tendency to respond by expansion in this direction was apt to be interrupted by periods of weakness associated with internal dissensions and with new incursions of desert pastoralists. The internal history of Kanem–Bornu and of the Hausa states is thus less important for the history of West Africa as a whole than that of Ghana, Mali and Songhai.

The Sefawa *Mais* (kings) were converted to Islam about the end of the eleventh century, soon after their monarchy had been firmly established in Kanem, when, in consequence, it could begin to offer some attraction and security to Muslim traders and travellers from the Fezzan and Ifriqiya. By the thirteenth century, the kingdom extended northwards to the oases of Bilma and Djado and further, towards the southern Fezzan, and it had established good relations with both Ifriqiya and

Egypt. To the south, however, it did not extend beyond the southern shore of Lake Chad.

There followed a period of increasing chaos, in which the royal family split into rival and often warring factions, and the kingdom was subject to growing pressure from invasions by the Bulala, pastoralists from the desert not unlike the Zaghawa or the earliest Kanembu themselves. Ultimately the Sefawa kings rescued themselves from this situation by virtually abandoning Kanem, and re-establishing their government in Bornu, where the Kanuri people and language were emerging from mixing between the Kanembu and the local Negroes. In the sixteenth century, they were strong enough to reconquer Kanem and make the Bulala tributary. Consequently, relations with North Africa, now (except for Morocco) under the Ottoman Turks, could be stabilised. Since Bornu was now a strong and stable state, these proved much more beneficial for it than did Songhai's contemporary relations with Morocco. *Mai* Idris Alawma (*c.* 1575–*c.* 1610) was able to secure firearms and military instructors from the Turks, then at the peak of their military career. Rather like the monarchs who were his contemporaries in western Europe, he thus became infinitely more powerful than all potential rivals, and he used his power not only to bring Hausa and other peoples to the west and south of Bornu under his protection, but also to establish in Bornu itself the foundations for the first manifestly Muslim state in West Africa, in which the Islamic administration and law emanating from the court began to cut through the traditional jurisdictions of tribe, clan and family, to touch their members as individual citizens.

Bornu remained a strong kingdom throughout most of the seventeenth century. But by its close, and in the eighteenth century, its kings and ministers—like some other oriental potentates in history—had become more and more involved in the intricacies of their rich life at court, and were becoming less and less effective in governing the state and in defending it against invaders, particularly the Kwararafa from the south and the Tuareg from the north. Thus when, after the Moroccan conquest of Songhai, the commercial system of the western Sudan began to decay, it was the small Hausa states between Bornu and the Niger, rather than the larger, but increasingly effete, Sefawa kingdom, which were able to gain the most advantage from the eastwards shift in the trans-Saharan trade routes.

Traditionally there are supposed to have been seven original Hausa kings, who shared a common ancestry, each ruling a small state around the walled city which was his capital. However, one of the original seven kingdoms, Rano, seems never to have been of much account, being overshadowed by nearby Kano. Two others, Daura and Biram, are important mainly for their role at the beginning of Hausa history, for their monarchies are regarded as the earliest, from which the other royal lines were descended. Daura survived into modern times in north-eastern Hausaland, but Biram, further east, was eventually absorbed in western Bornu.

By the time that Hausaland had become reasonably well known to the outside world, for example in Leo Africanus's *Description of Africa* (1526), the important states were Gobir, Katsina, Kano and Zaria. Of these Gobir, fronting the desert in the north, was the least advanced, while the others, and especially Katsina and Kano, had received a great stimulus from the arrival in their land, from the fourteenth century onwards, during the time of Mali's ascendancy in the west, of Mande merchants and settlers (known as 'Wangarawa' by the Hausa) and of the Islam that they brought with them. Quite possibly it was the experience and example of these Mande that turned the early city-states of Katsina and Kano, and of Zaria further south, into kingdoms which, though still somewhat small in territory, were to be of major historical importance. Islam clearly played its role here—even if the bulk of the people remained essentially animist, and if its main value was simply to provide a universal tradition to which kings and traders who now had important contacts with a wider world could usefully belong. However the introduction of the Hausa to international trade had quite remarkable results. Their new access to markets stimulated a great development of their agriculture, and of industries like weaving, leather manufacture, and metal working. By the seventeenth century at least, Hausa merchants were developing trade routes of their own to the south and south-west which, in the region of modern Ghana, competed effectively with those developed by the Mande.

Thus although the Hausa kingdoms themselves remained rather small states, often challenging each other, politically subject to domination by Mali and Songhai, in the west, and by Bornu, in the east, and apt to be threatened by attacks from people like the Kwararafa, they began to develop a considerable influence through the increasing activity of their traders and settlers, and the consequent spread of their language and culture. Together with the spread of more political influences from Bornu and Songhai, these factors occasioned the emergence of a number of so-called 'illegitimate' Hausa states, the *Banza Bakwoi* as opposed to the true *Hausa Bakwoi*. Kebbi, Zamfara, Gwari and Yauri, all to the west or south-west in an area of mixed Hausa and Songhai influence, are accounted among the *Banza Bakwoi*, as also—more doubtfully, for reasons which will become apparent in chapter 3—are Kwararafa, Nupe and the Yoruba states.

3

Wider consequences of the growth of empire and trade in the Sudan

In this chapter it is proposed to outline some of the wider effects of the growth of major kingdoms and centres of trade in the western and central Sudan from about the tenth century onwards. It is appropriate to begin with some of the more immediate effects of the emergence of the states of ancient Ghana and Mali. However, one of these, the emergence and dispersion of the Fulani people, was to have very wide consequences indeed.

The emergence and dispersion of the Fulani

There has been much speculation about the origins of the people known in English as the Fulani. (This is in fact a variant of the Hausa name for them. They call themselves Fulbe, the singular of which is Pulo—from which derives the name Peuls, by which they are usually referred to in the French literature.) This speculation arises for three principal reasons. First, the Fulani are by and large lighter-skinned than the generality of the West African Negroes, and even when, as is sometimes the case, they are very black, their physique still tends to set them apart from other West Africans. They are taller, and they tend to be long-headed whereas other West Africans are broad-headed. Secondly, they are the only West African people to have pastoralism as their fundamental way of living. Thirdly, although they and their long-horned Zebu cattle are dispersed throughout the savanna zone, the Fulani have tended to keep socially as well as politically separate from other West African peoples.

These characteristics have naturally led many commentators to conclude that the Fulani do not spring from a West African Negro stock, and to suppose that they must originally have been an immigrant 'Nilo-Saharan' or even 'Hamitic' people. Such a theory would certainly account for their distinctive physique, and for their pastoralism and their possession of Zebu cattle (which they almost certainly must have been responsible for introducing into West Africa). Yet it has long been recognised that their language is a West African Negro language, belonging to the particular group of languages spoken in the far west close to the sea, the 'West Atlantic' group, by people like the Wolof and Serer. It is apparently most closely related to one of the Serer dialects.

It is not yet possible (and may never be possible) for historians to solve the problem of the origins of the Fulani, because there is virtually no historical record of them before about the fourteenth century, when their ethnic, linguistic and cultural identities were already established. But it seems highly probable that the formation of these is to be associated with the emergence and development of the Soninke kingdom of Ghana, and that their subsequent expansion throughout the savanna is connected with the rise of Mali. About, let us say, the seventh century A.D., the ancestors of the present-day Fulani were probably pastoralists living with agricultural Soninke, and possibly also with Wolof and Serer, in the region of Aukar or Hodh. The establishment of the Soninke kingdom, with its emphasis on agriculture, would have thrust the pastoralists outwards, and the rise of the Almoravids must have tended to push them to the south. Considerable numbers of Fulani seem, in fact, to have entered the kingdom of Takrur. By about the beginning of the tenth century, the kings of Takrur were what we should now call Fulani (though in fact the term Tukolor, meaning 'the people of Takrur', is in modern usage sometimes difficult to distinguish from Fulani—'Fulani' in the Senegal being generally known as 'Tukolor'). By this time, whatever their original language, they must have been speaking their present West Atlantic language, akin to the languages of their Serer, Wolof and Tukolor neighbours. About the end of the tenth century, when Takrur became Muslim, the ruling Fulani group was expelled. It settled in lands to the south-east, on the Futa Jalon uplands (which the Fulani still dominate), and also in lands to the east which were predominantly inhabited by Mande-speaking peoples.

The subsequent rise to power of the Mali state seems to have provided both political and economic causes for the further dispersion of the Fulani. They must have been unassimilable from the political point of view, so that there were strong reasons why the Mali kings would seek to move large concentrations of Fulani away from their homeland. At the same time, however, with the growth of trading cities eastwards across the Sudan, there must have been a growing demand for milk, hides and meat, and so growing markets for the Fulani herds, and an incentive for the Fulani themselves to move eastwards. And move eastwards they did, throughout the grasslands between about 5 inches of annual rainfall in the north, and 30 inches and the northern limits of the tse-tse fly in the south. By the fifteenth century, they were settled in great numbers in Macina and had begun to appear in Hausaland, where further great concentrations developed. By the sixteenth century they were in Bornu, and by the eighteenth century considerable numbers were settling as far east as Adamawa in northern Cameroon.

The migrating Fulani for the most part infiltrated between the villages and towns of agricultural Negro society, and remained distinct from it, dealing with its kings and chiefs only through their own virtually independent leaders or 'guides', the *ardos*. In some areas, however, notably in Futa Jalon and in Macina, they became numerically dominant. By the eighteenth century they had established kingdoms of their own, possessed of cavalry which, in the general disorder following the Moroccan invasion, allowed them to raid their neighbours with impunity.

Some individuals were attracted into the towns, where they became Muslims, even scholars and divines, particularly after the decline of Mande scholarship which was in evidence, especially in Hausaland, by the eighteenth century. For the most part, however, the Fulani remained traditionally animist until the close of the eighteenth century. But then, stemming in part from the ancient tradition of Takrur and in part from the introduction into West Africa of Muslim brotherhoods like the Qadiriyya and Tijaniyya, there was a remarkable flourishing of Islamic thought and energy in the far west, especially in Futa Toro (ancient Takrur) and Futa Jalon. Since this was the homeland of the Fulani of the dispersion, with which they still maintained family ties, the fact of this dispersion provided a conductor along which a great movement for Islamic conversion and revolution was able to spread with remarkable speed and with most far-reaching effects.

Developments on the fringes of the Mali empire

The expansion of the empire of Mali, and also, at the same time, of the Fulani, had the effect of thrusting a number of peoples southwards and westwards from the upper Niger valley and Futa Jalon into lands inhabited by peoples speaking 'West Atlantic' languages. In the coastlands north of the Gambia, the Wolof and Serer remained dominant. But from the Gambia southwards, the area of many rivers, creeks and off-shore islands which extends to as far as modern Liberia, was one of considerable ethnic and linguistic complexity. In among the many small 'West Atlantic' groups—such as the Dyola, the Pepel, the Bulom—who, though they possessed advanced agricultural societies, did not develop political institutions beyond the village level, there pressed refugees from the Sudan and Futa Jalon, and groups of Mande conquerors. Also the region as a whole began to be penetrated by Mande-speaking traders, who were probably attracted to it in the first place by the idea of trading with the coastal peoples for sea salt.

A major immigrant group of refugees were the Susu who, after the defeat of Sumanguru by Sundiata, and the growth of Fulani dominance in Futa Jalon, began to settle close by the coast to the north of Sierra Leone. This became one of two major wedges driven into 'West Atlantic' lands by Mande-speaking peoples, the other resulting from direct commercial and political expansion from Mali along the line of the Gambia. But with the growth of Mande power, almost the whole area became tributary to the Mali emperors, who organised it into provinces under dignitaries called *Farims*. The major exceptions were the immediate coastlands south of the Gambia, in which Mande interests remained essentially commercial, and Futa Jalon, where the Fulani were independent of Mali by the fifteenth century, subsequently extending their power into Futa Toro. With the decay of Mali power, the *Farims*, though maintaining a nominal concept of the suzerainty of the Mande *Mansa*, became virtually autonomous petty kings.

In the first half of the sixteenth century, the situation was further complicated by the invasion of what is now Liberia and Sierra Leone from the east by a group of conquerors called the Mane. In origin the Mane seem to have been Mande soldiers. It would seem that the rise of Songhai power under Sonni Ali must have acted in some way to cut off a sizeable group of such soldiers from their homeland, and that they then conceived the remarkable project of returning to Mande territory by a great march southwards to the coast, which they then followed westwards. According to their own tradition, they reached the sea close by a Portuguese fort. This could only have been one of the forts on the Gold Coast (the coast of modern Ghana) built by the Portuguese from 1482 onwards (see chapter 4), though this is almost incredible, especially since there is no confirmation of it either from Portuguese records or from the traditions of the peoples of modern Ghana. On the other hand, however, Portuguese documents do attest the presence of Mande *traders* on the Gold Coast by *c.* 1500.

However, there is no question that, by about *c.* 1545, the Mane had passed through what is now Liberia and were crossing the modern eastern border of Sierra Leone. They proceeded by isolating and overcoming in turn each local people they came across. They would take some of the conquered people into their own army, either directly, or as auxiliaries called *Sumbas*. Some of the Mane would stay behind in the conquered area and create a new political organisation, and ultimately, perhaps, depending on how many of them there were, a new society of mixed Mane and local origins. Other Mane, increasingly diluted with non-Mande recruits, would press on and repeat the process further west.

The results of this remarkable wave of conquest were very varied. They would seem to include the modern Kru people of Liberia, who retained their original 'Kwa' language; the modern Mende of Sierra Leone,

Mande-speaking, and presumably predominantly Mane in origin; the Loko, Sierra Leoneans of predominantly local stock who adopted a Mande language; and the Temne, who took Mane chiefs but largely retained their local 'West Atlantic' culture. On the political plane, the Mane created four new Mande-type kingdoms in Sierra Leone, the kingdoms of Bullom, Loko, Boure (or Sierra Leone) and Sherbro, in which Mane kings ruled over the local peoples, who were collectively known as Sapes.

Mande trade and its political consequences

West and south-west of the centres of Mande power in the empire of Mali, the expansion of Mande trade was accompanied, as we have just seen, by conquests, considerable population movements, and settlement. To the south-east and east, however, the major influence of Mali outside its political frontiers was essentially commercial. The only new settlement was that of small groups of traders who went to live with the peoples with whom they were trading, and who, by and large, acknowledged the rulers and the laws of these peoples. But the expansion of Mande traders from about the thirteenth century onwards often had important political as well as economic consequences, and the lines of their expansion to the east and south-east seem to have been determined to some extent by the existence of what were probably very much earlier colonies of agriculturalists speaking variant languages of the Mande group.

A line of such colonies of Mande-speaking peoples stretches eastwards from the region about Jenne, through the lands of the inhabitants of the Volta basin who speak 'Gur' languages, to the western borders of Hausa country about Bussa. These doubtless provided a means of support for the Mande traders and propagators of Islam who contributed so much to the development of the Hausa states, Katsina and Kano in particular.

Another line of settlements of Mande-speaking peoples reaches south-south-east from Jenne towards the Akan peoples, the peoples speaking languages of the 'Kwa' language group who inhabit the larger part of modern Ghana south of the 'Gur'-speakers of its northern territories. It was doubtless through these settlements that Mande traders came to learn of the gold resources possessed by the Lobi of the Black Volta and, beyond them, of the greater gold wealth and of the kolas available further south in what we now call Ashanti and Gonja. Jenne, which, unlike Niani, Timbuctu and Gao, the other major towns of the Mali empire, lies not on or very close to the great highway of the Niger, but on its southern tributary, the Bani, seems to have been developed from about the twelfth century particularly as a base for trade towards Lobi and Ashanti. The

Mande merchants who developed this trade were Dyula, Islamised Mande akin to the Soninke.

The Dyula began to establish merchant quarters, or even separate townships, alongside the villages or towns inhabited by the principal pagan chiefs, rather in the same way, perhaps, as the early North African merchants had built their town adjacent to the pagan capital of ancient Ghana. By about the beginning of the fourteenth century, their coming, and the opportunities for trade they brought with them, were having important effects on the Akan peoples just north of the forest in modern Ghana. The kingdom of Banda had emerged, with its twin-city capital of Begho guarding a gap in the Banda hills through which the trade route ran to the southern gold-fields. A little to the south and east, another Akan state, Bono, with its capital at Bono-Mansu (near modern Techiman), was becoming even more rich and powerful through its control of the trade paths leading north from the gold diggings in the forest.

The forest itself is likely to have been only thinly peopled before this time. The Portuguese author, Pacheco Pereira, writing at the beginning of the sixteenth century when his countrymen were in contact with Mali and also settled on the Gold Coast itself, records a story that suggests that the Dyula, or their fellow traders of Banda and Bono, may have originally dealt with the forest goldminers by dumb barter. But increasing knowledge of the forest's wealth in gold must have made it less unattractive to the Akan peoples of its northern fringes, and have stimulated their expansion to the south. Initially their movement seems to have followed the northern edge of the forest as it slopes south-eastwards to the gap through which the Volta reaches the sea, so that the first organised Akan communities in the south may have been those on the coast. But the arrival of the south-east Asian foodcrops would have made the forest itself a less difficult environment. By about 1500, there were clearly important centres of Akan culture and statedom around the gold-rich valley of the River Ofin, centres which the early European traders on the coast were to know as Akany and Twifu.

These are significant names for, just as Akan is today the generic name for the dominant peoples of southern Ghana, so Twi is the name for the dominant dialect of their language. The royal families of many of the major Akan states of modern times trace their ancestry back to Twifu and Akany, and these early homes of Akan political organisation, trade and industry clearly derive in their turn from earlier developments in Bono and Banda which were sparked off by the arrival of the Dyula traders from Mande.

Political reflections from Kanem–Bornu and Hausaland

However, the commercial influence stemming from Mandeland was not the sole major force of change reaching from the Sudan towards the Gold Coast. The state-forming processes in the north-east which resulted in the emergence of the Sefawa monarchy in Kanem and Bornu, and in the Hausa kingdoms, seem to have set in train a series of repercussions which also reached as far as modern Ghana. The evidence for these is sketchy, consisting mainly of legends and traditions of origin among the ruling families of peoples living as far to the west as the Gã and the Dagomba and Mamprussi (in the south-east and north-east of modern Ghana respectively), to the effect that their ancestors came from the east or north-east. One of these legends, the story of Kisra, has already been mentioned in chapter 1. Sometimes these stories are presented in terms which lead us to suppose that whole peoples (for example, the Gã and the Adangme of the Accra plains) settled their present country from the east. In other cases (specifically, for example, in Dagomba), the stories clearly relate to the coming of small groups of military conquerors, who created kingdoms by bringing the small village and kinship groupings of earlier inhabitants under one single government.

In general, what seems to have happened is that groups of the conquerors who established monarchies among the Kanembu, Kanuri and Hausa, and who, in due course, lost their original identities in these peoples, pressed on to repeat the process of state formation further afield. In terms of contemporary ethnic geography, the first result was the emergence of kingdoms like that of the Jukun (or Kwararafa) on the middle Benue; Nupe, close by the Benue–Niger confluence; and the kingdoms of Borgu and Bussa to the north-west of Nupe. From the bases established in these kingdoms, local adventurers seem to have sallied out to repeat the process of state formation even further afield.

East of Borgu and Bussa, groups of horsed invaders entered the lands of the Gur-speaking peoples south of the Niger bend, and so (as has been seen in chapter 2) provided the basis for the Mossi raids on the rich commercial cities of the declining Mali empire. By the beginning of the fifteenth century, the re-establishment of Sudanic military strength in the Songhai empire under Sonni Ali and *Askia* Muhammad had finally repelled the raids of the Mossi. They and their more southerly kinsmen, the ancestors of the present day Dagomba and Mamprussi, settled down as the aristocracy which ruled and received tribute from the Gur-speaking natives in a number of kingdoms. Like the Norman conquerors of Normandy and of Anglo–Saxon England, the newcomers married more and more with the local people, and eventually found it most convenient to adopt their languages in place of their own.

Further south still, other invading horsemen from Borgu and Nupe must have pressed into Yorubaland in a number of waves, establishing walled cities, like those which lay at the centres of the Hausa states, from which they gradually established dominion over the local inhabitants. These, like the Hausa, were heirs to the rich Nok culture, and the Yoruba cities soon became flourishing centres of industry, in which craftsmen working in stone, terracotta[1] and metal, especially brass or bronze, were producing marvellous works of art for the palaces and religious cults of the kings. Thus arose the Yoruba civilisation traditionally associated in its earliest stages with the city of Ife, which has produced some of the finest sculpture in brass and terracotta in Africa—or, indeed, in the world. Associated with the Yoruba kingdoms was the Igala kingdom immediately to the east, and possibly more directly influenced from Nupe, its immediate neighbour to the north; and, to the south-east, the kingdom of Benin. The traditions of the arrival from Ife of the modern Benin dynasty, and, a little later, of the techniques of brass-casting, are thought to relate to the period around 1300. This suggests that the first Yoruba kingdoms may have been established by about the twelfth century or even earlier.

West and south-west of modern Yorubaland are the lands of other peoples speaking languages of the 'Kwa' group, such as the Egba, Egbado and Nago, and, beyond them the Egun, Aja, Ewe, Adangme and Gã. It was doubtless the ancestors of peoples like these who were formed into the modern Yoruba people by the founders of cities like Ife. The emergence of the modern Yoruba states, and the establishment of colonies of Yoruba west of Yorubaland proper, in northern Dahomey and Togo, seems to have set in train a series of repercussions which eventually reached as far as the Gã of the Accra plains. There may, indeed, have been along the coastlands a general westwards drift of people—of refugees from the Yoruba conquest, of Yoruba or Yoruba-style conquerors, or of varying mixtures of both—which has resulted in the somewhat confusing present-day pattern of peoples and languages along this coast. Support for this hypothesis comes from the existence of a series of now abandoned earthworks along a line running parallel to the coast from Ketu, in westernmost Yorubaland, to Tado on the River Mono and Nuatsi (Nuatje) in Togo. Some Gã, Adangme and Ewe traditions remember this as a line of emigration from the east, while Tado is recalled as a dispersion centre for the Aja of southern Dahomey, and Nuatsi for the Ewe of southern Togo and south-eastern Ghana. Over the centuries, there has certainly been much mixing of peoples in this area. Thus, for example, the Gã have both incorporated earlier inhabitants of the Accra plains, such as the Kpesi, who

[1] Terracotta (literally, 'baked earth') is a hard kind of unglazed pottery used to make ornaments or statuary.

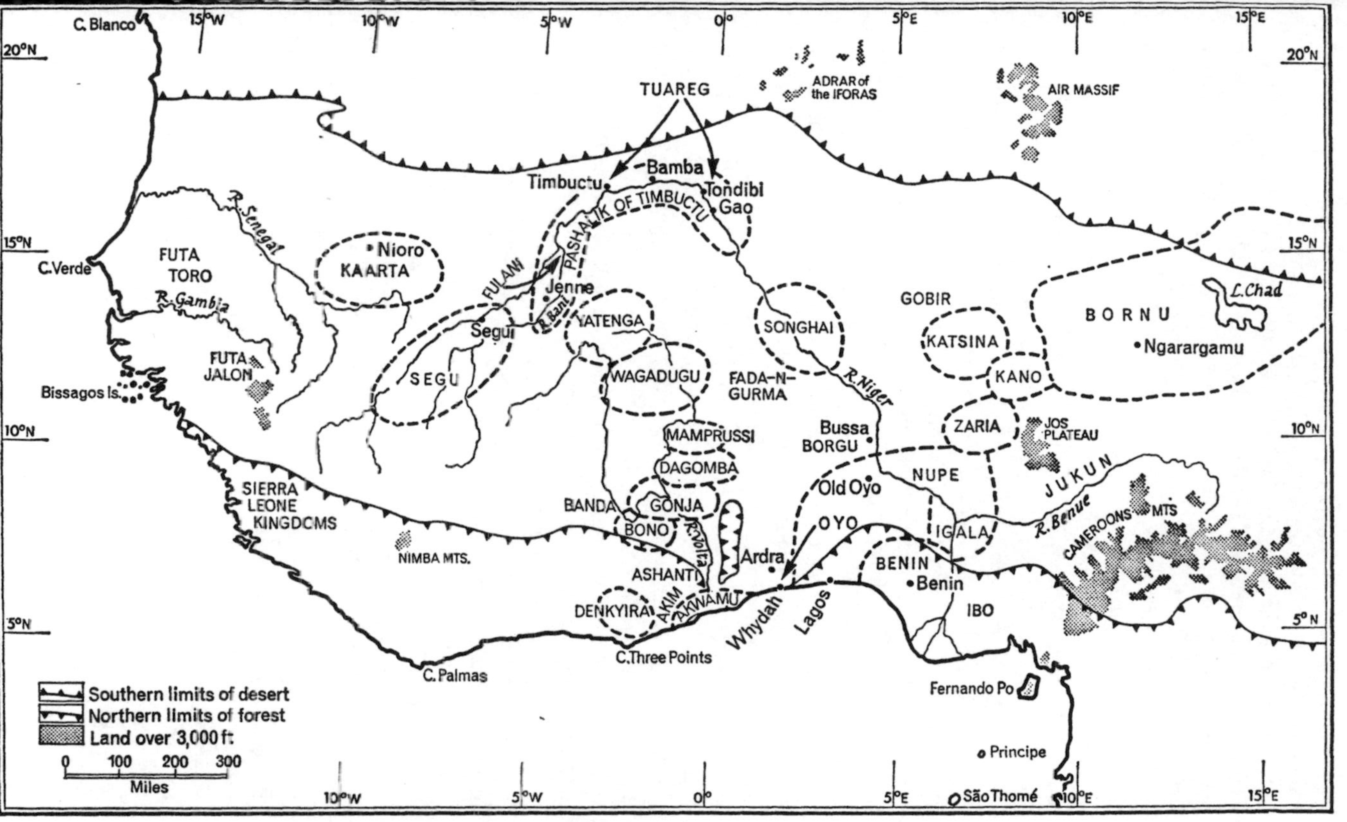

6 Major states in the seventeenth century

seem to have been early Akan, and they also maintain traditions of relationship with the peoples to the east, such as the Popos.

But westwards beyond the Aja, who clearly were subjected to a good deal of influence from the Yoruba (whose traders and cavalry alike were active in the wedge of savanna which reaches to the sea in Dahomey), these peoples did not create states of any size, but tended to live in comparatively small communities under rulers whose duties were as much religious and familial as they were political.

There was a somewhat similar absence of markedly political organisation further east, south of the Benue in what is now eastern Nigeria. It would seem that the state-forming impulses which operated to such dramatic effect in Yorubaland and elsewhere scarcely penetrated here (except for the late influence of Benin immediately to the east of this kingdom), though some of the peoples of this area, for example the Ibo, were second to none in fields like the development of agriculture, technology and art (which last have been most dramatically demonstrated by the recent discovery at Igbo-Ukwu of brass-work fully as fine as that of the Yoruba, though in a quite different tradition). By and large, however, their political organisations did not extend beyond clusters of villages, whose people claimed a tradition of a common ultimate ancestry, and who would have a meeting-place on common ground where disputes could be settled by a council under the presidency of the senior chief of the senior village, a place which would also serve as a centre of their common cults and as a market-place for the exchange of goods.

However, the Ibo village clusters did have one thing in common which was ultimately to have considerable economic and political significance. This was their belief in a supreme deity, Chukwu, and the recognition that the shrine and oracle where his wishes were made known was in the custody of one of their groups, the Aro people. When Ibo country began to be penetrated by long-distance trade routes, possession of the Chukwu oracle provided the Aro with a unique advantage which they astutely exploited to give them a general control of this trade.

However, as far as is known, long-distance trade of the pattern pioneered by the Dyula and later followed (as will be seen) by the Hausa, in which one group of merchants organised the whole movement of goods through foreign territories from their point of origin to their ultimate destination, did not develop in Iboland before the rise of the Atlantic slave trade in the seventeenth century. But when the idea of long distance trading did come, the Ibo clearly possessed a system of markets which enabled it to develop very rapidly, especially with the impetus given to it by Aro ambitions. It is possible, indeed, that, by being traded in stages by the merchants of one market area to the next, some commodities from eastern Nigeria, for example dried fish and sea salt, were already finding their way northwards towards the Sudan, and being exchanged for Sudanic goods.

A similar kind of local trading pattern may also have operated in the forestlands of what are today Liberia and the western Ivory Coast, a region for which the evidence suggests that long-distance trading was never well developed. However, compared with Iboland—or, for that matter, with the lands of the Hausa, the Yoruba and the Akan—this area, inhabited by peoples speaking languages akin to Kru, seems to have been very thinly populated. There is little evidence of significant commercial activity here much before the nineteenth century.

The spread of trade from Hausaland

It is now necessary to return to consider the development of trading routes controlled by traders from the Hausa cities. Political conditions in and around Hausaland were often turbulent. The early traditions of the northern Yoruba state of Oyo, for instance, present a picture of jostling military rivalries with the neighbouring states of Borgu and Nupe. Nevertheless, the existence of cities and organised kingdoms to the south-west of Hausaland seems to have provided conditions suitable for the spread of trade by itinerant Hausa merchants operating in much the same way as had the Mande Dyula. We know, for example, that merchants from Kano were trading for kola-nuts to as far as Gonja, between Dagomba and the forest in modern Ghana, by about the middle of the fifteenth century.

Information about the spread of trade more directly to the south of Hausaland is rather less precise. But we know that until about 1600, at least the more northerly Yoruba kingdoms, such as Oyo, were looking to the north for their essential supplies of salt. Equally, the Yoruba and other southerly states of what is now Nigeria must have looked to the north for their supplies of both brass and bronze, and of horses. The latter were important for military purposes in states like Oyo and Nupe; and at Benin, where the effective military use of horses was inhibited by the forest, lack of fodder, and the tse-tse fly, the prestige of the king and his nobles was in part symbolised by their possession of horses. By as late as the early eighteenth century, what would seem to be Muslim Hausa traders were in evidence on the coast of Dahomey. But to a large extent it would appear that in and around Yorubaland there needed to be only minimum penetration by Hausa traders to set in motion a comparable expansion of trade by merchants of the Yoruba themselves. By the late fifteenth century, it is apparent that the Portuguese merchants on the coast by Lagos and Benin were in fact trading with the southern fringes of a Yoruba commercial system.

In Gonja, the Hausa traders were competing directly with Mande traders who already possessed established colonies in the area. The heart of Gonja was an unproductive territory providing only a sparse subsistence for groups of Akan and Gur-speaking inhabitants. But, lying between the kingdom of Dagomba in the north (which at Daboya controlled the only good inland supply of salt in the region), and the Akan states which exported gold and kola-nuts in the south, it was a region of considerable strategic importance to long-distance traders. By the end of the sixteenth century, it would seem that the Mande traders, who had hitherto dominated the trading network centering on Gonja, were facing increasing difficulties. Dagomba and Bono were now both powerful kingdoms, able to dictate the terms on which salt, gold and kola-nuts could be obtained. There was now also direct competition for the trade of the area from Hausa merchants. Their competitive position may well have been stronger because of the relative political and economic stability of their homeland at a time when the Mande trading system was upset by the divisions in the Songhai government and by the Moroccan invasions.

In this situation the local Mande in Gonja appear to have decided to redress the balance in their favour by calling in a body of soldiers from the Mande homeland around Segu. Under a series of leaders called Jakpa, this military force proved adequate to force Dagomba to relinquish its hold on Daboya, and to move its capital from close to the White Volta to its present site at Yendi; to defeat and to restrict the power of Bono to the south; and to establish a new Gonja kingdom in which kings and horsemen of Mande origin ruled a heterogeneous population of Gur and Akan subjects.

But by this time—about the middle of the seventeenth century—the operations of trade carried on from totally new trading centres, established on the coast by merchants who had come to West Africa by sea from western Europe, were beginning to bring about a totally new situation which was to become of ever-increasing importance in determining the economic and political development of the Guinea peoples. Ultimately, the arrival of the Europeans was to have the most far-reaching consequences for the whole of West Africa.

4

The beginnings of European enterprise

Until the fifteenth century West Africa had been connected to and influenced by the world outside Africa only indirectly, through its relations with the peoples of North Africa. This situation began to be altered as a consequence of the European exploration of the West African coast. Between 1434 and 1482, seamen from the nations of western Europe, principally from Portugal and Castile, explored the whole coastline from Cape Bojador to the mouth of the Congo and beyond. Exploration was quickly followed by the establishment on the coast of European trading stations, and by the beginning of the sixteenth century, direct commercial relations had been opened by sea not only between West Africa and Europe, but also between West Africa and the newly discovered American continent. The consequences for West Africa of this direct contact with the outside world were truly momentous. Hitherto the most influential and the richest territories of West Africa had been the lands of the Sudan which faced north to the Sahara. The Guinea lands had been a hinterland difficult of access and remote from the major currents of world history. But now Guinea became the front door to West Africa from the outside world, and its peoples were given the opportunity—which many of them took—to eclipse those of the western and central Sudan in wealth and power. Many millions of West Africa's people were transported across the Atlantic to provide a labour force for European colonies in America. Finally, by the end of the nineteenth century, almost the whole of West Africa, Sudan as well as coastal districts and forest country, had been brought under the rule of European governments.

But when Europeans first came to West Africa by sea they had no thought for any of these things. In general the European exploration of the coastline of West Africa was an early manifestation of a new awakening of European interest in the world outside Europe; more particularly it was a development from long-standing European interests in the Mediterranean.

Europe's trade with Asia

For many centuries the well-to-do classes of western Europe had looked to Asia for their supplies of spices, sugar, silk, precious stones, ivory and other rare commodities which Europe did not produce itself. European merchants purchased such commodities in markets on the shores of the Eastern Mediterranean and the Black Sea, to which they had been brought by Asian merchants. But these commodities did not reach those markets in bulk consignments direct from their place of origin, which was usually in India or farther east. For example, a merchant in Malaya might purchase silk from a merchant in China, and might dispose of some of it, together with a consignment of spices, to a merchant from India. The Indian merchant might sell part of the silk and spices he had bought, and perhaps some sugar as well, to a trader from Egypt, who in his turn might sell part of his Indian consignment, together with ivory he had bought from East Africa, to a visiting European merchant. Thus by the time the goods got to Europe they had made a number of separate journeys, by sea or by land caravan or by a combination of both, each with its attendant risks of loss or damage. Duties and tolls had been levied on the goods each time they had been transhipped, and they had had to provide profits for a number of separate merchants. Asian products thus reached Europe in comparatively small quantities and at high prices. European demand for them steadily increased as the Middle Ages developed, yet it was not a simple matter for the European merchants to secure larger supplies.

From about the close of the eleventh century onwards, the markets of Syria, Egypt and Asia Minor, from which western Europe drew its supplies of Asiatic produce, were almost without exception in Islamic hands. Religious differences did not in practice act as a bar to trade between Christian and Muslim, but they did make it impossible for merchants from Christian Europe to attempt to venture directly to the sources of supply beyond the Mediterranean and Black Seas. This was in part because the merchants who controlled the trade routes in the Indian Ocean and surrounding countries were also Muslims, but principally because the Islamic world feared that even peaceful, commercial penetration within its borders by Europeans would be subversive of its religion and order. This fear was the more real because of the possibility that Europeans might join with the isolated Christian kingdom of Ethiopia to attack Islam from two sides at once. Yet at the same time as the Christian traders were denied access to the commercial world of Islam, they learnt from their dealings in Egypt, Syria, and Asia Minor, and from the travels of men like Marco Polo, how rich in the goods they wanted were the lands of farther Asia. They realised how rich they themselves might become if they could cut out the Islamic middlemen and themselves import goods in bulk directly from the markets of India and China.

The merchants who brought the Asian produce into Europe came from the maritime city-states of northern Italy. In return they supplied the Islamic countries with timber, iron and Christian slaves. This trade was equally lucrative in each direction, and there was strong competition for it between the Italian commercial states. As the thirteenth and fourteenth centuries progressed, by far the largest share of the Mediterranean trade was secured by Venetian merchants. For a time their principal rivals, the Genoese, managed to hold their own in the trade with North Africa, but by the end of the fourteenth century the Venetian traders were paramount in North Africa as well.

As opportunities for the employment of Genoese capital and initiative in the Mediterranean declined, so the more adventurous Genoese merchants began to look for new opportunities in the west. Their sailors and geographers were highly skilled. They knew about the trans-Saharan trade with the Sudan and the gold-lands of West Africa. They knew that with suitable ships and sufficient experience they might gain access by sea not only to West Africa but also, by circumnavigating Africa, to the rich trade of the Indian Ocean. About 1270, Genoese sailors sailing south-west into the Atlantic reached the Canary Islands; in 1291 a Genoese expedition set out to sail round Africa and, although it did not return, possibly succeeded in reaching the Red Sea.

But the decline of the power of Genoa in the fourteenth century made it increasingly difficult for her to support and follow up such ambitious ventures, with the result that many of her enterprising citizens sought new patrons and new opportunities. Sailors and geographers from Genoa and other Italian towns began to transfer their skills to the service of the new nation-states of western Europe; their merchants began to invest their capital and experience in the expansion of these nations' trade. Nowhere were the Italians more welcome than in the new Christian kingdoms of the Iberian peninsula.

Iberian expansion: Henry the Navigator

In the eighth century the whole of the Iberian peninsula had been conquered by the Muslims of North Africa. But the Christians had fought back, and by the middle of the thirteenth century had confined the forces of Islam to the small emirate of Granada. In the process of reconquest a number of Christian kingdoms had emerged, the chief of which were Aragon, Castile and Portugal. Aragon was the least likely to take advantage of Italian schemes for expansion to the south and west: she looked eastwards across the Mediterranean and her interests lay in that direction. On the other hand, not only did Castile and Portugal already possess an interest in trade with North Africa, and so indirectly with West Africa, but their seamen and fishermen were beginning to venture out into the broad Atlantic. Castile was the richer and stronger nation, but her rulers were too concerned with the presence of Granada as their neighbour to give much support to more distant ventures. In Portugal, however, conditions were different. At the end of the fourteenth century a new dynasty, the house of Aviz, had come to power and had succeeded in asserting the independence of the Portuguese nation against the pretensions of Castile. With no Muslim danger on the borders of its own territory, the house of Aviz was prepared to carry the Iberian crusade against Islam across to Africa.

During the fifteenth and sixteenth centuries this expansive, anti-Islamic impulse of the rulers of Portugal took two forms. The first was an attempt to conquer Morocco. It was not a success, and it is of little concern here except for the fact that, after the Portuguese capture of Ceuta in 1415, a younger son of the Portuguese king, Prince Henry, was appointed governor of the town, and so placed in an unusually favourable position to acquire knowledge of the West African lands across the Sahara with which Morocco traded. Within a few years, Prince Henry was devoting the major part of his energies to organising the systematic exploration of the west coast of Africa by Portuguese ships. This enterprise continued without a break until the year of his death in 1460, and thus earned him the name of Henry the Navigator by which he is known to history.

Both the intention and the execution of the Portuguese voyages owe much to the Italian, particularly the Genoese, example. As we have seen, Genoese seamen initiated the exploration of the Atlantic, and Genoese merchants first conceived the notion of establishing direct commercial relations with the Indian Ocean by sailing round Africa (which was Henry's ultimate aim). Like the Italians, Henry was keen to join forces with the Christians of Ethiopia against Islam. The early Portuguese explorers learnt from the Italians the arts of accurate navigation and of mapping the coastlines they discovered. Italian navigators and seamen sailed in, and sometimes commanded, Portuguese vessels, and Italian merchants invested capital in Portuguese expeditions. What was new in Henry's enterprise was that it was supported by the rulers of a united nation, and that it was deliberately and systematically planned and directed. The Portuguese voyages of African exploration begun by Henry and continued after his death were not isolated ventures into the unknown. They were ordered as part of a master plan, and the results and experience of each voyage were carefully assessed, and compared with all available information from Arab and other sources, so that each new expedition set out better informed and equipped for its task than the one before.

Henry knew that it might be many years before Portugal could gain the necessary knowledge and experience successfully to run ships regularly along the long and possibly dangerous sea-route into the Indian Ocean, or to establish lasting and beneficial contact with Christian Ethiopia. But in the meantime there was a more easily attainable objective. The Portuguese knew that the Muslim states of North Africa did not actually control the gold-producing lands of West Africa with which their merchants traded so profitably. Henry hoped, therefore, that his ships might outflank the area of Muslim rule in north-western Africa and establish direct contact with the Negroes of West Africa. The peoples of West Africa might then be converted into Christian allies for the assault against Islam, while their valuable trade would be diverted directly to Portugal.

The Portuguese purpose in undertaking the exploration of the West African coast may thus be briefly summarised as follows. First, to direct the trade of West Africa and then of the Indian Ocean into channels which would not be under the control of the Muslim merchants of the Levant and North Africa, but which would bring it directly to Europe to the profit of Portugal. Secondly, to find or to convert and create Christian allies in Africa to join with the Europeans in a joint onslaught against Islam.

Portuguese exploration of the coast of West Africa

The progress of Portuguese exploration was slow at first. Madeira was discovered in 1418, but Portuguese ships did not pass beyond Cape Bojador, the extreme southern limit of normal European navigation, until 1434. The Azores were first sighted in 1439, and in 1441 Cape Blanco was rounded and the little island of Arguin just to the south of it was discovered in 1443 by Diniz Dias and Nuno Tristão. So far the Portuguese had found little that was of very great value. The coast was arid and inhospitable, and its few inhabitants were Muslims. However, the sea just off the coast offered rich fishing grounds which the Portuguese began to exploit. In addition, it had proved possible to purchase small quantities of gold which Saharan merchants had secured from trading with Mali. Arguin was therefore selected as a convenient base for the fishing fleets and for the trade of the coast, which it was hoped might be developed inland to cut the caravan route between Mali and Morocco. The building of a fort on the island was commenced in 1448.

In 1444–5 the mouth of the Senegal and Cape Verde were reached by Diniz Dias, and the Portuguese had passed beyond the desert to Guinea, to the green and fertile land of Negroes who, though under Islamic influence, were not themselves Muslims.[1] A few Negroes were captured and taken back to Portugal. The intention was to show Henry that his captains had indeed passed beyond the confines of Muslim Africa, and to provide a first batch of pupils for training in Christian and European

[1] The name 'Cape Verde', of course, means 'the green cape'; it should be compared with Cape Blanco, 'the white cape' on the desolate, sandy Saharan coast.

ways. However, some Portuguese merchants looked at the captives with different eyes. Hitherto they had stood aloof from Henry's voyages because they could not see much commercial profit in them. Now, however, they realised that they could enrich themselves by capturing Negroes or buying them from Muslim merchants, bringing them to Portugal and selling them to work as slaves in the thinly populated southern districts of the country which had recently been reconquered from the Moors. Thus one of the first major commercial results of an enterprise which had as one of its aims the conversion of the Negroes to Christianity was the development of a trade which sold them into servitude to Europeans.

When Henry died in 1460, his captains were abreast of Sierra Leone. Without Henry there to spur it on, his enterprise at first languished, and no major voyages of new exploration seem to have been undertaken between 1460 and 1469, though the Cape Verde islands were colonised and developed into a base for the trade in slaves and some other commodities with the adjacent mainland. However, the appetite of the Portuguese traders had been whetted, and in 1469 a Lisbon merchant, one Fernão Gomes, persuaded the king of Portugal to grant him a five years' monopoly of the trade of the Guinea coast beyond the Cape Verde islands on condition that he explored a hundred leagues (i.e. nearly 400 miles) of new coastline each year. Gomes's contract was subsequently extended until 1475, by which time his ships had reached Fernando Po and crossed the equator. In so doing his captains, João de Santarem and Pero de Escobar, had discovered that between the mouths of the rivers Ankobra and Volta lay a country in which gold and gold-dust were evident in such abundance that they gave it the name of Mina, 'the mine', or, as later Europeans came to call it, the Gold Coast.

Importance of the Gold Coast to the Portuguese

The discovery of the Gold Coast meant that the Portuguese were within measurable distance of achieving the economic purpose which had brought them to West Africa, for the gold of the Gold Coast came from Akany and Twifu and adjacent districts of the forest which were one of the sources of supply for the Sudanic and the trans-Saharan trades in gold. The Portuguese appreciated that if they could establish a firm hold of the trade of the coast they should be able to direct into their own hands a considerable portion of the gold which had hitherto gone to Muslim North Africa. At the same time as their enemies would thus be weakened, the Portuguese would be assured of adequate funds to complete their ambitious design of establishing the sea-route round Africa to the east.

An immediate consequence of the discovery of the Gold Coast was that Gomes's contract was not renewed after 1475, and the Portuguese crown

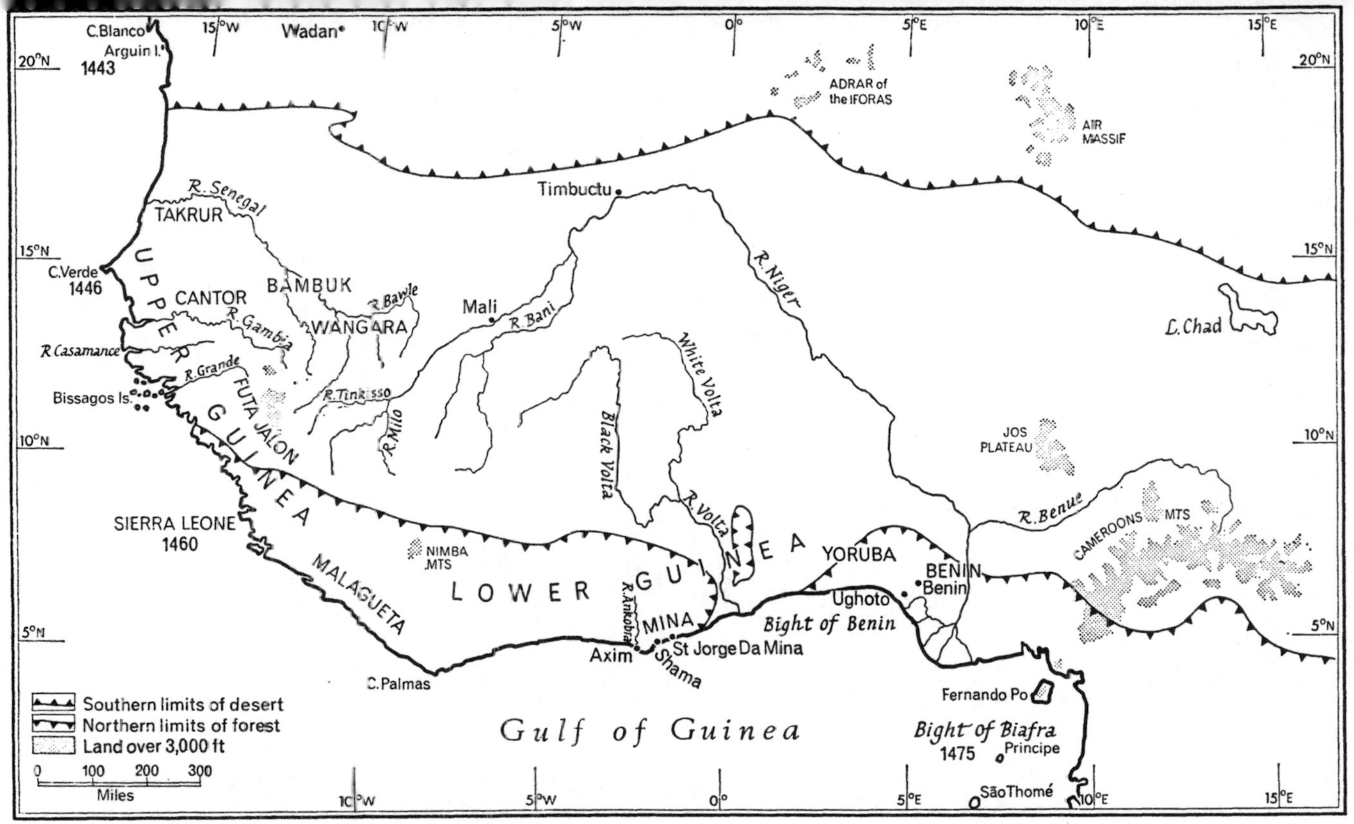

7 The Portuguese in West Africa

resumed direct supervision of the Guinea trade and the conduct of further voyages of exploration. These voyages, which led, via the discovery of the Congo by Diogo Cão in 1482, to the rounding of the Cape of Good Hope by Bartholomeu Diaz five years later, and ultimately in 1497 to the first direct sea voyage from Europe to India under Vasco de Gama, hardly concern the history of West Africa, except that one of the results of the successful entry of the Portuguese into the rich trade of the Indian Ocean was that they then became somewhat less interested in African trade.

The countries of the Indian Ocean and further Asia possessed a highly organised network of maritime trade which made it easy for the Portuguese to secure commodities for which there was a demand in Europe, and to secure these in the preferred qualities and quantities. But the coastlands of West Africa which the Portuguese had come to by sea had no maritime economy, and they were usually the economically least developed parts of the country. Only between the Senegal and Sierra Leone, and on the Gold Coast and in what is now south-western Nigeria, were the Portuguese in contact with peoples who had developed exchange economies on any scale. But in these territories, merchants were, by and large, involved in a trading system which looked northwards to the Sudan; it certainly did not look southwards to the sea. The Portuguese were not strong enough to extend their power inland in an attempt to reverse the flow of trade. They had either to generate new trade, or to compete as best they could with African merchants in a trading system which was ultimately directed from the Sudan.

The peoples of the West African coastlands had in fact available for trade with the Portuguese relatively few commodities for which there was a worthwhile demand in Europe. Furthermore, since Portugal herself was not a great manufacturing country, her merchants experienced some difficulty in supplying the Guinea peoples with the cloth, hardware, beads, iron and other metals for which they were willing to exchange their own produce. The principal commodities of West African trade which were available in the coastlands were gold, ivory, peppers, kola-nuts and, in some areas, slaves. But the market for Negro slaves in Europe was not large, and there was no European demand for kola-nuts. The West African peppers were not the same as the East Indian pepper to which Europeans were accustomed, and the Portuguese soon ceased dealing in them. The Portuguese were always willing to trade for ivory, but it took some time for the coastal peoples to arrange for it to be regularly available at the coast in attractive quantities.

It was West African gold, and in particular the gold of the Gold Coast, which chiefly interested the Portuguese. Western Europe was chronically short of the precious metals. Its wars were becoming increasingly costly and its new nations were finding them increasingly difficult to finance. Its foreign trade was expanding, and gold and silver were essential media of exchange, especially for the trade with eastern Asia, whose sophisticated peoples evinced relatively little taste for the European exports of the period. Although gold could be obtained at many points on the West African coast, it was only on the Gold Coast that the supplies were large and regular. The other gold-producing areas were too far in the interior for more than a trickle of gold to escape to the coast away from the established Sudan and trans-Saharan trades.

King John II decided that Portugal should have a permanent base on the Gold Coast. In 1482 an expedition was sent out under Diogo d'Azambuja to erect a strong stone fort there and, despite opposition from the local Akan people, the castle of São Jorge da Mina was successfully built at the place now known as Elmina. This castle was intended to serve as something more than a fortified warehouse where Portuguese traders could safely keep their stocks of merchandise and their purchases of gold during periods when no Portuguese ships were in the offing. In addition, Elmina was to be the headquarters of a royal governor and a garrison, whose job it was to ensure that only properly licensed Portuguese merchants were allowed to trade with the Gold Coast.

Portugal's rivals in the trade with West Africa

It was necessary to watch for interlopers because the Portuguese were not the sole pioneers of European sea trade with West Africa. Throughout the course of their exploration of the coast, the Portuguese ships had been followed, at times perhaps even preceded, by ships from other western European nations. Little is known of these voyages because for the most part they were individual ventures, lacking the planned royal support that was so characteristic a feature of the Portuguese enterprise. But we know that Frenchmen and Castilians were active in the Canary Islands by as early as the beginning of the fifteenth century, and there is certain evidence of a large Castilian expedition trading to Guinea, probably to the Senegambia, in 1453–4. There can be no doubt that the Portuguese were worried about foreign competition in the trade with West Africa, for on no less than three occasions (1451, 1455 and 1456) Henry the Navigator went to the trouble of securing from the Pope bulls reserving to himself and Portugal a monopoly of the exploration and trade of the West African coast.

The discovery of the Gold Coast led to renewed activity on the part of merchants from other countries, from Castile in particular. The king of Portugal was at this time laying claim to the throne of Castile. The two countries were at war between 1475 and 1479, with the result that the Castilian authorities were almost for the first time prepared to give full support to their merchants in their struggle to invade a sphere in which the Portuguese claimed a monopoly. Outstanding differences between the two countries were officially settled in 1479 by the Treaty of Alcaçovas, by which, in return for Portugal's renunciation of claims to Castile and the Canaries, the Castilian authorities agreed not to dispute or disturb Portuguese possessions on the West African coast and in the Azores, Madeira and the Cape Verde Islands. Nevertheless, individual Castilian merchants continued to compete with the Portuguese in West Africa until about 1492, when Columbus's discovery of America provided them with a new and exclusively Castilian outlet for their enterprise. Thereafter, three Papal bulls of 1493, and the Treaty of Tordesillas between Castile and Portugal in 1494, proclaimed that Castile should have a monopoly of the European exploitation of the New World (except for Brazil), and Portugal of Africa and Asia. But the Treaty of Tordesillas concerned Portugal and Castile alone, and the seamen of other nations were not prepared to accept the authority of the Pope to limit the sphere of their activities. By the early 1530s, French and English seamen and merchants were active all along the West African coast.

The early French and English voyages to Guinea, such as those conducted under the auspices of Jean Ango and William and John Hawkins, were individual trading ventures. A group of merchants would raise the capital to send out one or two ships to trade in West Africa and, if their venture were successful, they might repeat it. But neither country attempted during the sixteenth century to establish a position in West Africa to rival that of Portugal. Until 1598, Portugal was the only European country to possess a footing on West African soil. Individual French and English merchants were not strong enough to establish permanent bases on the coast in the face of established Portuguese resistance. It is true that on the not infrequent occasions when Portugal protested at French and English invasions of her monopoly, neither the French nor the English governments took effective steps to restrain the West African activities of their merchants, but on the other hand they offered them little consistent encouragement. On political grounds both countries were more interested in using their limited maritime resources to challenge the power of Spain in America, and in fact, after about 1570, French and English seamen in general came to find the plundering of Spanish treasure fleets and colonies a more lucrative occupation than trade with Guinea.

In the sixteenth century, then, the French and English (the former were the more active before, the latter the more active after, about 1560) exerted little influence in West Africa to compare with that of the Portuguese. From the Portuguese point of view, the French and English voyages were more of a nuisance than a challenge, a nuisance which reduced the profits they would have got had they been complete monopolists of the sea trade of West Africa, and which forced them to spend an increasing proportion of the profits they did make on naval patrols and other defensive measures. For the coastal Africans, the French and English voyages offered occasional opportunities to sell their wares at prices higher than the Portuguese were willing to pay, and therefore served to make them increasingly discontented with Portuguese domination. But the French and English remained occasional visitors to West Africa; only the Portuguese attempted to exert a lasting influence over the land and its peoples.

The Portuguese in West Africa

Even the Portuguese were not so much interested in West Africa as in its trade. The areas actually occupied and governed by the Portuguese in the fifteenth and sixteenth centuries were small. Their typical settlement was a coastal trading post or an off-shore island. Nevertheless, the commercial, and sometimes the religious, influence of these settlements was very wide.

In attempting to assess the nature and extent of this influence it is convenient to adopt the seventeenth- and eighteenth-century division of the West African coast into Upper Guinea (approximately from Cape Blanco as far as Sierra Leone) and Lower Guinea (from Sierra Leone to the Cameroon). Lower Guinea was subdivided into four sections each named after a principal export: the Grain Coast (so called from the 'grains of paradise' of malagueta pepper), which corresponds to the coast of modern Liberia; the Ivory Coast and the Gold Coast; and the Slave Coast, the coast between the River Volta and the Niger delta.

Portuguese influence in Upper Guinea was slight north of the Senegal. The trade of this inhospitable and scantily populated land was insignificant, and the only permanent settlement maintained by the Portuguese was the fort at Arguin. Even when the Portuguese maintained a satellite trading post inland at the caravan centre of Wadan (*c.* 1487–1513), the hostility of the Saharan traders prevented more than a small part of the caravan trade from West Africa to Morocco being diverted to Arguin. As the Portuguese found that they could secure the commodities they wanted more easily by direct trade with the Negroes farther south, Arguin was allowed to fall into decline.

Portuguese influence in the southern half of Upper Guinea south of the River Senegal was great and extended for a considerable distance inland. This was due to a favourable combination of circumstances. The Senegal and Gambia rivers, and to some extent the lesser rivers and creeks of the coast south of the Gambia, provided good routes into the interior. Except in Takrur, the local peoples were Negroes who were under no great degree of Muslim influence and were organised in small political groups that, with the decline of the Mali empire, offered little resistance to Portuguese commercial penetration. Finally, just off the coast lay the Cape Verde Islands, eminently suitable for the establishment of a purely Portuguese colony which would serve as a firm base for the penetration of the mainland. Portuguese colonists were early attracted to settle in the islands by the grant of large estates and of the privilege of trading freely with the mainland. While official Portuguese embassies penetrated inland to Mali (1534) and possibly even as far as Timbuctu (1565 ?), the colonists of the Cape Verde Islands were establishing trading agents at numerous points on the coast and up most of the many creeks and rivers between the Senegal and Sierra Leone. In this way Portuguese influence rapidly reached as far inland as the Mande markets of Cantor on the upper Gambia, and up the Senegal almost as far as the alluvial gold-workings of Bambuk (the Wangara of the Arabs).

From a commercial point of view the results of their influence were not displeasing to the Portuguese authorities, since a fair trade in gold-dust, pepper, gum arabic and slaves developed in return for Portuguese imports of cloth and hardware. But in other respects Portuguese influence between the Senegal and Sierra Leone developed characteristics unacceptable to the Portuguese government. The Portuguese agents on the mainland were expected to assimilate the Africans to Portuguese and Christian ways, but this did not happen. The traders tended to settle down, marry African wives, and establish a mulatto society that was free from the more annoying restrictions of both European and African life. This society attracted to it a motley crowd of undesirable fugitives and exiles from Portugal and other European lands. It exerted no Christian influence on the Africans and when, during the sixteenth century, merchants from other European countries began to appear on the scene, it was quite prepared to forget the interests of Portugal and to provide agents for the trade of the foreigners. The Portuguese government tried to check this deterioration in Portuguese influence by revoking the mainland trading rights of the Cape Verde islanders in 1518, and by supporting the work of Catholic missionaries from Portugal, but they were too late. Except for the region around the Portuguese settlement of Cacheu, the coastal districts between the Senegal and Sierra Leone had become a happy hunting-ground for the more disreputable traders of many European nations.

The Portuguese had little contact with the Grain and Ivory Coasts principally because, since they lacked natural harbours, the strong off-shore current and frequent storms of the region made it unsafe for sailing ships to venture close to them for any length of time. Consequently the peoples of this part of West Africa remained remarkably free from European influence right up to the nineteenth century.

On the other hand, the Gold Coast was the scene of the greatest Portuguese commercial activity in all Guinea. In addition to their headquarters at Elmina, the Portuguese built forts at Axim and Shama, which, like Elmina Castle can still be seen today, and also at Accra, though here the local Gã captured and destroyed their fort in 1576. By the early years of the sixteenth century, the officials and traders in these forts were sending to Portugal each year gold to the value of £100,000 or $400,000 in the money of the time (equivalent to one-tenth of the world's supply of gold), which they had received in return for imports of cloth, hardware, beads and slaves. (In view of what was to happen later, it may seem strange that the Portuguese were *importing* slaves into the Gold Coast. But this was undoubtedly the case in the sixteenth century, presumably because the upcountry merchants needed labourers for the mines and porters to carry back with them the much bulkier goods they had received in exchange for the gold-dust they had brought to the coast. As will be seen, the Portuguese brought the slaves from the area of Benin and the Niger delta.)

But though Portuguese trade with the Gold Coast was great, Portuguese influence there was limited. The attitude of the coastal states towards the Portuguese virtually restricted their power to within gun-shot of their forts and ships. The coastal peoples welcomed the Portuguese only for the trade they brought and the profits they themselves could make from this trade. They insisted that trade between the Portuguese and the inland countries, where most of the gold was mined, should pass through their hands, and they actively opposed Portuguese attempts to establish direct contact with the interior. They strongly objected to the Portuguese claim to a monopoly of their trade with Europeans, and particularly to the Portuguese habit of sending punitive expeditions against states who traded with other Europeans. They feared lest the Portuguese should use their forts as bases for the extension of their political and Christian influence into the country, so that they would become utterly under Portuguese control. They therefore insisted that the ground on which the forts were built belonged to them, and that the Portuguese rights were those of lessors only.

Nevertheless, the attractions of trade with the Portuguese were so great that an increasing number of Africans, from the inland as well as the coastal states, left home to work in new towns that began to grow up beneath the walls of the forts, Elmina in particular. These people were subject to the jurisdiction of no traditional African chief, the men of the Portuguese garrisons chose wives from among them, and in course of time communities developed which were almost as much European and Christian in character as they were African and animist, and which were governed according to a rough European pattern by chiefs of their own who were responsible to the Portuguese commanders of the forts.

The Portuguese did little trade between the Volta and Lagos. This part of Guinea offered no gold; consequently the Portuguese did not bother to solve the difficulties involved in establishing permanent contact with its peoples across the heavy surf and the lagoons characteristic of this part of the coast. The Portuguese were active, however, on the coast from Lagos (situated by the only permanent entrance to the lagoons) to the Niger delta and, initially, especially at Benin. There were a number of reasons for this. In the first place, this coast with its numerous creeks and rivers, was easily penetrable by, and offered safe anchorages for the Portuguese ships. Secondly, the Portuguese seem to have found an active local trade in progress—no doubt because this region formed part of the Yoruba trading system. Except in respect of peppers and ivory, there was no European demand for the principal commodities of this trade. But the Portuguese discovered that some of these, notably, it would seem, *akori* beads,[1] cloth and slaves, were in demand on the Gold Coast. The Gold Coast peoples' interest in *akori* and in cloth from what is now Western Nigeria (and also, for that matter, in cloth and clothing which the Portuguese brought them from Morocco) suggests strongly, in fact, that at least some quantity of these commodities had been reaching the Gold Coast along established African trade routes before the Portuguese arrived on the scene. Since Portugal herself was not a great supplier of manufactured goods, the commodities she herself could offer on the Gold Coast were either little attractive to its exporters of gold or had to be purchased by her at a cost from other European countries. The Portuguese were therefore naturally attracted to the scheme of exchanging their European goods for Nigerian produce, and re-selling the latter on the Gold Coast, for in this way they gained two opportunities for profit instead of only one.[2]

The third reason which the Portuguese had for interesting themselves in the coast between Lagos and the Niger delta was that it was dominated by Benin, the only considerable West African state of the time which was close enough to the sea for them to deal with directly. The Portuguese, still looking for potential allies in their struggle against the world of Islam and at first unaware of the distance that lay between Benin and Muslim territory (which they underestimated) or of the size of the Benin kingdom (which they may have overestimated), could see considerable political and

[1] It is not entirely certain what these *akori* beads were. In the sixteenth and seventeenth centuries, the name *akori* was most probably applied to beads of bluish-green stone or glass which were manufactured somewhere in what is now Nigeria. Later, on the Gold Coast, the term *akori* or *aggrey* came to mean almost any highly valued bead.

[2] It might be added that trading in this way as intermediaries was typical of Portuguese enterprise in the sixteenth century, not only in Africa, but even more in Asia, where there was a demand for very few of the goods that Europe then had to offer, and where consequently the Portuguese had to husband their gold and silver.

economic advantages to themselves if they could bring the kingdom and its trade under their influence and control. Accordingly in 1486, they established a post at Ughoto (Gwato), whch became the port for Benin City (about twenty miles distant), and sent out missionaries in an attempt to convert the king and his principal men to a Christian way of life.

The post at Ughoto was maintained for a few decades and then abandoned. This was not, as has been argued, because of the high death rate which the Portuguese experienced from the fevers of the area. A mission was maintained in the nearby satellite kingdom of Warri until the late seventeenth century. Commercial factors must have played some part in the decision. In 1506, for instance, the Portuguese had decided to cease buying West African peppers, because they now had assured supplies of the East Indian pepper which Europe preferred. Furthermore the Portuguese were undoubtedly hampered by the strict control exercised over trade by the king of Benin. Thus, for example, there was a refusal to allow the export of male slaves, doubtless because they were so valuable to the royal power and to the country's own economy. Indeed, the paramount reason for the withdrawal of the Portuguese from Benin was probably that its monarchy and its government were too independently minded and too strong to be made subservient to their economic and political purposes.

Although there was obviously more hope that the Portuguese might be able to dominate the smaller and weaker kingdom of Warri, the Portuguese on the whole found it more sensible to conduct their trade (increasingly a trade for slaves) with the whole coast from Lagos to as far as the Congo from bases in the islands of the Gulf of Guinea which they had begun to settle about 1493. The colonisation of São Thomé and Fernando Po and the two lesser islands in the Gulf of Guinea—O Principe (Prince's Island) and Annobon—was encouraged by means similar to those which had been used in the Cape Verde Islands. It was hoped that if the settlers were allowed to trade freely with the mainland, the islands would develop a valuable trade with Portugal. At first few Portuguese cared to settle so far afield in the tropics, but the situation was altered when it became apparent that a combination of heavy rainfall and a rich volcanic soil had made the islands extremely suitable for the growing of sugar and some other tropical crops which found a ready sale in Europe. By the 1520s the settlers had developed first-class sugar plantations, and they were in fact neglecting the trade with the mainland except to secure slaves to work on their own plantations. The Portuguese sugar planters enjoyed a period of great prosperity until, about 1570, the large slave population on the islands began to get out of control. Many of the planters then began to transfer their activities across the Atlantic, to the coastal plains of tropical Brazil, which were just beginning to be colonised by the Portuguese.

However, the islands, São Thomé in particular, remained important to the Portuguese because they then reverted to something like the role originally intended for them, becoming collecting points for the slaves which were sent to Brazil.

But by this time—the end of the sixteenth century—the Portuguese were no longer the only Europeans who wished to establish permanent contact with West Africa. First the Dutch, then the English and French and some lesser European nations were anxious to break in on the Portuguese monopoly and establish trading bases of their own on the shores of West Africa. A new era was beginning in which these western European nations were to regard West Africa primarily as a source of slave labour for the plantations they were setting up in the West Indies and other tropical parts of the New World, and in which they were to compete bitterly among themselves for this trade.

5

European competition for trade in the Guinea coastlands in the seventeenth and eighteenth centuries

The beginnings of the Atlantic slave trade

The Portuguese were not the only Europeans to realise that they could achieve fame, wealth and power by establishing direct sea communication with the rich trade of the Indian Ocean and further Asia. Christopher Columbus, a Genoese mariner who may have been a member of the Portuguese expedition which built Elmina Castle in 1482, and who was certainly well aware of the profits to be gained from direct sea trade with lands outside Europe, conceived the idea that a route to Asia more direct than that which the Portuguese were seeking round Africa could be found by sailing westwards across the Atlantic. Having after some difficulty persuaded Queen Isabella of the newly united monarchies of Castile and Aragon (which henceforth were to constitute the kingdom of Spain) to provide him with ships and men, in 1492 Columbus set out and, after a voyage lasting 33 days, discovered islands which he supposed to be the easternmost islands of Asia. But by about 1504 subsequent voyages of exploration, by Columbus and others, had shown that Columbus had reached, not the easternmost East Indies, but islands lying off a continent the existence of which had hitherto been unappreciated by Europeans, a continent which was soon named America.

Just as Portugal, whose sailors had by this time established their sea route to Asia round the Cape of Good Hope, claimed exclusive rights in the lands discovered on the way, so Spain claimed a monopoly of the exploitation of the West Indies and of the American mainland discovered by her explorers. At first the value of the new lands seemed small. Their comparatively simple peoples afforded no opportunity for rich trade of the kind that Columbus had been seeking. However, some of the larger West Indian islands showed signs of being rich in gold, and they were swiftly conquered by Spanish adventurers determined to exploit this wealth. The result was disappointing: relatively little gold was found, and, in the process of extracting what there was, the native population of the islands was almost exterminated. Some were killed in the conquest, others died from the effects of new diseases introduced from Europe by the conquerors, but many of them died simply because they were not accustomed to the labour demanded of them by the Spaniards in their search for gold. Having squeezed the islands dry of such mineral wealth as they possessed, the Spaniards then turned to the conquest of the adjacent mainland, and there, by the middle of the sixteenth century, they found themselves in possession of the richest source of precious metals then known to Europe, the silver mines of Mexico and Peru.

Spain now had within her grasp the means to make herself the richest and most powerful state in all Europe. But her conquests were of little value unless she could be assured of an adequate supply of reliable labour both to work the mines and to replace the depleted population of the West Indian islands, which, though not rich in minerals, possessed soil and climate ideally suited to the cultivation of tropical crops greatly valued in Europe. The population of America was small and, as experience in the West Indies had shown, her peoples were not accustomed to intensive labour. The Spaniards realised that they would have to supplement the American resources of labour, and they turned to West Africa for a supply of slaves. The Negroes were used to the work required for sustained agriculture in the tropics; winds and currents made the voyage from West Africa to America relatively easy for the sailing ships of the period; and the Portuguese merchants, who were already trading in West African slaves, were ready to exploit a new market for them since the demand for slaves in their own possessions was limited.

Thus, in about 1530, commenced the trans-Atlantic slave trade, the carriage by Europeans of African slaves across the Atlantic for sale in the Americas, a trade which was to be the most important single external influence on the life of West Africa for the next three and a half centuries. But the nature and scale of the trade in the sixteenth century were very different from what they were later to become. The number of slaves imported into America was strictly regulated by the Spanish authorities and, since Spain herself possessed no trading bases in West Africa, the trade was done by means of contracts (*asientos*) granted by the Spanish government to merchants who were either Portuguese themselves or who had Portuguese agents. With a few minor exceptions, of which the slaving voyages of the Englishman John Hawkins between 1562 and 1568 are perhaps the best known, the supply of slaves to the European colonists in America in the sixteenth century was entirely in Portuguese hands. The capacity of the Portuguese to carry slaves across the Atlantic was undoubtedly limited by the shipping resources available to the sixteenth century, but the demand itself was not great. The mines needed relatively few labourers, and the plantations of Spanish America and Portuguese Brazil were as yet only in their infancy. The best figures we have suggest that the total number of slaves taken to the Americas in the sixteenth century was only about 125,000 (about 75,000 to the Spanish colonies and 50,000 to Portuguese Brazil), a small figure when it is considered that the tiny island of São Thomé may have absorbed 60,000 slaves during the same period, and a small figure too in relation to the totals of later centuries. The development of plantations in the Americas, especially by the Portuguese in Brazil, was considerably stepped up in the first third of the seventeenth century, but even so the first hundred years of the trans-Atlantic slave trade saw no more than about 200,000 Africans landed in the Americas. As will be seen in chapter 6, very much larger numbers were carried across the Atlantic during the late seventeenth and eighteenth centuries, when the slave trade was at its height.

The Dutch entry into Atlantic trade

The wealth which Spain drew from the Americas soon attracted the attention of maritime adventurers from other seafaring nations of western Europe. Spain's claim to the exclusive exploitation of America was no more respected by other nations than Portugal's claim to a monopoly of the sea trade of West Africa. But the English and French, the principal challengers of Spain's power in America in the sixteenth century, were no more successful in securing footholds in America than they were in West Africa. For the most part they contented themselves with plundering attacks on Spanish colonial settlements and on the Spanish fleets bringing the silver from the American mines to Europe.

Spain's position as the paramount European power in America and Portugal's as the paramount European power on the coasts of Africa and in the Indian Ocean were not seriously challenged until after 1580, in which year the kings of Spain became rulers of Portugal as well, and thus masters of all Europe's imperial interests overseas. In 1572, the Dutch people of the Netherlands had revolted against Spanish rule, and thereafter they successfully maintained their independence despite all Spanish attempts to subdue them. Now, the Netherlands merchants had been the principal distributors in north-western Europe of the spices and other oriental goods which the Portuguese brought from Asia. At the close of the sixteenth century, as part of his campaign to bring his rebellious Dutch subjects to heel, Philip II of Spain closed the ports of Portugal and Spain to ships from the Netherlands. But the only result was to determine the Dutch to extend their war against Philip to the high seas, and to attempt to destroy the Portuguese and Spanish monopoly of Europe's trade with the outside world.

The most valuable and vulnerable part of this trade was the Portuguese commerce in spices in the Indian Ocean, and at first the Dutch concentrated on this. By 1610, Portuguese naval power in the Indian Ocean had been destroyed and the Dutch had secured complete mastery of its trade. Although from 1598 onwards the Dutch had established a few small posts on the coasts of Guinea and the Caribbean, no comparable attack on Spanish and Portuguese interests in America and West Africa was made by them until after 1621, when the Dutch West Indies Company was formed. As its name suggests, this company was primarily concerned with the Americas, but, as we shall see, its activities there had major repercussions in West Africa.

The Company continued the French and English tradition of attacking and plundering Spanish shipping in American waters to such good effect that, by about 1630, Spain had finally lost command of the sea. The Dutch then embarked on the conquest of Portuguese Brazil, and by 1637 a large part of the colony was in their hands.

The Dutch commander, Maurice of Nassau, judged that the best way for the Dutch to profit from their conquest of Brazil was to encourage the activities of the Portuguese planters settled there, who were successfully growing sugar and other valuable tropical crops for export. But the planters could not prosper unless they had a regular supply of slaves from Africa. Maurice therefore set about the capture of the Portuguese trading posts in West Africa, and by 1642 Arguin, Goree, São Thomé, Loanda, and all the Portuguese forts on the Gold Coast were in Dutch hands.[1]

In 1640 the Portuguese asserted their independence of Spain, so that the Dutch no longer had any justification for attacking Portuguese possessions. Although the Dutch attempted to keep all they had taken, in 1648 the Portuguese recaptured São Thomé and Loanda, and by 1654 they had finally expelled the Dutch from Brazil.

Nevertheless, the Dutch West Indies Company, retaining Arguin, Goree and posts on the mainland opposite that island, and all the strongest forts on the Gold Coast, remained by far the strongest European power on the coast of Guinea. It was also the most active and best organised agent in the Atlantic slave trade. It was no longer feasible for the Dutch to sell slaves to the Portuguese planters in Brazil, because Portugal could and did supply their needs from Loanda and São Thomé, but since Spain still had no trading posts in West Africa and refused to buy slaves from the Portuguese (who were regarded as rebellious subjects of the Spanish king), the Dutch company found a ready market for its slaves among the Spanish settlers in America. In addition, the Dutch destruction of Spanish sea power in American waters had enabled English and French colonists to flout Spanish claims, and settle on those of the

[1] Goree is an island in the lee of Cape Verde and was the seventeenth- and eighteenth-century strategic equivalent of Dakar, of which mainland port it now forms part. Loanda was the principal Portuguese settlement in Angola, south of the Congo.

West Indian islands which were either unoccupied or only thinly settled by the Spaniards. From its experience in Brazil, the Dutch company was able to teach these settlers how to grow sugar for export to Europe, and it provided them, on easy terms, with the capital, equipment, and slaves required to set up their plantations.

Curaçao and other Dutch possessions in the Caribbean became bases for a flourishing Dutch trade with the European colonists in the West Indies and the tropical areas of the American mainland. Spanish, English, and French planters bought their slaves, plantation stores, and other requirements from Dutch merchants because only the Dutch were in a position to supply them efficiently. At the same time the Dutch secured the business of marketing the settlers' crops in Europe. This business was extremely profitable because the European market for West Indian produce was continually increasing, especially that for sugar, since the custom of drinking sweetened coffee and tea was becoming more and more widespread.

European competition for Atlantic trade

Although the Dutch trade with the Spanish colonies was contrary to Spanish law, there was little the Spanish government could do about it. Spain was incapable of supplying all her colonists' needs herself, and her naval power was too weak to prevent the Dutch traders doing much as they pleased. However, from 1650 onwards, the English and French governments did take active steps to confine the trade of their colonies to their own merchants and shipping.

By this date the bulk of Europe's trade with the outside world was being carried in Dutch ships. Englishmen, Frenchmen and other Europeans who wanted Asian, American, or African produce found that they could most expeditiously buy it from Dutch merchants. Now, the economic theory of the seventeenth century laid it down that a nation's wealth, and therefore its power, was determined by its possession of gold and silver. The statesmen of England and France became seriously worried at the prospect that all their nations' stocks of the precious metals would pass to the Dutch to pay for the tropical produce their peoples wanted. Since the amount of gold and silver in the world was limited, England and France would become progressively poorer and weaker, and the Dutch progressively wealthier and stronger. The English and French governments therefore decided that they must increase their nations' share of Europe's overseas trade, not only so that the English and French stocks of gold and silver would cease to diminish, but also so that they would actually increase, because England and France would then be in a position to sell tropical produce to other, less fortunate, European peoples. Consequently, during the seventeenth century the English and French governments fostered the development of national trading companies to compete with the Dutch for overseas trade, particularly in those parts of the world, like Asia and Africa, where the commodities which Europe wanted were bought from native producers or merchants. In America, however, the commodities Europeans required were for the most part produced on plantations owned and managed by European colonists, and other measures were needed to counter the virtual monopoly which the Dutch had built up of the trade of the English and French colonies. The value of such colonies in the eyes of the English and French governments was that they should provide protected markets for home exports, and a means of obtaining tropical produce without the disbursement of gold and silver to alien producers or merchants. So from 1650 onwards both the English and French governments began to enact and enforce laws requiring that the trade of their colonies should be exclusively conducted by the merchants and shipping of their own nations.

This new attitude towards the trade of the English and French plantation colonies in America and the West Indies had important results for West Africa. The plantations were dependent on West Africa for their supply of slave labour, and their demand for slaves was continual and increasing. The demand for slaves was continual because the useful life of a slave on a plantation was at most thirty years, and the slave population of the plantations did not maintain its numbers by natural increase. The state of servitude did not encourage men to marry and raise families, and in any case men outnumbered women as plantation slaves by about two to one. The demand for slaves was increasing because both the plantations and the plantation colonies steadily grew in number to meet Europe's growing demand for the sugar, tobacco, coffee, indigo and other crops that they grew. Since the Dutch, who up to 1650 provided most of the slaves, were no longer to have any share in the trade of the English and French colonies, England and France needed to enter the slave trade on an ever-increasing scale.

European competition for the slave trade

The demand for slaves tended always to exceed the supply, and it was thus clearly profitable for English merchants, for instance, to endeavour to sell slaves to French or Spanish planters as well as to their own colonists. Consequently, from about 1650 onwards, the Atlantic slave trade became highly competitive. In addition to English, French, Dutch and Portuguese slave-traders, merchants of other countries, such as Sweden, Denmark and Brandenburg, began to engage in the business of buying slaves in West Africa and selling them to European planters in the

West Indies and America. Unlike England and France, these countries were not great colonial powers possessing important plantation colonies in America. Such small West Indian possessions as they owned served principally as distributing centres for the slaves they sold to the planters of other nations. These lesser competitors in the slave trade were thus not operating in quite the same manner as England and France, but were rather following the Dutch example of a few years earlier. Indeed the Danish and Brandenburger slaving companies secured much of their capital and experience from Dutch sources, since the monopolising nature of the Dutch West Indies Company and the success of English and French measures in reducing the Dutch share in Atlantic trade had induced some Dutch merchants to seek investments and employment outside the Netherlands.

The newcomers to the slave trade—the English, the French, the Danes, the Swedes, and the Brandenburgers—all found that they could compete effectively with the Dutch in West Africa only if they formed national trading companies, variously called West African or West Indian companies, which were granted charters giving them a monopoly of their nation's trade with West Africa. The first really effective English company, the Company of the Royal Adventurers trading into Africa, was first chartered in 1660, and in 1672 was succeeded by the Royal African Company; the first effective French company was the French West Indies Company, chartered in 1664. It is true that there had been earlier English companies, with a monopoly of English trade to West Africa, chartered in 1588, 1618 and 1631, and that there had been four companies with a monopoly of French trade with West Africa chartered between 1634 and 1658. But none of these earlier English and French West African companies had been a lasting success, and none of them had had, as did the English companies of 1660 and 1672 and the French company of 1664, the provision of slaves for the West Indian plantations as a principal object. Individual merchants were not supposed to trade to West Africa unless they were members of, or licensed by, the appropriate national company.

Trade was officially restricted to the monopoly companies because only large and powerful companies could afford to build, maintain, and garrison the forts on the coasts of West Africa which were deemed essential in the seventeenth century for the conduct of the slave trade. The European traders secured their slaves by buying them at the coast from African merchants who obtained the bulk of them from the interior. Since it was in practice impossible to ensure that slaves and ships both arrived at the coast at a steady rate, depots of some kind were needed where stocks of slaves and of the trade goods that were offered in exchange for them could be kept. These depots needed to be fortified and garrisoned during the seventeenth century so that they could be defended against attacks by the armed forces of a rival slave-trading company or nation.

Between about 1640 and about 1750, a great number of European forts and trading-posts were established on the shores of West Africa, and their ownership was constantly changing as the slave-trading nations fought with each other to enlarge their shares in the trade. But this European struggle for bases in West Africa was only a part of a very much wider competition for trade and empire in the Atlantic. It must not be forgotten that the purpose of the slave trade was to provide the European colonies in the Americas with the slaves needed on their plantations, and the real prizes in the European imperial wars of the period were not bases in West Africa, but colonies and trade in America.

This struggle for Atlantic trade and empire had two main phases. The first was in outline a successful attempt by England and France to destroy the Dutch hold on Europe's overseas trade. The second phase was a bitter and protracted fight between England and France to achieve the ascendancy in world trade and empire which the exhausted Dutch had been forced to relinquish. The two phases overlapped, but it is convenient for West African history to say that the first phase ended with the Treaty of Utrecht in 1713. By this treaty, among other things, England secured the *asiento*, the contract to supply the 4,800 slaves a year that were officially allowed to be imported into Spanish America.[1] By 1713 the French had replaced the Dutch as the strongest European power on the shores of Upper Guinea, and the English were strongly established in competition with the Dutch on the Gold Coast.

The French on the Senegal, *c.* 1630–1758

The French concentrated in West Africa on the exploitation of the extensive area accessible from the sea by the River Senegal. French posts at the mouth of the Senegal were first established in the 1630s, and in 1659 the island of St Louis was selected as their headquarters. A fort was built and a town soon grew up around it. In 1677, Arguin and Goree were captured from the Dutch. Arguin was now of little commercial importance, but Goree was rapidly developed as the principal French maritime base in West Africa.

Under the energetic direction of André Brue between 1697 and 1720, French explorers, traders and missionaries used St Louis and Goree as bases for the extension of French influence over a wide area. The French penetrated inland as far as Bambuk (the Wangara of the Arabs), while to the south trading-posts were established at Albreda on the Gambia and at Bissau and Bulama on the coast of what is now Portuguese Guinea. The

[1] The *asiento* was relinquished by England in 1750.

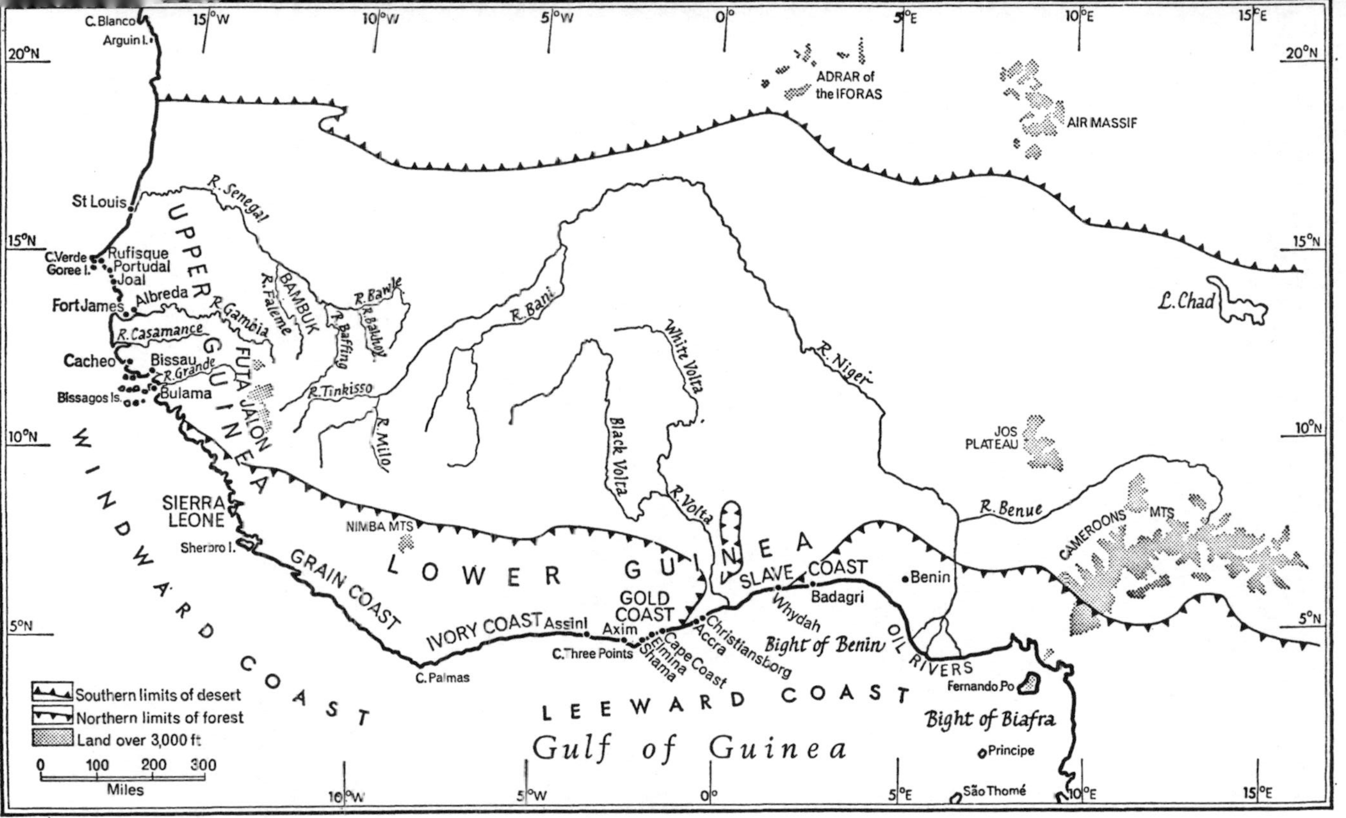

8 Europeans in West Africa, *c.* 1640–*c.* 1750

commercial results of this expansion proved rather disappointing. A trade in gum, wax, ivory, hides and slaves was developed which at its peak was worth about £500,000 or $2,000,000 a year. But the profits from this trade were inadequate to sustain the efforts of maintaining French interests over so great an extent of territory, and this was one of the reasons why none of the French West African companies ever remained solvent for very long. Between 1664 and 1758 there were no less than six such companies in succession. A more particular reason for the repeated failures of the French West African companies was that they never managed to secure enough slaves for the French West Indian plantations. The peak French exports from Africa during the first half of the eighteenth century were probably of the order of 9,000 slaves a year (compared with a British peak for this period, in the 1740s, of about 25,000). The Senegambian region was not a very good one for the European slave trade. In the first place its population was not very great, especially in the north along the Senegal valley, where the French penetration was strongest. Secondly, the more the French penetrated here, the more they met with effective competition from long-established African traders, Mande and Fulani (or Tukolor). Indeed, it proved impossible for them to maintain their inland stations for any length of time, and the more they tried to do so, the more costly it was in manpower and money. It may be doubted in fact whether the French ever succeeded in getting more than about 1,000 slaves a year from the Senegal region, to which the greatest efforts of their companies were directed. It was easier and cheaper to look elsewhere for slaves, and having failed to establish themselves permanently on the Gold Coast, the French slave-traders began to traffic more and more on the Grain and Ivory Coasts and, especially, on the Slave Coast (as well as farther afield, in the Congo and Angola).

Trade on the Windward Coast

From Goree to about Sherbro Island, the slave trade flourished, but neither the West African companies of France and England nor of any other nation ever succeeded in securing a major share of it. A multiplicity of coastal inlets and off-shore islands offered a wide choice of secluded anchorages for any independently owned ship which chose to slip in to do business with the established mulatto traders of the region. As has been seen in chapter 4, although these traders commonly spoke Portuguese and were often in part of Portuguese extraction, they owed allegiance to no European nation and resented any attempt to control their activities. Consequently, this part of the Guinea coast was a happy hunting-ground for slave-traders of many nations, men who were not connected with any of the great national trading companies, and whose trading methods were often of the crudest. Only a very elaborate and expensive system of forts and coastal patrols could have secured the control of this trade in the interests of any one nation or company, and such a system was not in evidence in the eighteenth century. The greater part of the coast was claimed by Portugal, but Portuguese authority was continuous and effective only in the immediate neighbourhood of their settlement at Cacheu. The French posts at Bissau and Bulama soon proved unprofitable and were abandoned. There were usually English settlements on the Sierra Leone river and on or near Sherbro Island, but these were bases for independent merchants unconnected with the English West African companies. The only exception to this pattern of independent trade was on the River Gambia, which afforded a channel for the trade of the interior which was relatively easy to control, and inferior in importance in this region of West Africa only to the Senegal. It was on James Island, not far from the mouth of the Gambia, that the English had erected their first fort in West Africa as early as 1618, but the English companies' hold on the river was not strong enough to prevent the French from establishing a rival trading post at Albreda, on the northern bank of the river, close to James Island.

Trade on the Grain and Ivory Coasts

The major trading companies paid relatively little attention to the Grain and Ivory Coasts during the seventeenth and eighteenth centuries. Malagueta pepper was no longer valuable in world trade. A brisk trade in ivory during the seventeenth century brought about such a swift decline in the number of elephants in the coastal zone that the trade itself had begun to decline by the beginning of the eighteenth century. The strong off-shore current, frequent storms, and the lack of safe anchorages and landing-places which had kept the early Portuguese voyagers away from the coast, were still deterrents to shipping. Consequently the rather thin population, which had played relatively little part in the indigenous development of trade in West Africa, remained little involved in trade with Europeans, and without much stimulus to organise itself for it on any scale sufficient to warrant much in the way of permanent trading posts. A French post was established at Assini, in the extreme east of the Ivory Coast and close by the Gold Coast, at the end of the seventeenth century, but it was abandoned within a few years. Nevertheless, from about the end of the seventeenth century onwards, the growing demand for slaves in the Americas was such as to encourage the ships of individual European merchants to pay more attention to the Grain and Ivory Coasts. The volume of their slave trade here proved erratic, but occasionally they were able to do profitable business.

The Gold Coast

The situation on the Gold Coast was very different: it continued to be one of the major scenes of European activity in West Africa. The gold trade continued. By about the beginning of the eighteenth century, it was probably worth as much as £250,000 or $1,000,000 a year, though by the end of the century it was declining, less because of any fall in the yield of the diggings, it would seem, than because the increase in the strength and prosperity of the Akan states meant that their people required to keep a higher proportion of the gold for their own purposes. However, in the latter part of the seventeenth and in the earlier eighteenth century, the gold trade was still a major lure for the European merchants. Furthermore, its continuance over so many years had made the Gold Coast peoples better organised for trading with the Europeans, and more dependent on the imports these brought, than most West Africans. Thus, when slaves became a major demand of the Europeans, their merchants were both willing and quickly able to organise a steady supply of them.

European trade on the Gold Coast continued in the spirit of bitter competition that had commenced when the Dutch had seized the Portuguese forts. By the early years of the eighteenth century, there were on the Gold Coast about twenty-five major stone or brick-built forts, together with about the same number of smaller trading posts or 'lodges', crammed together on only about 250 miles of coastline. Both the Dutch West Indies Company and the English Royal African Company had their African headquarters here, the Dutch at Elmina, and the English only some ten miles distant at Cape Coast Castle. As well as these two, Swedish, Danish and Brandenburger companies also had forts on the Gold Coast at some time or other in the seventeenth and eighteenth centuries. Of the major European slave-trading nations, only the Portuguese (after their expulsion by the Dutch in 1637–42) and the French never managed to establish themselves on the Gold Coast.

Between 1637 and about 1720, as the European nations fought each other for sea trade and empire and their companies competed with each other in West Africa, the Gold Coast forts were continually changing hands. Thus, for example, the original English headquarters at Kormantin (their first fort on the Gold Coast, begun in 1631) was taken by the Dutch in 1665, while Cape Coast Castle had passed successively through Swedish, Danish and Dutch hands (as well as being for a time in African occupation) before finally falling to the English in 1664. But by about 1720, the position had stabilised. The trade of the central part of the coast, on which gold-dust could be bought, from about Axim to Accra, was controlled by Dutch and English forts which were more or less evenly dispersed along its length. However, the position of the English, with only eight major forts, was weaker than that of the Dutch, who had thirteen, which by and large were stronger and better garrisoned, and who were also in the process of taking over three forts on the western coast from a now bankrupt Brandenburger company. The Swedes had been expelled altogether, and Danish activities had been limited to the eastern end of the coast where, from headquarters at Fort Christiansborg at Osu, close by Accra, they were developing a new chain of small forts, primarily for the slave trade alone, to as far as Keta.

For the rest of the eighteenth century, the main competition, for gold as well as slaves, was between the Dutch and the English. At the beginning of the century, the Dutch took a half or more of the trade, and the English share was about a third. But the English steadily gained ground and by about 1785, when the major part of the Gold Coast trade was the export of about 10,000 slaves a year, more than half of it was in English hands, and the Dutch share was very small.

This English success was in part only a reflection of the fact that the English had replaced the Dutch as the leading commercial nation of western Europe, but it was also facilitated by a reorganisation of the system of English trade with West Africa. Until it was finally liquidated in 1795, the Dutch West Indies Company retained its legal monopoly of Dutch trade with West Africa. In practice, however, more and more of the Dutch West African trade in the eighteenth century was done by 'interlopers', i.e. individual merchants illegally competing with the company. The interlopers benefited from the pioneer work done by the company in building forts to organise and protect Dutch trade. But they made no contribution towards the cost of maintaining the forts and their garrisons, which accordingly absorbed an increasing share of the company's declining profits. The net result of the activities of the Dutch interlopers was therefore to weaken the position of the Dutch nation as a whole in the European trade with West Africa. On the other hand, in 1750 the English, who for some time had been licensing individual traders, finally took them into partnership. The Royal African Company, the London company which had possessed the official monopoly, was dissolved, and replaced by an association, called the Company of Merchants Trading to West Africa, with membership and a share in the management open to merchants from the growing out-ports like Bristol and Liverpool. The new company did not itself engage in trade, but concerned itself solely with the general furtherance of English commercial interests in West Africa, in particular with the upkeep of the English forts, towards the cost of which it received an annual grant from parliament. This English recognition of the value of the independent trader was greatly to the English advantage when the slave trade was extended to the coasts east of the Gold Coast.

Trade on the Slave Coast and in the Gulf of Guinea

The European nations which entered the slave trade from about 1640 onwards to cater for the greatly increased demand for slaves brought about by the extension of sugar planting in the West Indies, first looked for slaves to those parts of the West African coastline where the inhabitants were already accustomed to trade with Europeans. Thus the Dutch began by capturing most of the Portuguese trading-posts; the French by taking the Dutch bases in Upper Guinea; the English by building forts on the Gold Coast to compete with the Dutch. But when the demand for slaves continued to outrun the supply, attention began to be given to those parts of the coastline where European trade had hitherto been little developed. The coast east of the Gold Coast received early attention, since the prevailing winds and currents required ships leaving the Gold Coast to proceed eastwards close to the shore to about as far as Fernando Po before they could set course for Europe or America. By the end of the seventeenth century the coast between the mouth of the Volta and Lagos was already known as the Slave Coast, and during the following century slave-traders of many nations became active in the Oil Rivers (as the mouths of the Niger were then known) and as far as the Gaboon river and beyond. The Portuguese had never paid much attention to the Slave Coast, and, after the cessation of the Benin pepper trade and the emigration to Brazil of the Portuguese planters on São Thomé and the other islands of the Gulf of Guinea, they had done very little trade on the shores of the Gulf. The greater part of the slaves they supplied to Brazil were taken from Angola.

The slave trade which developed on the Slave Coast and on the shores of the Gulf of Guinea was conducted by individual European merchants and small companies rather than by the large national monopoly companies that had developed the earlier trade on the Gold Coast and in Upper Guinea. The idea that large profits could be made by selling slaves to Europeans spread eastwards among the coastal Africans just about as quickly as the eastwards extension of the European trade. Consequently, slaves tended to be available at the coast in numbers large enough to supply all the European merchants who sought to buy them. Thus the building and maintenance of coastal forts to protect each nation's share of the trade became an unnecessary expense. At the same time the African kings and merchants who were growing rich from the slave trade realised, from the example of what had happened on the Gold Coast, that when Europeans were allowed to build strong forts, control of the trade and often of the coastal trading communities was apt to pass into their hands. They were keen that Europeans should buy their slaves, but they wanted a much larger share in determining the conditions on which trade was done.

No permanent fortified bases were built by Europeans on the shores of the Gulf of Guinea. They still needed depots where slaves could be collected and trade goods stored, but this need was often met by the device of mooring hulks in the river mouths. Since there were no expensive forts to maintain and garrison, there was no need for the European slave-traders to band themselves into large monopoly companies; any individual trader was rich enough to provide an old ship to serve as a hulk. Since the European traders operated as individuals and possessed no easily defended bases, they were dependent on the goodwill of the local rulers, and were required to make them presents and to pay duties on their trade.

The circumstances in which trade was conducted on the Slave Coast lay about halfway between those obtaining in the Gulf of Guinea and those on the Gold Coast. The trade was extended to the Slave Coast before the position of the great national West African Companies had been much undermined by the activities of the independent traders, and by the early years of the eighteenth century, French, Dutch, English, and Portuguese companies had all acquired bases on this coast. But the local chiefs did not allow the companies to build strong stone or brick forts on the shore where they could be covered by fire from the guns of their ships. They insisted that the European establishments should be made of mud and thatch, and that they should be built close to their palaces in towns a few miles inland where they could be under their supervision.[1] Thus, whereas at Elmina, Axim, or Cape Coast the agents of the European companies had asserted their control over the trading towns which grew up under the walls of their forts, on the Slave Coast these agents were legally responsible to the native authorities for what they and their fellow-countrymen did. As more of the trade became done by individual merchants, so the role of the companies' agents became more like that of consuls, representing the interests of their nations to the local African authorities.

The British Colony of the Senegambia, 1763–83

Having between them ruined Dutch trade, between 1689 and 1815 Britain and France fought on opposite sides in seven major wars, which had as one of their principal objects the achievement of ascendancy in world trade and empire. The important campaigns were fought in Europe, in America, in India, and on the high seas. West Africa was never more than a subsidiary theatre of war. However, during the Seven Years' War the British captured all the French posts in Upper Guinea.

[1] It would in fact have been difficult for the Europeans on the Slave Coast to have erected stone or brick forts by the sea. The shore was a sandbar, lacking rock to provide either sure foundations or building material.

By the Treaty of Paris in 1763, Goree was returned to France, but Britain retained her other West African conquests. In the following year these were joined with the British posts on the Gambia, hitherto administered by the Company of Merchants, and constituted into the crown colony of Senegambia.

The crown colony of Senegambia is significant as the first attempt made by a British government to assume responsibility for the administration of an area of African territory and its inhabitants. Hitherto British interests in West Africa had been the responsibility of the trading companies, and these had administered only within the coastal forts. The new colony was given a constitution modelled on that of the English colonies in North America, with a royal governor, a nominated council, and an elaborate judicial system, but its administration proved a complete failure. In the first place, its elaborate constitution and machinery of government were ill adapted to a territory few of whose people were used to British ways. Secondly, it had been a serious error of judgement to allow the French to return to their stronghold of Goree. It had been intended that revenue for the upkeep of the expensive crown colony administration should come from duties levied on the colony's trade, but soon the greater part of the trade was in the hands of the French merchants of Goree, who evaded payment of duty. The British administration in Senegambia was thus forced to use the greater part of its limited resources in ineffectual attempts to keep out the French, and the commercial development of the colony, especially in the interior, was neglected. At length, during the War of American Independence (1778–83), the French recaptured St Louis and most of their other former posts on the mainland. Although the British retaliated by taking Goree, at the Peace of Versailles in 1783 Britain's holdings in Upper Guinea were once again restricted to the Gambia, which was restored to the care of the Company of Merchants. The terms of the peace promised Britain a share in the gum trade of the Senegal in return for a French share in the trade of the Gambia, but in practice the French traders were much more successful on the Gambia than the English were ever allowed to be on the Senegal.

The British become the dominant power in trade with West Africa

The real significance for West Africa of the Anglo-French wars of the eighteenth century was not the abortive colony of Senegambia, but the fact that Britain emerged from them holding at least as large a share of the maritime trade of West Africa as all the other European nations combined. Britain's dominance of the trade was already apparent even before the beginning of the French Revolutionary and Napoleonic Wars (1793–1815), during which her blockade of the European coastline virtually halted the activities of all her rivals in the African trade except Portugal and the new United States. On the eve of these wars, in the mid-1780s, at least a third, and possibly nearer a half, of the whole Atlantic slave trade was already in the hands of British or North American merchants. It is not easy to give very precise figures, because estimates vary, but it would seem that about this time British ships were taking an average of something like 38,000 slaves across the Atlantic each year. Estimates for the other slave-trading nations are rather less certain, but the French share seems likely to have been around 25,000 a year, that of the Portuguese possibly about 20,000, and that of all other nations combined probably not more than about 10,000. These are estimates for slaves arriving in the Americas from all parts of Africa. But most of the Portuguese slaves, and about half of the French slaves were being taken from coasts south of the Cameroons, i.e. from outside West Africa. On the other hand, at least two-thirds of the British slave trade was with the West African coast from the Senegal to the Cameroons. Thus as far as the *West* African trade is concerned, it may be said that Britain's share was at least 26,000 slaves a year, compared with perhaps 12,500 a year for the French, and no more than about 14,000 a year for all the other European and American trading nations combined.

Britain's dominance of the maritime trade of West Africa was a reflection of her great and rapidly increasing strength in the whole field of Europe's overseas trade. Each of the Anglo-French wars of the eighteenth century led to a great increase in the size of Britain's mercantile marine and in the extent of her overseas trade, and also to a destruction of the shipping and trade of all the other seafaring nations of western Europe, which tended unavailingly to side with France in the hope of checking the growing maritime strength of Britain. This process reached its culminating development during the wars of 1793–1815, when French trade with West Africa was brought to a complete standstill. About 1798, Britain may have been transporting as many as about 50,000 slaves a year across the Atlantic, and then had only two effective rivals, Portugal, an ally of Britain in the wars, which was taking about 25,000 slaves a year (but mainly from outside West Africa, from the Congo and Angola), and the traders of the new United States of America, transporting about 15,000 slaves a year.

The profits from Britain's increasing foreign trade played a large part in providing the finance for her industrial development, and this in its turn occasioned further expansion of her overseas trade and shipping. Britain's loss of her thirteen North American colonies did not halt this process of commercial growth. Indeed, it seemed to suggest that the growth of British commerce was to some extent independent of the fact that most of the Anglo-French wars also resulted in an enlargement of

Britain's territorial empire in America, the West Indies and Asia. The value of Britain's overseas trade in general, and of her trade with North America in particular, increased more rapidly after 1783 than it had done while the thirteen colonies were still within her empire. Englishmen accordingly began to doubt the idea, which had lain behind the European empire-building of the previous two centuries, that the possession of colonies was essential for the successful development of overseas trade. Indeed, during the hundred years following 1783, they tended to argue that Britain's commercial interests would be best served if the number and extent of her colonies were kept as small as possible. The administration and defence of colonies absorbed money which could be more profitably invested in trade: the only colonies that were really useful were those which provided strategic bases from which the British navy could protect the expanding stream of British merchant shipping in the oceans of the world. Thus we find that although during the Napoleonic wars Britain once again conquered the French colonies in Upper Guinea, they were all returned to France after the peace of 1815.

When the nineteenth century dawned, Europe's trade with West Africa was practically identical with the trade in slaves, and by far the greatest number of slaves were being exported by British merchants. These facts are important for two reasons. In the first place, the British nation believed that its trade would prosper without the extension of British rule over non-European territories and peoples, an opinion with which the British merchants in West Africa, viewing the results of the unhappy Senegambia experiment in colonial administration, were strongly inclined to agree. Secondly, in 1808 Britain made participation in the slave trade illegal for her subjects, and shortly afterwards determined that the West African slave trade should be stopped altogether. The result of these decisions was the relatively rapid destruction of the trade which had provided the basis of the relations between Europeans and West Africans for the previous two centuries, and a new era opened for West Africa. But before this can be considered, it is necessary to turn to deal more directly with what was happening to the peoples and states of Guinea during the era of the slave trade.

6

The slave trade and economic change

The broad effect of the Atlantic slave trade seems to have been to create the conditions for a commercial revolution in Guinea comparable to the earlier commercial growth which had taken place in the western and central Sudan following the stimulus afforded by trans-Saharan trade. In this, the fact that it was a *slave* trade was of far less account than the fact that it represented a really great increase in international trade. It just so happened that the principal external commercial demand on West Africa in the seventeenth and eighteenth centuries was for labour, for slaves to work on the American plantations.

The trans-Saharan trade had involved the export of Negro slaves to the Muslim countries of North Africa and the Near East, but the scale of this northwards export of slaves was nothing like the scale of the Atlantic trade as it had developed by the end of the seventeenth century. To move large numbers of men across the arid and inhospitable desert posed very serious problems; to move them across the ocean by ship was relatively much easier and cheaper. It may be doubted whether at any time it was ever possible to move more than about 10,000 slaves a year across the Sahara, and by and large it must always have been more profitable for the trans-Saharan traders to concentrate on articles of small bulk and high value, rather than on slaves who consumed scarce and expensive resources of food and water.[1]

It is therefore necessary to begin this essay on the economic effects of the Atlantic slave trade on West Africa by trying to establish just how many of its people were removed by the trade.

The volume of the Atlantic slave trade

It is not possible to assess the volume of the Atlantic slave trade with anything approaching absolute certainty, since nobody really appreciated the value of accurate statistics of trade (or of other economic activities) much before the nineteenth century. Thus, although the data available for the trans-Atlantic slave trade are appreciably better than those for the

[1] It has been estimated that the death rate for slaves crossing the Sahara may have been as high as two in five.

trans-Saharan trade, estimates of its total volume vary quite widely. Until very recently, the most commonly accepted figures for the total number of Africans landed in the Americas were of the order of 14 or 15 millions—some, indeed, were even higher than this. Now, however, Professor Philip D. Curtin has made a very careful analysis of such data as are available in Europe and the Americas, and has concluded that the total number of African slaves reaching the New World over the whole period of the Atlantic trade is unlikely to have been more than about 9,300,000. To this figure he would add a further 175,000 for slaves landed in Europe and in the European-held islands off the Atlantic coasts of Africa (Madeira, the Azores, the Canaries, the Cape Verde Islands, and São Thomé and the other islands of the Gulf of Guinea), making a total of nearly 9,500,000. He believes further that the available shipping resources would not have permitted the carriage of a very much greater number than this.

This total can be broken down in a number of ways; first of all, by periods. The slave trade began on a small scale in the later fifteenth and in the sixteenth century, was built up in the later seventeenth century to reach its peak in the eighteenth, and was finally extinguished during the third quarter of the nineteenth century. Curtin's data suggest that the total number of Africans taken to the Americas prior to 1600 was about 125,000, to which may be added about 150,000 taken to Europe and the Atlantic islands, giving a total for the Atlantic trade in the fifteenth and sixteenth centuries of about 275,000. The annual average for this period of about 150 years would therefore be about 1,800, and for the sixteenth century alone about 2,400. In the seventeenth century, Curtin's figure for the total number of Africans reaching the New World is about 1,280,000, to which a further 25,000 or so should be added for slaves taken to Europe (by now a negligible quantity) and to the Atlantic islands (a trade which had practically ceased by the middle of the century). The annual average for the seventeenth century as a whole would thus be about 13,000 a year. However, this statistic conceals the escalation noticeable after the Dutch entry into Atlantic trade in the second quarter of the seventeenth century. In the last fifty years of the century, the number of slaves landed in the Americas was about a million, or an average of about 20,000 a year. Between 1701 and 1810, by about which time most European nations were outlawing the slave trade, the total number of slaves landed in the Americas was about 6,265,000, or an average of about 57,000 a year, and between 1811 and the end of the trade in the 1870s, the estimated total is 1,628,000, or an average of about 27,000 a year. Curtin's estimates are summarised in Table A on p. 83.

But these are estimates for the number of slaves successfully landed overseas. From the African point of view, it is more important to gauge

TABLE A *African slaves landed overseas*

	Slaves landed in		
	Europe & the Atlantic islands	The Americas	Approximate annual average
Up to 1500	33,500	—	670
1501–1600	116,400	125,000	2,400
1601–1700	25,100*	1,280,000	13,000
1701–1810	—	6,265,000	57,000
After 1810	—	1,628,000	27,000
Total	175,000	9,298,000	

* Almost entirely to the Atlantic islands during this period, and all except about 5,000 before *c.* 1650.

the numbers leaving the shores of Africa. The mortality on the slave ships was considerable, though probably hardly higher for the slaves than for the crews—or, indeed, for any voyagers across the oceans in the small sailing ships of the period, where the cramped conditions encouraged the spread of disease, where there were few or no fresh foodstuffs, and where storms or unfavourable winds might easily occasion desperate shortages of provisions or of fresh water. In addition, of course, a proportion of the slave ships setting out from Africa never reached their destinations, being wrecked or lost at sea. Curtin's data suggest that in the eighteenth century about 16 per cent of the slaves shipped from Africa never reached the Americas, and he believes this to be a representative figure for the whole period of the slave trade. To allow for this loss, it is necessary to increase the figures for slaves landed in the Americas by approximately one-fifth to arrive at an estimate for the numbers of slaves *leaving Africa.* This provides the estimates given in Table B.

TABLE B *Slaves exported from Africa*

	Estimated numbers of slaves taken from Africa as a whole	Approximate annual average
Up to 1600	330,000	2,200
1601–1700	1,560,000	15,600
1701–1810	7,520,000	68,400
After 1810	1,950,000	32,500
Total	11,360,000	

At this point in the discussion, it is necessary to take into account the manner in which the export of slaves was distributed in Africa, for by no means all the slaves were taken from the part of the continent with which this book is concerned. Considerable and, as time went on, increasing numbers were taken from the coasts south of the Cameroons, especially from the Congo and Angola, and even from Moçambique. From the figures so meticulously assembled by Professor Curtin, it is possible to deduce that about a third of the slaves in the Spanish American colonies and about 70 per cent in Portuguese Brazil came from outside West Africa, that about a quarter or a fifth of the slaves transported by English-speaking traders were taken from coasts south of the Cameroons, and about a third of the slaves shipped by other traders, principally the French. This would tend to the conclusion that *West* Africa provided about 55 per cent of all slaves taken to America, and this agrees well with the figure of 60 per cent suggested by Curtin's data for the eighteenth century, in which century, of course, most of the slaves were transported.

Effects of the slave trade on the population of West Africa

For the eighteenth century, then, we might approximately estimate the loss of population to West Africa occasioned directly by the slave trade as being about 60 per cent of the number of slaves leaving Africa as a whole, that is at about 4½ million men and women. West Africa's share of the exports in the sixteenth and seventeenth centuries is unlikely to have been substantially different, so that for these two centuries we can estimate, though with somewhat less confidence, a population loss of about 1,100,000. But for the nineteenth century West Africa's share is likely to have been substantially less than 60 per cent. The measures then being taken against the Atlantic slave trade were far more effective north of the equator than south of it, and West Africa's share of the total exports may possibly have been only about a third, or only of the order of about 650,000 people. The total loss of population to West Africa over the whole period of the slave trade might therefore have been of the order of 6¼ million men and women.

There are, of course, considerable areas of uncertainty both in the basic data and in the calculations that have been applied to them. Professor Curtin thinks that his figures could be out by ± 20 per cent, but that they are more likely to prove to be too large than too small. It may therefore be permissible to present Table C as the best guess that can at present be made as to the likely maximum drain on the population of West Africa directly occasioned by the Atlantic slave trade.

In terms of individual human suffering, the involuntary emigration of some 6 million human beings from West Africa, 4½ million in the

TABLE C *Possible loss of population to West Africa occasioned directly by the Atlantic slave trade*

	Per cent of total for all Africa as given in Table B	Loss of population	Approximate average annual loss
Up to 1600	60	200,000	1,340
1601–1700	60	940,000	9,400
1701–1810	60	4,510,000	41,000
After 1810	33	650,000	11,000
Total		6,300,000	

eighteenth century alone, was a crime and a disaster of major proportions, but in quantitative terms it is not very easy to assess what effect the loss of men and women on this scale might have had on the population of West Africa. To begin with, we lack population data for tropical Africa for any period before the early days of colonial administration. Even the early colonial figures for African populations were at best estimates, sometimes hardly more than informed guesses, and there is often considerable argument as to the accuracy even of recent censuses. It seems reasonable to assume, however, that the total population of West Africa in the mid-1960s was about 88 million.[1] The totals of the official estimates for the various territories *c.* 1940 and *c.* 1910 were about 44 and 33 million respectively, but recent demographic inquiries suggest that these estimates are likely to have been on the low side, perhaps by as much as 10 per cent. If therefore we want to have some idea of what the population of West Africa may have been during the period of the Atlantic slave trade, it seems best to work backwards from notional figures of 88 million for *c.* 1965, 48 million for *c.* 1940, and 36 million for *c.* 1910. These suggest that the compound growth rate for the West African population between about 1940 and 1965 was of the order of 2.4 per cent a year, and that the rate between about 1910 and 1940 was of the order of 1 per cent a year. These are high growth rates, but they are not impossibly higher than the rates commonly assumed by demographers for the population of Africa as a whole for these periods. Before the twentieth century, population growth rates, not only in Africa, but throughout the world, were very much lower. The figures commonly accepted for Africa as a whole are of the order of 0·19 per cent per annum for the nineteenth century, and 0·11–0·12 per cent per annum for earlier centuries except the

[1] This figure includes an allowance for the population of Nigeria of 47½ million, compared with the official figure of 57½ million derived from the unhappy 1963 census (see chapter 13); some unofficial estimates go as high as 49 million.

eighteenth when, because of the slave trade, the population of Africa as a whole is assumed to have been more or less static.

It seems reasonable to apply growth rates of these orders to estimate, on the basis of the twentieth-century figures, what the size of the West African population might have been during the slave trade era. Leaving the possible effects of the slave trade out of account, it would seem reasonable to suppose that between about 1500 and 1800, there would have been no major factor to interfere with a gradually increasing rate of population growth. After the introduction of tropical American crops at the beginning of this period, the range of foodstuffs available to West Africans did not change, and there was no radical change either in the relevant technologies, in the available medical knowledge, or in the fundamental social bases of the vast bulk of the people. From about 1810 onwards, with the diminution and final extinction of the export slave trade and, especially from about 1880 onwards, with the coming of colonial rule and the introduction of new technologies and medical knowledge, there should have been a gradually accelerating increase in the rate of population growth.

Estimating on this basis, it seems possible that *c.* 1500, when the Atlantic slave trade was just beginning, the population of West Africa may have been of the order of 20 million, and that *c.* 1700, when the trade was beginning to reach its peak of intensity, it may have been of the order of 25 million. Such estimates, of course, can only be very rough guides; the figures here are, if anything, on the conservative side. If the population were in fact somewhat larger than has been suggested for these dates, then, of course, the effects of the slave trade on it would be less than is suggested. But even on the basis of 20 million for *c.* 1500 and 25 million for *c.* 1700, it can readily be seen that the rate of loss due to the operation of the slave trade in the sixteenth and seventeenth centuries should have been very much smaller than the natural growth rate. It is unlikely, perhaps, to have had very much more effect than to give net growth rates in the sixteenth century of the order of 0·10 per cent and in the seventeenth century of the order of 0·12 per cent, instead of rates of the order of 0·12 per cent and 0·15 per cent respectively that could be assumed had there been no export of slaves.

In the eighteenth century, the effect of the export slave trade on population growth must have been very much more serious. If at the beginning of the century, the population were 25 million, then an average loss of something like 41,000 men and women a year throughout the century would be equivalent to a rate of loss of just over 0·16 per cent a year (i.e. a loss every year of 16 persons out of every 10,000). Though less than the likely rate of population growth through natural increase in the second half of the century, which may have been of the order of 0·19 per cent a year or more, such an average rate of loss due to the slave trade would appear to have been marginally higher than the likely natural rate of increase of population in the first half of the century. In the earlier part of the eighteenth century, therefore, the slave trade might have caused an absolute, if small, decrease in the total population.

However, there may well have been no such absolute decrease, because only a third of the slaves exported were women. Since West African societies were polygynous, the number of children not born in West Africa because of the enforced emigration of their mothers would have been less than would have been the case had as many women been exported as were men. The conclusion then is that, when the slave trade was at its height in the eighteenth century, West Africa's loss of manpower was more or less equivalent to the natural increase of population, and that at worst the total population remained static. (To this one might add, of course, that had there not been this artificial check to population growth in the eighteenth century, the population of West Africa *c.* 1965 might possibly have been nearer 118 than 88 million. But if this were so, then population pressures which are manifest today in certain parts of West Africa would be both more acute and more widespread.) In the nineteenth century, with a declining slave trade and with a gradually increasing rate of natural growth, the population would have begun to grow again, and at increasing rates, perhaps reaching between 0·3 and 0·4 per cent per annum by the 1850s.

It will be apparent that no allowance has been made in these estimates for any loss of life due to the operation of the slave trade within West Africa itself: for example, deaths directly or indirectly caused by raiding for slaves, and deaths on the way to the coast or while awaiting shipment. It is unlikely, however, that such losses would significantly affect the conclusions, especially bearing in mind that the slave trade figures may err on the side of overestimation, and those for population on the side of underestimation. There is no evidence to suggest that at any time the operations of the slave trade within West Africa caused anything like the devastation and loss of life that sometimes resulted from the Arab slave trade of the nineteenth century in parts of east and central Africa, where the business of slaving in the interior was sometimes conducted by men who were strangers to the societies within which they were operating. It would be difficult to show that the loss of life among slaves, or in the processes of obtaining slaves, was significantly greater than that occurring among free men generally, or that due anyhow to warfare, judicial executions, human sacrifices and other accepted practices.[1]

However, it is by no means sufficient to consider crude averages for the

[1] See below, p. 95. It might be added that the movement of slaves through West Africa down to the coast must have served to spread disease, but perhaps not appreciably more so than the movements of traders which had begun before the slave trade.

whole of West Africa over long periods, for on some parts of the coast at some periods the incidence of the Atlantic slave trade could be far higher than the average. Thus it is clear, for example, that in the eighteenth century, more than half of *all* the slaves taken from Africa to the Americas were taken from the coast from modern Liberia to the Cameroons, and, indeed, that the Slave Coast and the Niger delta region alone were then providing about a third of *all* slaves exported from the whole of Africa. This uneven distribution of slaving operations may be demonstrated by estimated figures for the decade of the 1780s (Table D). These show the slave trade at or about its peak, and may be more accurate than many slave trade estimates, because this was the time when, with abolition of the trade in the air, both its opponents and its proponents were actively collecting information about it.

TABLE D *Approximate average numbers of slaves taken each year from the different coasts during the 1780s*

	Annual numbers	Approximate percentages
West African coasts:		
Senegambia	2,200	
Sierra Leone region	2,000	7
Grain and Ivory Coasts	4,000	
Gold Coast	10,000	9
Slave Coast to Benin	12,500	14
Niger delta and Cameroons area	22,000	25
All other parts of Africa	40,300	45
Total	93,000	

If the losses caused by the Atlantic slave trade did have a very damaging effect on the population of West Africa, one might expect that this would be most noticeable in the lands adjacent to the 1,000 miles of coast from the Gold Coast to the Cameroons. But today the territories of modern Ghana, Togo, Dahomey and Nigeria stand out as one of the most densely populated blocs of West Africa (and West Africa as a whole is the most densely populated part of tropical Africa). Although there has been some recent migration to the coastlands from the interior, visitors to these coastlands from Ghana to Nigeria in the eighteenth and early nineteenth centuries commonly also commented on the density of their populations at that time. This tends to confirm the belief that in West Africa the rate of population loss due to the export slave trade may not have been crippling in its immediate effects. It suggests, moreover, that part of the explanation for the high contribution to the slave trade of lower Guinea was simply that this was the most densely populated area of West Africa within easy reach of the coast. It is even conceivable that it may have been more profitable for some parts of this area to have exported the equivalent of its natural growth of population rather than to have kept it at home.

Such a hypothesis is not as wild as it might seem at first sight, because it must also be remembered that the parts of West Africa which contributed most slaves to the Atlantic slave trade were also those parts of the Guinea coastlands which were most advanced in their economic organisation (and those which contained some of the most developed political organisations also). In seeking to assess the effects on West Africa of the export trade in slaves, we must take into account other factors than simply the loss of population.

The growth of trade in Guinea

In the first place, the European slave-traders were *traders*, who bought their slaves from coastal African merchants. The capturing or kidnapping of slaves by force by Europeans did occasionally occur, especially perhaps in the early stages of the trade. But it was extremely rare, because it naturally led to estranged relations with the coastal Africans. In any direct confrontation on shore before the nineteenth century, these could always bring stronger forces to bear than the small numbers of Europeans available. The forcible capture or kidnapping of slaves by the Europeans thus in the long run always meant fewer, not more, slaves available for transport to and sale in the Americas.

In return for the slaves they bought, the Europeans provided West African traders with many kinds of goods: textiles (woollens and linens manufactured in Europe; cottons manufactured, before the nineteenth century, mostly in India; and silks manufactured either in Europe or in Asia); all kinds of firearms, gunpowder and shot; knives and cutlasses; many kinds of European-made ironmongery and hardware; iron, copper, brass, and lead in bar form; beads and trinkets; spirits (rum, brandy, or gin, according to the country of origin of the trader); and many kinds of provisions.

These imports clearly had value to the West Africans, for otherwise they would not have been willing to exchange slaves for them. It is true that there are different ways of assessing this value. It can be argued, for instance, that the import of European spirits, a significant proportion of the total trade, was harmful to West African society, and that it might have been better if the Africans had kept to their traditional beers and palm wine, but this would be a value judgement which clearly did not find favour with many Africans at the time. It may be that the import of guns and ammunition made it easier for Africans to kill other Africans or to capture them for sale as slaves. But it was probably also a factor enabling some of them to establish stronger and more effective governments over larger areas. It may be pointed out that the growing imports of cloth, hardware and metals tended to weaken or to destroy African village industries making these things. But Africans would not have bought these imports if they had not been cheaper or better or more widely available than their own manufactures.

It is not very easy to place a monetary value on the imports which West Africa received in return for its exports of slaves. In the first place, there are two different ways in which the European goods may be priced. There are the prices which the European merchants had to pay in Europe or elsewhere to obtain them, and there are the monetary values which they placed on them when selling in Africa. By the end of the seventeenth century, European merchants were coming to accept a convention by which the selling price in Africa was commonly about twice the buying price in Europe. Since they had to pay for shipping and storage, and for insurance or to cover themselves against various risks or losses (which could be heavy in seventeenth- and eighteenth-century conditions), and also to show a profit, this may not have been an unreasonable mark-up. Presumably also, they could not in the long run charge more for their imports than the Africans were willing to pay, and the Africans would determine this in relation to what they were accustomed to pay for their own locally made cloth, metals, cutlasses, etc. So, from the point of view of the history of West Africa and its imports (as opposed to that of Europe and its exports), it seems more sensible to accept as the standard the prices placed on European imports in Africa rather than those applying in their countries of origin.

The values placed on African slaves in terms of European trade goods varied quite widely. The best prices were paid for what were termed 'prime slaves', that is, healthy males between about 12 and 35 years of age, the kind of slaves who might be expected to be most useful as plantation labourers in the Americas. Slave-traders would try and make up their cargoes as much as possible from this group, but if prime slaves were in short supply, they would also buy children, older or less fit men, or women up to the age of about 25 (after which age the effects of child-bearing were deemed to make them unsuited for plantation labour), and the prices of these would rise accordingly. The numbers of slaves available for sale in any one place at any one time, and also the number of slave-ships seeking cargoes, were subject to considerable fluctuations, and these naturally occasioned considerable fluctuations in prices. By and large, however, since the American demand for slaves was always increasing, and the African supply tended to lag behind the demand, the prices paid for slaves were always tending to increase.

Concentrating on the eighteenth century, when the slave trade was at its height, it might be said that, in terms of the current prices placed on European trade goods in Africa, the average value of a prime slave in the early years of the century may have been about £15 (or $60), and in the closing years at least £25 ($100). Since the number of slaves exported from West Africa in the second half of the century (as opposed to the numbers from Africa as a whole) was not significantly greater than the number in the first half, and assuming that only half the exports were of prime slaves (which is reasonable, bearing in mind that approximately one third were women), the average price per slave, irrespective of sex, age, or condition, over the century as a whole might be about £15 ($60). On this fairly conservative basis, the contemporary value of the goods received by the West African economy in exchange for slaves exported to America in the eighteenth century would be of the order of at least £66,000,000 ($264,000,000). In annual terms, the smaller numbers of slaves exported at lower prices in the early years of the century might be valued as at least £450,000 ($1,800,000) a year, and the larger number at higher prices in the closing years as at least £1,000,000 ($4,000,000) a year.

Such sums may seem small by present-day standards. But by eighteenth-century standards and in relation to the economic development of West Africa, they were far from negligible. At the beginning of the century, for example, England, the major trading power of the time, with a population perhaps a third of West Africa's, was importing about £6,000,000 ($24,000,000) of goods a year. As late as the 1850s, the explorer Barth reckoned the state revenue of Kano, then a rich West African state, at about £20,000 ($80,000) a year, and the value of its exports of cloth and slaves together with that of its imports of kola and salt at about £130,000 ($520,000) a year, adding that 'a whole family in that country may live with ease, including every expense' for about £4 or £5 ($16 or $20) a year.

There can be no doubt that in the eighteenth century West Africa's involvement in the slave trade was big business, contributing substantially to the growth of her trade. It must have greatly stimulated trade generally, though especially in lower Guinea. The slaves had to be fed and cared for while still in African hands, thus providing new markets for local production. The European slave-traders brought considerable new business to African merchants and producers, since they had to buy provisions for the slaves on the voyage across the Atlantic. The slave trade brought increasing numbers of Europeans to the shores of West Africa, so that there was a growing number of buyers for her gold, ivory, gums, woods, palm oil and many other things besides the slaves and their provisions. Taking exports and imports together, the new international trade of West Africa by sea that had been engendered principally by the demand for slaves in the Americas may have increased from not far short of £2,000,000 ($8,000,000) a year at the beginning of the eighteenth century to something over £4,000,000 ($16,000,000) at the end. This must have been a very considerable stimulus to the internal economic development of Guinea, and one more than comparable to the earlier stimulus of the trans-Saharan trade in the Sudan.

The number of professional traders must have considerably increased. Buying and selling slaves necessitated more professional merchants, in part because establishing the prices of slaves or of European imports—or, indeed, of any goods for sale in West Africa—in terms of the currencies used, some of which were themselves commodities of trade, was a complex and professional business. The use of these currencies—such as gold-dust on the Gold Coast, cowrie shells and metal bars on the Slave Coast, bars of iron in Sierra Leone, pieces of cloth on the Ivory Coast and in the Cameroons—must have increased and spread. The merchants, the officials who were increasingly needed to regulate trade in each state, the soldiers in the armies who captured the slaves, indeed many new kinds of professional men, had less time available to grow their own food, to make houses or clothing, and so stimulated other peoples' production for exchange. West Africa indeed became a land renowned for its markets.

The growth of slavery

This veritable commercial revolution must also have stimulated the growth of a slave class in West Africa itself. There seems in fact to have been a close connection between economic development and the growth of slavery within West African society. It has already been noted that, by about 1500, the Portuguese found that there was a demand for slaves on the Gold Coast, and that the value of slaves was also appreciated at Benin, where the export of male slaves was prohibited. This situation contrasts with that found among the coastal peoples of upper Guinea. Early Portuguese accounts of these peoples afford practically no evidence for the existence of a slave class. Its development seems to have been mainly a consequence of their own demand for slaves, of the growth of Mande commerce, and of the Mane conquests.

Questions of the origin and the social and economic role of slavery in West Africa tend to be confused by the indiscriminate use of the single word 'slave' to cover a number of social and economic conditions, few of which approximated to slavery as it was understood, for example, on American or West Indian plantations. In one sense, indeed, only kings were wholly free men—that is, not subordinate to any other earthly control. All men and women under their jurisdiction might be spoken of as 'slaves', whereas 'subjects' would be the more appropriate word. Great men would seek to attach themselves directly to the protection of a king, lesser men to greater men, and so on, so that each man would in some sense regard himself, and be regarded, as 'slave' to another. But this was more properly 'clientage' or 'serfdom', not slavery. On another level, it might be said that the only 'free men' in West African society were the family or household heads. These were responsible to greater men, ultimately to chiefs or kings, for their wives and children, and for other members of the family or household who were not kin, but who had in some way attached themselves to it or been impressed into it. Such men and women would be called 'slaves', but were more properly 'servants'. There were also people who had been pledged to others by their kin—or had pledged themselves, even—in respect of a debt or some other obligation, or merely to learn a trade or to acquire some skill or education. These too might be referred to as 'slaves'.

All these various kinds of 'slaves'—subjects, serfs, servants, pledges or pawns, apprentices—would have well-recognised rights in society. Almost invariably, too, there would be a recognised procedure by which they could return to the status of 'freemen'. Their condition was far removed from the abject status of the slaves on the trans-Atlantic plantations. In practice, these were virtually unprotected by law, and were chattels, the absolute property of their masters, who could buy, sell or maltreat them more or less as they pleased, much as they might the cattle they might also employ on their fields.[1]

The commercial revolutions initiated in Guinea by the Atlantic slave trade, and in the Sudan by the trans-Saharan trade, seem undoubtedly to have influenced the formation in West Africa of a new way of looking at men and women which approximated more closely to the idea of chattel slavery, and to have led to the emergence of what might be termed a slave class. The new idea developed that men and women could be valued not only in respect of the social status—royalty, elder, family head, freeman, retainer, etc.—to which they had been born or to which they had become attached, but also in economic terms.

This was not due simply to the growth of the *slave trade*, dominant though this became in Guinea, and important though it was throughout West Africa in spreading the idea that men and women could be viewed not only as members of society, but also as property which could be priced in terms of money or other commodities, and which, as with other property, might be exchanged, bought or sold. The growth of *trade* generally increased the need for the organisation of labour in ways and in quantities which were foreign to the traditional organisation of society in kinship groupings, and suggested too that labour itself had an economic value.

[1] It may be appropriate to note that *chattel* originally meant *cattle*, which, in effect, the slaves on the plantations were virtually replacing; both words come from the Latin word which gives us *capital*, i.e. 'chief property'.

Labourers were needed in growing numbers for a variety of purposes. In Guinea, where animal transport was impossible because of the tse-tse fly and because of the lack of fodder in the forests, porters were needed to carry the ever-growing flow of trade goods. Labourers were needed to grow foodstuffs and to produce other commodities for the developing towns and markets, and to bring them to the markets; to maintain the paths; to build and maintain and to run the houses of the class—merchants, rulers, officials—which was becoming increasingly wealthy as a result of the growth of trade. These demands for labour could not always be met, or could not wholly be met, within the traditional social system. Today, of course, they are met by a system of wage-earning, but, as with societies everywhere, the development of this and of the full-fledged monetary economy which is its prerequisite, could only be gradual. The more immediate recourse was to a slave economy.

It is apparent that the exchange economies of the major states of the western and central Sudan were to a considerable extent dependent on slave labour by about the fourteenth century. It would appear, too, that with the extension of trade from the Sudanese centres, elements of a slave economy had reached as far south as the Gold Coast and the Benin region by the beginning of the sixteenth century, even if they were not yet apparent in the coastlands of Upper Guinea. With the growth of trade on the coasts following the great European demand for slaves in the seventeenth and eighteenth centuries, the growth of a slave economy was consolidated in every part of West Africa which was reached by the major trade-routes. Thus by the beginning of the nineteenth century, for example, we know that some of the great men of the Ashanti kingdom possessed estates or whole villages of people engaged in productive labour for exchange and for the profit of their masters or of the state.

Against this background, it becomes easier to see how the African societies were able to meet the European demand for labour in the Americas. Principal men of enterprise at all levels of society, from family heads to kings, became increasingly aware of the economic value of their servants, pawns, serfs and subjects, and became increasingly keen to add to their numbers to the greatest possible extent. All possible means to this end were exploited. The evidence suggests that rather less than a third of their slaves were acquired through what might be described as 'normal' social processes: becoming slaves because they had been convicted of crime, had become debtors, or simply because they were poor, and so had been sold by relatives (or had even sold themselves). Rather less than a third again seem to have been unfortunate people, who had no powerful friends or had become detached from their families or were strangers, who were more or less kidnapped. The remainder, perhaps nearly 50 per cent, were in origin prisoners of war.

Before the growth of the slave economy and the slave trade, prisoners taken in war might have been retained by their captors as servants or serfs. Thus they would gradually have been absorbed into their captors' society, acquiring rights in the process, possibly even ultimately the status of freemen (which would certainly go to their male children by local wives). Alternatively they might have been used as human sacrifices, or they might have been held to be ransomed back by the society from which they had been taken. Now, however, there were new and often attractive alternatives: slave labour in their captors' economy, or sale to the slave traders. In the eighteenth and nineteenth centuries, Europeans sometimes argued that West African wars were often deliberately fought to secure men and women for human sacrifices or slavery. However, both Ashanti and Dahoman kings are known to have specifically denied this, arguing that monarchies had to maintain their interests and their power, that war was a common result of this, and that the acquisition of captives by the victors was a likely consequence of any war.

There would seem to be much to be said for this point of view. Nevertheless there can be no doubt that the principal men of many West African societies were becoming increasingly rich and powerful through their acquisition of growing numbers of slaves. Conversely, of course, life for ordinary men and women, unless they bound themselves to powerful patrons, was becoming less safe and secure, and increasing insecurity and acquisitiveness must certainly be put to the debit side of the slave-trade account. It is also apparent that the newly emergent rich and powerful men were more and more aware that they had a choice of retaining their slaves—as servants, labourers, artisans, soldiers, traders, etc.—in their own service, or of selling them to buy other things of value to them. This was basically an economic choice, a decision as to which choice seemed more valuable and remunerative. In so far as they were inclined to place growing numbers of their slaves on the market, and, indeed, to regard slaves increasingly as marketable commodities, they were also helping to build up, closely associated with themselves, an increasingly rich and influential merchant class. The growing business of the export–import trade was in fact very closely associated with the growth of political power. Kings and their officials were often themselves the principal merchants, or they employed as traders their junior kinsmen or their own most trusted slaves. They certainly determined the conditions under which trade was carried on, required a percentage of the profits for themselves, or demanded fees, duties or presents from the traders—on the coast, from European as well as African merchants. The growth of long-distance trade in Guinea, as well as in the Sudan, was closely associated with the rise of major kingdoms, and the history of some of these forms the subject of the next chapter.

7

The political development of lower Guinea from the sixteenth to the eighteenth century

By the sixteenth century, when European merchants were developing their trading activities along the West African coasts, the idea of political statehood had already taken firm root among some of the peoples of lower Guinea. It has already been seen that the good organisation of the kingdom of Benin seemed to the early Portuguese pioneers to provide an opportunity for the spread of their influence. It has been suggested, moreover, that it was in fact the very strength of the kingdom that led the Portuguese to abandon their plans to infiltrate it. On the Gold Coast, the existence of organised states, containing established merchant communities and an accepted body of law and custom to regulate trade, undoubtedly contributed to the success of the European traders there, both when, as at first, they sought gold and, later, when they demanded slaves also. Behind Benin and the states of the Gold Coast littoral were yet other states, the Yoruba kingdoms and the Akan states of the interior, capable of supplying the coastlands with regular supplies of the commodities which interested the Europeans, and providing them with assured markets for their own goods.

Until about the end of the seventeenth century, however, the scale of the commercial operations engendered by the presence of European traders on the coast was such that the interior was hardly known to the outside world. The two-way flow of goods was assured, so that the Europeans had no need to penetrate beyond the immediate coastlands, and the interior communities were content to do their business by sending their traders to lodge with merchants at the coast who acted as agents for, and intermediaries in, the trade with the Europeans. With the great increase in trade following the phenomenal growth of the Atlantic slave trade from the latter part of the seventeenth century onwards, the situation began to change.

In the Oil Rivers east of Benin and Warri, where hitherto there would seem to have been little overtly political development, new city-states emerged which were specifically directed towards trading with the Europeans, and more than able to hold their own with them. On the Gold and Slave Coasts, however, earlier political developments had already produced a multiplicity of small kingdoms. With the growth of their commerce, the influence of the Europeans in these states greatly increased, with the result that the African political systems became weakened, divided, or otherwise subverted to the European influence. The growing weakness of the coastal kingdoms created a problem for the kings and merchants of the interior communities. With the growth of trade on the coast, their own commercial activities were becoming increasingly directed to the south, rather than to the north, to the older trading system of the Sudan. This still remained important to them, but they were becoming more and more involved in the coastal trade, which by and large was becoming capable of providing them with imports more cheaply than the northern trade routes, and which in one case, namely guns and ammunition, afforded supplies of a desired import which the northern traders could not effectively provide at all. But with the growth of European influence on the Gold and Slave Coasts, its kingdoms were becoming less satisfactory as intermediaries in the trade between the interior and the Europeans. Their laws and governments were less effective in ensuring the security required for the inland merchants to operate satisfactorily, and the European traders were more and more able to decide the terms of trade in their own favour.

The kings and leading men of the interior responded to this situation by organising more powerful and extensive governments, and by seeking to extend their own systems of law and order down to the coast itself. Thus between about 1670 and 1700, the Europeans on the coasts were forced to take cognisance of a series of powerful states of the interior, such as Denkyira, Akwamu and, ultimately, Ashanti in the hinterland of the Gold Coast; and Oyo and Dahomey behind the Slave Coast. But since these states were well organised to bring trade to the coast, so that there was no incentive for the Europeans to penetrate inland, and they were also sufficiently strong and determined to keep the Europeans out, there is relatively little in the way of contemporary accounts of the rise and of the organisation of the states of lower Guinea in their prime to rival the accounts available from Arabic sources for many of the great states of the western and central Sudan. Much has to be inferred from their own traditional oral histories, which rarely afford more than an outline of their political history, the names of the kings and bare statements of their more important achievements, and from the essentially commercial correspondence of the Europeans on the coast who were viewing events in the interior from a distance.

The kingdom of Benin

However, Benin, close by the sea, and already a considerable kingdom when the Portuguese arrived, is a notable exception to the general rule. The most detailed accounts of Benin in its prime in fact came mainly from Dutch visitors of the period *c.* 1600–*c.* 1640, when Dutch merchants were anxious to increase their share in West African trade, and thus keen to find out as much as possible about the political conditions governing trade on the coast. By this time the power of Benin was effective in the west to at least as far as the fishing and trading settlement at Lagos, while in the east Benin influence extended to the Niger, and included Warri (though the establishment of the Portuguese here was doubtless a factor tending to convert this Benin principality into an independent kingdom). The east–west extent of the Benin kingdom was thus something like 200 miles. The extent of its power to the north is more vaguely known, and there was probably no need for definite limits to be fixed until the rise of Oyo power made it advisable for a boundary to be agreed at Otun, in Ekiti country, about 100 miles from the sea.

From the sources available in the middle of the seventeenth century, the Dutch author Olfert Dapper put together an account of Benin, from which it may be said that Europeans of the early seventeenth century seem to have been as impressed by Benin as earlier Arabic writers had been by ancient Ghana and Mali. Dapper's account begins with a description of the capital, Benin City. Together with its palaces, it was said to have a perimeter of some 24 miles, and 'thirty main streets, very straight and 120 feet wide'. The palace of the *Oba*, the king, a collection of buildings surrounded by a wall, occupied as much space as the town of Haarlem in the Netherlands, and contained 'five galleries most of which are as big as those on the Exchange Building at Amsterdam'. These galleries were supported by wooden columns on which were fixed the brass plaques so famous in Benin art, on which, says Dapper, their 'victories are depicted'. The houses of ordinary people, of wood and palm-thatch, were only of one storey, but they were arranged 'in good order'. Furthermore, 'in the houses of the gentry there are long galleries, and many rooms whose walls and floors are of red earth. These people are in no way inferior to the Dutch as regards cleanliness; they wash and scrub their houses so well that they are polished and shining like a looking glass.'

Indeed the general picture is of a very well-ordered community, reminiscent of the Mali visited by Ibn Battuta three centuries earlier. Thus care was taken to provide supplies of good clean water for travellers on the road to Benin City from its port at Ughoto, and in general it was a country of 'people who have good laws and a well organised police; who live on good terms with the Dutch and other foreigners who come to trade with them, and show them a thousand marks of friendship'.

Trade with the Europeans was under the strict control of the *Oba* and his ministers, and the general impression given is one of a strong and effective government organised under its divine monarchy.

By the beginning of the eighteenth century, however, things had changed. The Dutch merchant David van Nyendael visited Ughoto and Benin City in 1702, and wrote a long and very interesting description. In many respects he says much the same as Dapper had done, though with considerably greater detail, but both Benin City and Ughoto had suffered seriously from civil wars and were in a half-ruined state, and it seems that there had been a lessening in the power of the monarchy and in its control over trade. Benin traditions for the period covering the second half of the seventeenth century, between the date of Dapper's information and the time of Nyendael's visit, are unfortunately rather vague and difficult to interpret. But this in itself is significant, suggesting that the kingdom was passing through a period of unusual strain. The period is characterised by an uncertain succession, a number of short reigns and the only deposition in Benin history, and by conflict between the *Obas* and the chiefs who represented the interests of the people of Benin.

The constitution of Benin was complex, and doubtless one always subject to change. There was probably always a possibility of conflict between nobles and chiefs, who were the hereditary or chosen representatives of the people, and kings, whose office was sacred and who were responsible to the gods and their ancestors; and the risk of such conflict would be increased by the tendency of the kings to create classes of officials responsible directly to themselves. It may well never be known what the dissensions of the later seventeenth century were about. But it seems possible that one of the factors involved was a commercial one. With the growing preoccupation of the European merchants in West Africa with the trade in slaves, the prohibition on the export of male slaves must have placed Benin at a growing disadvantage in its foreign trade compared with neighbouring states. The kingdom must have been becoming relatively poorer, and the members of its merchant community more and more dissatisfied with a royal control of trade which they would have viewed as prejudicial to their own interests.

It is significant that, shortly before the time of Nyendael's visit, the royal prohibition on the export of male slaves was rescinded. It should also be noted that the time of troubles in Benin corresponds with the period in which one of the Yoruba kingdoms, Oyo, was establishing its hegemony over its fellows, and opening up direct relations between Yoruba traders and the European merchants on the coasts. It seems likely that earlier trade between the coast and Yorubaland had been conducted largely via Benin, which controlled the coast as far west as Lagos, and possibly beyond (to Badagri, or even, perhaps, as far as Whydah). If so, then the growth of Oyo power, and the development of direct trading contacts between Yorubaland and the Europeans on the coast, must also have been an economic factor contributing to the difficulties which Benin seems to have experienced during the later seventeenth century.

The rise of the Oyo empire

Originally Oyo was simply one of a number of small kingdoms based on the walled cities of Yoruba settlement in the boundary land between forest and savanna in what is now the south-west of Nigeria and south-easternmost Dahomey. These states were essentially independent of one another except that they all acknowledged the ritual supremacy of Ife. Ife was regarded as the first Yoruba settlement, and all the Yoruba kings traced their descent from its first mythological king, Oduduwa, who—according to one legend—was the son of God sent to earth to rule the Yoruba from Ife. Accordingly the other Yoruba kings regarded the *Oni* of Ife as a ritual superior with a right to confirm their own succession to office. (The dynasty of Benin also traced its descent from the marriage between an Ife prince, who had been invited to Benin by its traditional nobles, and a local woman, and its kings also sent to Ife for confirmation of their accessions.)

Oyo was the northernmost of the Yoruba kingdoms, and initially unremarkable except that its position in the savanna—its capital was only about fifty miles from Jebba, where today the Niger is crossed by the railway—meant that its relations with the not dissimilar kingdoms of Borgu and Nupe were its main external preoccupation. In the sixteenth century, Nupe was an expansive state, and the Oyo kings were forced for a time to seek refuge in Borgu, with whose kings they were related by marriage. The danger then was that Oyo might become a Borgu satellite. Oyo seems to have survived the pressures on it from Nupe and Borgu only because its king, the *Alafin*, established a stronger position in relation to the council of nobles, the *Oyo Misi*, who traditionally represented the community as a whole, than was customary among the Yoruba, and through the development of a strong army based on the use of cavalry.

The importance of cavalry in its army suggests that at this time Oyo's trading relations were orientated northwards, for horses could only have come from the north. But around the beginning of the seventeenth century, there seems to have been a significant change. The tradition of the reign of *Alafin* Obalokun reports the introduction of good salt to

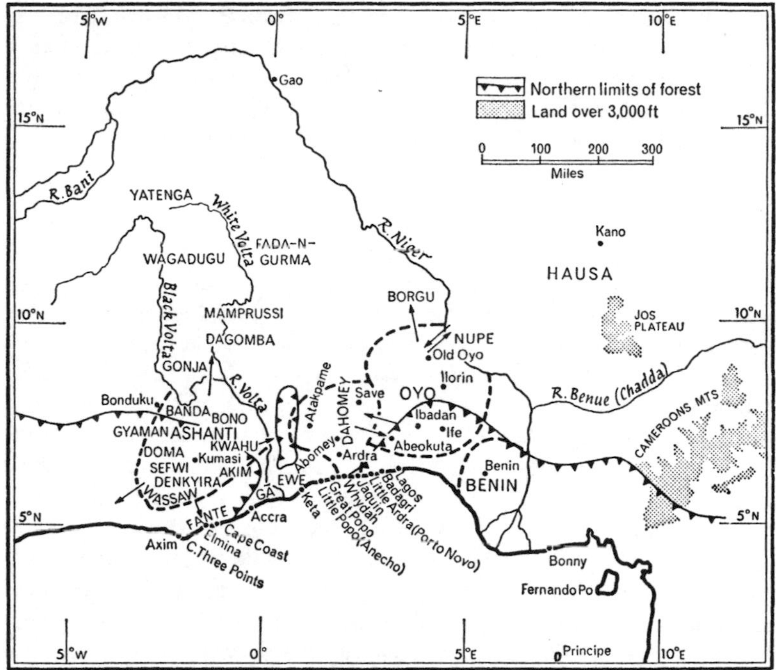

9 The states of the Guinea Forest, *c.* 1700–1900

replace the inferior product which was produced locally (from vegetable ash), a new contact of some kind with non-Negro peoples, and the beginning of Oyo wars of conquest to the south. Although both good salt and contacts with non-Negroes could be associated with trade stemming from the Sahara, the tradition that at this time Oyo also began to expand towards the south, towards forestlands unsuited to the use of cavalry (indeed, its armies seem not to have been very successful in their first southern campaigns), suggests most strongly that this was the time when this most northerly and militant Yoruba state began to feel the pull of the trade routes which were developing from the activities of the European merchants on the coast, and from their growing demand for slaves.

The forest must always have been a barrier to an army which had cavalry as its principal arm, but at this time the greater part of Yoruba country lay north of the forest proper, and Oyo seems quickly to have established a hegemony over many of the other kingdoms. The need for defining a boundary with Benin in the south-east has already been mentioned, but the main drive of Oyo expansion seems to have been to the south-west, along the southwards-sloping northern edge of the forest, which ultimately comes to an end at the coastline just west of Porto Novo. This was a coastline on which the European merchants were actively developing their trade in slaves during the second half of the seventeenth century, and by the 1680s at least, their reports make it evident that the campaigns of its cavalry had made Oyo the dominant power in this region.

The states of the western Slave Coast, the rise of Dahomey, and the fall of Oyo

The coast between Keta and Badagri, on which the Europeans had begun to establish trading-posts in the 1660s, was divided between about five very small African principalities. These may be essentially identified from west to east as Little Popo (modern Anecho), Great Popo, Whydah,[1] Jakin, and Little Ardra (modern Porto Novo). Though the Popos had links with the Gã further west, these were all broadly settlements of the Aja people, whose traditions looked back to the route of migration from Ketu through Tado to Nuatsi. Specifically the Aja regarded Tado as the point from which they had dispersed to establish their states, and the principal of these was Allada, or Great Ardra, with its capital about forty miles north of Whydah. The coastal states may originally, indeed, have been little more than provincial divisions of Allada under hereditary viceroys. The first European dealings with the Aja were certainly with the king of Allada. But Allada was a fair way inland, and the main European places of trade were established at the lesser towns closer to the coast. This gave the coastal rulers an economic advantage, and by the last years of the seventeenth century they were in practice acting independently of Allada except in so far as there was still some advantage to them in having their successions confirmed by its king. Increasingly, in fact, they were becoming the creatures of the European trading companies—Dutch, English, French and Portuguese—that were competing for the trade of the Slave Coast.

If Allada retained a theoretical overlordship over the coastal states, it was itself subject to an overlordship from Oyo which could be very practically demonstrated by forays of Yoruba cavalry. Oyo interest in the western Slave Coast was considerable because there can be little doubt that at this time it was Oyo's main trading outlet to the sea. It is probable, indeed, that a very considerable proportion of the growing number of slaves being exported through Whydah, Jakin and the other ports were in origin captives taken in the Oyo wars of conquest.

The deterioration in Allada's control over the Slave Coast, and the increasing *de facto* usurpation of power by the Europeans on the coast-

[1] Also spelt Ouidah, Fida, Juda.

line, brought about a general decline in the fabric of good government and public order on the Slave Coast which, however much it may have suited the slave-traders, clearly created difficulties for more northerly states, such as Oyo and the northernmost of the Aja kingdoms, Dahomey.

The origins of Dahomey lie in a dispute within the ruling family of Allada during the first half of the seventeenth century. It seems possible that one of the points at issue may have been the advisability or otherwise of developing trade with the Europeans. If this was so, then the unsuccessful party would have been that which had argued that to develop trade with the Europeans would bring in political dangers to the state of the sort that could be seen to be weakening the states on the Gold Coast just to the west. Be this as it may, the losers in the dispute emigrated to the north, establishing themselves at Abomey, some 50 miles beyond Allada, where they set about building a new kingdom of their own by conquering the surrounding peoples. In so doing they developed a kind of monarchy which was very different from the normal Aja concept, one in which the king was an absolute monarch commanding the allegiance of all his people as individual subjects, and backing this up with a monopoly of force in the shape of a standing army. Elsewhere among the Aja, and also among their Yoruba neighbours (even in Oyo), the king, despite his supposedly divine origin, could only rule with the consent of the elders of the people; he had no direct access to individuals except through the elders and the heads of families, and little in the way of a permanent military force subject to his sole control.

The autocratic and forceful Dahoman monarchy looked with disfavour on the growing disorder to the south, and between 1724 and 1734 King Agaja engaged in a number of campaigns by which the whole Aja country was brought under his direct control. One consequence of this was the cessation for the time being of the export of slaves from the Slave Coast. In part this was because the European merchants had tended to take sides with the southern states in the wars against Dahomey, so that it was not easy for them to come to terms with the new political authority. In addition, however, the Dahoman kings seem to have had much the same attitude towards slave-trading as had the monarchs of Benin in the sixteenth and seventeenth centuries. Though desirous of getting supplies of European goods—particularly, perhaps, of guns and powder—on favourable terms and without them being subject to exorbitant profits and dues by the coastal merchants and kings, they regarded their war captives and other slaves as constituting an essential part of the economic and military strength of their state, and initially Agaja forbade their export altogether.

But this attitude could not last. In the first place, if Dahomey did not export slaves, it had practically nothing else with which to buy the European goods it wanted. Consequently by the time of Agaja's successor,

Tegbesu (1740–74), the slave trade was in full spate, but as an activity in which the interest of the state was uppermost, and both African and European traders were very much under royal control. Another factor at work was a second, and more important consequence of Agaja's conquest of the other Aja kingdoms, namely a series of Oyo invasions.

Oyo's great commercial interest in the western Slave Coast has already been noted. The *Alafin* clearly regarded the king of Allada as a subordinate king responsible for ensuring a free flow of Yoruba trade to and from the coast. Now, however, the king of Allada had been swept aside by a junior king with independent ideas. One of Allada's responses to invasion by Dahomey had in fact been to appeal to its overlord at Oyo for aid, and Oyo's reaction to the new situation on the Slave Coast was to mount a series of attacks on Dahomey. These continued from 1726 to 1747, and they ceased only when there was no question but that Tegbesu had accepted that Dahomey was tributary to Oyo.

However there remained continued friction between the two states along the frontier between them. Refugees from the Dahoman conquest of Allada, including the royal family, took refuge at what is now Porto Novo, which Oyo regarded as being under its special protection. This then was a source of dispute, as also was the growing Oyo tendency to route Yoruba trade away from Dahomey to Porto Novo and to the developing new port of Badagri farther east (and, to some extent, farther east still, to Lagos). This provided the cause for a number of Dahomey raids against Porto Novo and Badagri.

Nevertheless Oyo continued to exact tribute from Dahomey until about 1818, and when finally Dahomey became fully independent, this was a consequence of the collapse of the Oyo empire rather than of any new accession of strength by Dahomey. For a period of some thirty years in the middle of the eighteenth century, the *Alafins* were completely dominated by the leader of their state council, the *Basorun* Gaha, who seems to have acted more despotically towards the other Yoruba kings than custom demanded. *Alafin* Abiodun (*c.* 1774–89) regained control both of his throne and of his empire, but after him there came a general reaction to control from Oyo throughout Yorubaland. When, about 1817, a rebellious Oyo general called in Fulani aid from the north, the whole empire rapidly collapsed in a series of wars in which traditional kings and ambitious generals all sought to outdo each other, a tragedy which was to the profit of no one except the slave traders eagerly awaiting human cargoes by the beaches of Porto Novo, Badagri and Lagos.

The states of the Gold Coast

The states on the Gold Coast, Gã and Adangme in the east, elsewhere Akan, with which the Europeans had been trading, and on whose shores they had begun to build forts, for nearly two centuries before they became seriously interested in the Slave Coast, were for the most part but little larger or more powerful than the Slave Coast states. By the time that, following the Dutch expulsion of the Portuguese, the European trade had become highly competitive and increasingly directed towards the export of slaves, the Europeans recognised about a dozen separate African jurisdictions on the 200 or so miles of coast between the mouths of the Ankobra and Volta rivers.

The European forts on the coasts, and the African settlements that developed around their walls, became centres of economic and political power which were often stronger than the traditional capitals of the states, which were usually some miles from the sea. At some of the coastal towns, for example Axim and Elmina, where only one European trading company was established, its representatives became *de facto* rulers, dispensing justice over the Africans and taking the place of the traditional kings in confirming the local leaders in office. In some cases, for example Accra, the traditional kings themselves moved down to the coast, seeking the protection of the forts against enemies in the interior. Some African merchants on the coast became so essential as intermediaries in the trade with Europeans, and so wealthy as a result, for example John Konny in Ahanta and John Kabes at Komenda, that they became more powerful than the traditional kings. Where more than one European company was established on the coast of a kingdom, this kingdom might become in effect divided into two states, as happened, for example, at Komenda.

But though the European presence led to decline and disintegration among the coastal polities, the Europeans did not replace the governments of these states with administrations of their own; their direct power hardly extended beyond the range of the cannon on their forts. They were merchants who wanted trading profits, not administrative responsibility and expense. Furthermore, they were not strong enough. Even their forts were, in the last resort, dependent on the goodwill of the local people, on whom they relied for food and water and the provision of all kinds of services. There were at least a dozen occasions on which, because of some local quarrel or because of particular weaknesses on the part of their garrisons, European forts were captured, and either occupied or destroyed by Africans; on as many occasions, Africans besieged forts and virtually held their inmates to ransom. Konny took over the forts of the Brandenburgers when their company went bankrupt, and only after some years were the Dutch, to whom they had been sold, finally able to gain possession. It was Kabes who, having quarrelled with the Dutch, made it possible for the English to establish a rival fort at Komenda.

There was thus a lack of security in the coastlands which became a matter of concern to growing new states in the hinterland which developed out of the important political and economic nucleus of Akan settlement in the forestlands known as Twifu and Akany. This controlled the important gold-bearing lands around the Ofin valley; its people, called 'Accanies' by the Europeans, were the principal traders with the coast. The growth of the coastal trade in the seventeenth century, following the breaking of the Portuguese monopoly, and the development of the intensive European competition for the slave trade, provided a powerful incentive for the increase and centralisation of political power. A number of ambitious and influential families broke away from the Twifu–Akany nucleus and, with traditions of government developed there from experience in the earlier Akan states, such as Bono and Banda, north of the forest, began to create powerful new forest kingdoms. The plurality of European posts on the coast provided competitive outlets for their trade, which they could turn to their advantage. In particular, it was now possible for them to exchange their gold and slaves for the guns and gunpowder through which they could increase the power and extent of their monarchies. Portuguese policy had been not to sell arms which might increase African power; the Dutch, English and Danes, vying with each other to obtain as much trade as possible, came to have no such scruples. In some cases, indeed, they were willing to use the arms trade to help come to commercially profitable understandings with the new African powers of the interior, each of which was seeking to gain as much as possible of the trade with the coast for its own rulers and merchants.

By the latter part of the seventeenth century, the immediate hinterland, and all its trade with the coast, was controlled by three major states. The best known of these was Akwamu, which had expanded from a small kingdom behind the coastal states of Agona (Akan) and Accra (Gã) to control all the trade routes leading inland from the coast between Winneba, in Agona, and the Popos. Beginning with the conquest of Accra in 1677–81, the coastlands themselves had either been made tributary or subjected to the rule of viceroys from the Akwamu royal family. On its western frontier, Akwamu was competing for trade and influence with Akim, and, by intervening in the coastal state of Agona, had succeeded to a considerable degree in cutting it off from direct access to the coast. Akim at this stage was appreciably less powerful, and less centralised, a kingdom than Akwamu. It had accordingly tended to ally itself with the third major state of the hinterland, Denkyira, further to the west. Since Denkyira's direct political power did not actually reach to the sea, less is known of its early history than is the case with Akwamu. Nevertheless by the 1690s Denkyira seems to have conquered or made tributary all the chiefs and people of the hinterland from just beyond the River Tano, in the west, to the River Pra, in the centre of the Gold Coast. Twifu had been reduced to vassalage, and Akany was being directly threatened. Denkyira merchants dominated the trade of the whole western half of the coast, and all the European companies trading here had thought it necessary to establish direct relations with its king.

However, a number of factors prevented the three states of Akwamu, Akim and Denkyira consolidating their hold on the Gold Coast. One was that the Fante states on the central part of the coast, on which were the important European trading posts at Komenda, Elmina, Cape Coast and Anomabu, began to see the need for united action, at least in military matters, and between 1706 and 1720 came together to form a confederation with a central assembly of chiefs and a single commander-in-chief (*Brafo*) for their military forces, which, taken together, were not inconsiderable. Secondly, neither Akwamu nor Denkyira were able to create a central administration capable of permanently holding together their extensive conquests. Akwamu viceroys consolidated their local power by marrying into the families of conquered kings, and when, in 1730, Akwamu was defeated in war by Akim, its empire quickly dissolved into a number of independent principalities. Denkyira seems to have had even less idea of imperial administration, contenting itself merely with levying tribute on the kings it had conquered. When it had great need of money, its demands for tribute could be excessive, serving only to provoke revolts. This was the case in 1698, when demands for funds to help fight Akany led to the declaration of independence by the young kingdom of Ashanti, which then went on to expand its dominions until they embraced practically the whole territory of modern Ghana.

The rise of Ashanti

The origins of the kingdom of Ashanti lie with the northwards emigration of a number of small kin-groupings from the region of Twifu and Akany to settle around Tafo in country inhabited by groups of Brong (i.e. northern Akan, the people who had created Bono) and Dormaa people. Doubtless this emigration had something to do with the transformation of the Twifu–Akany nucleus that was connected with the growth of trade with the coast, a transformation probably involving an increase of population, and certainly producing political stresses, stresses which also led to the rise of Akwamu and Denkyira. The area in which the ancestors of the Ashanti (more properly, Asante) nation settled was of some commercial significance, for Tafo was the junction for the two major trade routes to the north: the north-western route through Bono and Banda and so, ultimately, to Jenne; and the north-eastern route via eastern Gonja to Hausaland.

Possession of Tafo doubtless provided the early Ashanti with the means for prosperity and an increase in numbers, and so for expansion which led them to incorporate into their own communities the lands and people of neighbouring settlements. The early Ashanti states were, however, severally small and weak, and their rulers seem quickly to have appreciated the need for mutual cooperation and support if they were to succeed in establishing themselves in Brong and Dormaa lands, and also if they were to maintain their identity in face of Denkyira, the powerful and ambitious state to the south of them. They were aided in this by the fact that almost all of them belonged to the same Akan clan, the Oyoko, and out of this a sense of common nationhood could be developed. That in fact it was developed, was due essentially to the leadership provided by the kings of the state which was to be known as Kumasi.

Nevertheless the early Ashanti were not able to escape becoming tributary to Denkyira, and about 1680 or 1690 the *Kumasihene* (king of Kumasi) Osei Tutu seems to have realised that something more than cooperation between independent states was necessary if the Ashanti people were to escape permanent domination by Denkyira. Osei Tutu's early career is of some interest. He had been sent as a hostage to the court of Denkyira, but had fled from it to Akwamu, with which the Ashanti seem to have been developing ties of friendship in an attempt to offset their domination by Denkyira. It was from Akwamu that he returned to assume the stool of Kumasi, and he seems to have gained in Akwamu useful experience of its military and civil organisation, and to have returned to Kumasi with a party of Akwamu advisers and musketeers.

With the aid of an Akwamu priest, Osei Tutu impressed on all the Ashanti kings and people a number of concepts of national unity, chief among these a Golden Stool, in which it was asserted that there resided the spirit of the whole Ashanti nation, and of which the *Kumasihene* was to be the perpetual guardian. In this way the *Kumasihene* also became the *Asantehene*, the king of all Ashanti, in whom the kings of the other states, though remaining the natural leaders of their own peoples, merged some of their own sovereignty. A national army was built up on the Akwamu model, in which all the individual kings and their armies were subordinate to the *Asantehene*'s supreme authority.

When, in 1698, Denkyira demanded exorbitant tribute, this army was used to win Ashanti independence in a war which lasted to 1701. Ashanti was helped in this by aid, including the supply of guns and powder, from Akwamu, and by the failure of most of Denkyira's subject states to fight for their overweening suzerain. It is said, indeed, that they conspired to cut Denkyira off from supplies of arms from the coast, and Denkyira was supported only by its ally, Akim. Denykira's defeat meant the immediate collapse of its empire, the tributary states all asserting their independence. This led to a confused situation on Ashanti's southern and south-western frontier, which involved it in further wars, including a campaign against Akim in 1717 in which a section of Ashanti's army was betrayed by Akwamu, ambushed by the Akims, and its king killed.

However, Osei Tutu and his advisers had created a sense of nationhood strong enough to survive this disaster, and his successors were able greatly to enlarge his kingdom. In 1724 Ashanti was able to conquer the kingdom of Bono, which henceforth, as the subject state of Techiman, brought to Ashanti all the renown and wealth of this earliest of Akan states, with its mastery of the trade in gold, ivory and slaves to the north-west. It was subsequently possible greatly to extend the Ashanti empire through western lands further to the south which had been under Denkyira control. To the south-east was Akwamu, now a declining power increasingly anxious at the growth of strength by Ashanti, its one-time ally whom it had betrayed in 1717. Ashanti therefore did nothing to help Akwamu in 1730, when it was attacked by Akim and reduced to the status of a petty state. Akim itself was too divided to be a serious threat to Ashanti, and in 1741–2, it was overrun by Ashanti armies. As a result, northern Akim was annexed to Ashanti, which also assumed an overlordship over the eastern coastal states which had once been subject to Akwamu.

By 1742, the only part of the coastlands not dominated by Ashanti was the states of the Fante Confederacy. Fearing Ashanti invasion, the Fante sought to consolidate under their leadership the remnants of many of the states earlier defeated by Ashanti, such as Denkyira and Wassa. In fact, except in 1765, Ashanti mounted no direct attack on Fante during the remainder of the century. The explanation is partly that much of Ashanti's military energies were devoted to the consolidation of its hegemony in the north, where Gonja and Dagomba were successively made tributary. In addition, however, Ashanti's early successes had by about 1745 occasioned problems of internal organisation which became a matter of increasing concern for the *Asantehenes* of this time.

Osei Tutu, anxious to keep the nation together under Kumasi leadership, had initiated a policy by which territories conquered or made tributary by the national army were placed in the care of the traditional elders of the Kumasi state, which thus became larger and more powerful than the other constituent states of the original union. But by the 1740s the Kumasi elders seem to have become so powerful that they sought to dictate national policy. The *Asantehene* of the time, Opoku Ware, was only able to maintain his independence of action by seeking aid from the kings and armies of the other states. A struggle for power then emerged between these kings and the Kumasi elders which could well have destroyed the concept of a united kingdom initiated in Osei Tutu's time. It was not until the reign of Osei Kojo (1764–77) that a way was found out of this difficulty by beginning to create a new centralised administrative machinery of civil and police officers, chosen by the *Asantehene* not on any traditional grounds but because they would be loyal and efficient subordinates responsible to him alone.

The development of this royal bureaucracy gave Ashanti the inner strength which was so markedly lacking in some other Guinea kingdoms, notably Oyo, and also its own Akan predecessors, Denkyira and Akwamu. It enabled the kingdom to withstand all the many threats presented by revolts from its conquered or tributary states, or even the other foundation kingdoms, and to become a monolithic military power dominating the whole hinterland of the Gold Coast. By the middle of the eighteenth century, indeed, virtually all the slaves and gold reaching the Gold Coast had originated in territory under Ashanti control, and nearly all European imports were passing to or through Ashanti markets.

Ashanti's relations with the Fante Confederacy, the only part of the coastlands not subject to its domination, thus became of crucial importance, the more so as it was on the Fante shores that both the Dutch and the British trading companies had their headquarters and a concentration of their more important trading stations. The Dutch, increasingly outtraded by the British, inclined to the belief that their best policy was to develop close relations with Ashanti and to welcome an Ashanti hegemony over Fante. On the other hand, the British, doing more and more trade with Fante merchants, were more and more being drawn into the role of allies, and of potential protectors of the Fante should they be invaded. As to the Fante themselves, their basic interest was the same as Ashanti's, namely the maximum possible trade between the coast and the interior. But in this there lay a continuing cause of friction, for the Fante kings and traders wanted the maximum profits for themselves, while the Ashanti interest was to secure freedom and the maximum security for its own people going down to the coast.

In 1805 the Fante gave shelter to refugees from Ashanti jurisdiction. In 1806, the *Asantehene*, Osei Bonsu, responded with a full-scale invasion which quickly overran the Fante states, and which brought Ashanti arms into direct confrontation with the British at their fort at Anomabu. Thus was initiated a very significant crisis in West African history, a crisis in which for the first time a major African state was challenging a major European trading power for mastery of a trading frontier that was crucial to both parties. The crisis was the more vital because it was just at this time that the major European trading nations were agreeing to end the Atlantic slave trade, the trade that had dominated Afro-European relations for the previous two centuries, and which had done much to shape the political patterns of the Guinea peoples.

8

West Africa and the campaign against the slave trade

The British anti-slavery movement

It was not until the close of the eighteenth century that more than a small minority of Europeans began to realise that there was anything wrong in the business of buying slaves in Africa and carrying them across the Atlantic for sale in America. Men and women who were accustomed to seeing their own fellows executed for petty theft and imprisoned for debt, to the forcible impressment of men to serve in the navy, to flogging as an accepted means of maintaining discipline in the army and navy, and to the transportation of criminals as a normal means of peopling the colonies, were not likely to be troubled by the inhumanity and injustice involved in the slave trade and plantation slavery. In practice most Europeans saw and knew next to nothing of either the slave trade or slavery. There was now no demand for African slaves to work in Europe. Although the ships and men engaged in the slave trade began and ended their voyages in European ports like Liverpool, Nantes, and Amsterdam, slaves were on board only on the stage between West Africa and America. The only African slaves that were normally seen in Europe were the few brought as personal servants by American planters returning home on leave or retirement.

The Catholic Church forbade its members to engage in the slave trade (on the ground that it was wrong to buy and sell men and women who had been deliberately captured for slavery), but it did not prohibit the possession of slaves, and in practice traders from Catholic countries engaged in the slave trade equally with those from Protestant countries.[1] Some Protestant slave-traders and slave-owners salved their consciences by twisting the Calvinist doctrine that some men were inevitably destined for salvation and others equally inevitably for damnation, to mean that the black men were morally inferior to the whites, so that nothing that the white men did to them would effect their own chance of salvation. Other Protestant churches, like the eighteenth-century Church of England,

[1] Until 1789 the slave trade was illegal for Spanish subjects, and in fact few Spaniards engaged in it. However, when other nations began to cease trading in slaves, the Spanish trade, particularly to Cuba, rapidly increased.

were so much committed to the protection of the rights of established property-owners that when it was seen that men were buying and selling and owning slaves just as they bought and sold and owned cattle, they accepted the idea that slaves were property just as cattle were.

Indeed, when statesmen and other people of influence in the great imperial and mercantile states of western Europe thought about slavery and the slave trade, they tended to consider them both not from a moral point of view, but as a great property and a great commercial activity which were vital to national prosperity and strength. The West Indian trade contributed so largely to the wealth and strength of these states, and the West Indian planters were so influential in their councils, that their leaders in general accepted the planters' assertions that slaves were property, that sugar and other desired tropical crops could not be economically produced without slave labour, and that the slave trade was essential if this labour force were to be kept up to strength. The slave trade was a vested property interest which seemed as strong and as vital to the prosperity of the imperial and commercial nations of western Europe as slavery itself. The amount of capital invested in the trade was often considerable, and some great ports, like Liverpool in England, owed their development and prosperity almost entirely to it. The slave trade provided employment for numbers of trained seamen and work for shipyards, ship-chandlers and countless other businesses, all of which were valuable to naval strength in the many wars of this period.

In no country were the arguments in defence of the slave trade and of plantation slavery stronger than in Britain. But these arguments were all materialistic ones, and in Britain it was becoming possible to match them with counter-arguments that were equally materialistic. These centred on the fact that, by the end of the eighteenth century, Britain was so dominant in world trade that she had easy access to a number of other markets in Asia and America where, for a variety of reasons, sugar and other important tropical crops could be purchased more cheaply than they could then be produced on the British West Indian plantations. Since Britain was a nation increasingly devoted to making its living by selling its manufactures abroad, it could be argued that she should keep the cost of producing these to the minimum by seeking to buy foodstuffs for her workers and raw materials for her factories where these could be most cheaply obtained. It followed that she should abandon, rather than protect, uneconomic production in her West Indian colonies, and should instead cultivate free trade.

Thus towards the end of the eighteenth century, provided that it was well organised and strongly led by able men of good standing in public life, a campaign to convince the British people of the moral iniquity of the slave trade and of plantation slavery had an increasing chance of success.

From small beginnings in 1765, just such a campaign was developed by a small group of idealists with evangelical or Quaker connections, the most outstanding of whom were Granville Sharp, Thomas Clarkson and William Wilberforce. This group achieved three major successes. First, in 1772 the Lord Chief Justice of England, Lord Mansfield, was brought to declare that the state of slavery was so odious that it could only be supported by positive law, and that there was no such law in England. The result was that thereafter any slave who was in, or had been brought to, England automatically became a free man. Secondly, in 1807 an Act of Parliament made it illegal for British subjects to engage in the African slave trade. Finally, in 1833 another act was passed which abolished slavery throughout the British Empire.

The British navy and the slave trade

This book is concerned with this great campaign against the slave trade and slavery only in so far as its results affected West Africa. From this point of view, the abolition of slavery in England in 1772 is more important than the abolition of slavery in the British overseas territories sixty-one years later. The first led directly to the beginnings of the British colony at Sierra Leone in 1787, while the latter was of little consequence for West Africa, since in 1833 the British territories there were few and small and did not possess many slaves.

By far the most important measure from the West African point of view was the abolition of the British slave trade. This was not merely because the British share in this trade had been much greater than that of any other European nation, but because it led to a movement which resulted eventually in the complete cessation of the export of slaves across the Atlantic from West Africa. Of course, the British were by no means alone in outlawing the slave trade. It had already, in 1803, become illegal for citizens of Denmark to engage in it, and the United States, Sweden and the Netherlands each independently enacted similar laws which took effect in 1808, 1813, and 1814 respectively. But the British campaign against the slave trade was far more active and widespread than that of any other nation, and it had far more positive results in West Africa.

From the beginning, the British prohibition was stringently enforced by ships of the British navy, and the penalties imposed on British subjects caught trading in slaves were quickly increased, until in 1824 they became liable to the death penalty. Secondly, having agreed that it was wrong for Britons to traffic in slaves, the British government went on to the logical conclusions both that it was wrong for other peoples, whether white or black, to engage in the slave trade, and also that, if they did so, it would be harmful to the interests of the British traders in West Africa who were forbidden to deal in slaves. Diplomatic pressure was therefore brought to bear on the principal European and American nations which had not declared their slave trades illegal, with the result that France outlawed her trade in 1818 and Brazil in 1825, while Portugal (in 1815) and Spain (1817) were induced to introduce laws restricting their slave-traders to the seas south of the equator.

It soon became apparent, however, that apart from Britain, most of the nations which had enacted laws outlawing or restricting their slave trades lacked either the ability or the determination to see that they were obeyed on the high seas. Only Britain established a permanent naval patrol in West African waters specifically for the purpose of stopping the export of slaves, and although slaves were no longer carried in British ships, the numbers of slaves exported from Africa each year showed no immediate signs of decreasing to any substantial extent.

The next stage in the British campaign against the slave trade was thus devoted to efforts to get those states whose subjects still traded in slaves either to enforce their laws properly themselves or to allow the British naval patrols to do this work for them. In 1817, Spain and Portugal reluctantly allowed ships of the British navy the right to stop and search ships sailing under their flags which were suspected of carrying slaves. In return their naval vessels received the right to stop and search suspected British slave-traders. If slaves were found on board, such ships were taken to Sierra Leone or to ports in America, where Courts of Mixed Commission (that is, courts with Spanish and Portuguese as well as British judges) were established to adjudicate upon them. In 1831 France agreed to cooperate in a similar manner, while at the same time tightening up her own laws against the slave trade.

But these 'Reciprocal Search Treaties' did not work well. In practice only the British navy consistently maintained effective anti-slave-trade patrols and arrested slave-ships, and the other nations were apt to be so jealous of this interference of the British with their shipping that their judges in the Courts of Mixed Commission rarely agreed with their British colleagues on a verdict. Moreover, it was not difficult for slave-traders to secure papers purporting to show that their ships belonged to nations which had not signed Reciprocal Search Treaties with Britain. Above all, a slaving-ship could not be condemned unless there were slaves actually on board at the moment of arrest. By 1840, the number of slaves exported from West Africa each year was thought to be higher than ever.

Britain therefore began to negotiate a new series of treaties providing that ships could be condemned as slavers if they were found to be carrying equipment used in the slave trade, for example, handcuffs, or even utensils for feeding a larger number of persons than the ship's crew. France agreed to sign such a treaty in 1833 and Spain in 1835, while

Portugal was literally forced to sign in 1842. But the United States, which, since her war with England in 1812, was much more jealous of British interference with her shipping than any other power, and which until 1865 contained a powerful slave interest in her southern states, refused to sign either a Reciprocal Search Treaty or an Equipment Treaty until 1862.[1] Before this date her own anti-slave-trade patrols were ineffective, with the result that many slave-traders escaped arrest or condemnation by sailing under the American flag.

By the 1840s it seemed that the system of international treaties and British naval patrols was not going to be sufficient by itself to stop the export of slaves from West Africa. From 1808 until about 1870, a sizeable proportion of the strength of the Royal Navy was stationed in West African waters for the sole purpose of catching slave-ships. In the 1840s, when the patrol was at its most active, there were commonly about twenty warships and well over a thousand men employed in it. But even then it is to be doubted whether the patrol succeeded in capturing more than about one in every four of the slave-ships visiting West Africa. Quite apart from the loopholes in the treaty system, even a very much larger naval force could not have guaranteed to catch every slaver in West African waters. It was quite impossible to have a ship watching every mile of the coastline all the time, and the difficulties facing the patrol were considerable. The only British possession which possessed a base at all suitable for the ships patrolling the coast was Sierra Leone, at its northern extremity. Any slave ship arrested had to be taken to Freetown to be condemned, even if this meant a long and arduous voyage of 1,500 miles or more against the prevailing wind and current. The long periods of continual sailing in the tropics, and of boat-work close to an unhealthy coast, with few opportunities for shore leave, placed a heavy burden on the crews employed. In more than one year, more than one out of every ten men serving in West African waters died there; the average death-rate between 1825 and 1845 was about one in twenty, about three times as high as that on any other foreign station of the Royal Navy.

Though the treaties and the naval patrols failed to stop the transport of slaves to America, the existence of the British patrols at any rate made the slave trade a risky business. Between 1825 and 1865 no less than 1,287 slave-ships were captured, from which about 130,000 slaves were released alive. Nevertheless, the fact that during the same period well over a million slaves were successfully landed in America shows that so long as the institution of slavery continued in some of the American states, and so long as it was possible to buy slaves somewhere on the coast of Africa,

[1] The Anglo-French Equipment Treaty came to an end in 1845, in which year France agreed to maintain her own anti-slavery patrol in West African waters. This patrol was not very effective, however.

there would be lawless characters prepared to run the risk of losing their ships, and perhaps even their lives, by engaging in the Atlantic slave trade.

The positive West African policy of the British anti-slavery movement

It was not possible for Britain to secure the abolition of slavery throughout the Americas, but it did seem possible for her to take action which would tend to prevent slaves being presented for sale on the coasts of West Africa. From the very beginning of the British anti-slave-trade movement, its leaders had urged that it should include a positive policy towards West Africa as well as the purely negative policy of trying to stop the transport of slaves across the Atlantic. The positive policy recommended by Wilberforce and his colleagues can be summed up in three words: Christianity, commerce and colonisation. Efforts should be made to convert and educate the peoples of West Africa to the Christian way of life, to develop a healthy trade in commodities other than slaves, and to establish pioneer communities in West Africa which would demonstrate to her peoples good methods of agriculture, industry and government.

One of the reasons why it seemed desirable to foster and develop legitimate trade was obviously to provide compensation for the British merchants who had invested capital in trade with West Africa and who were now debarred from trading in slaves. At first only one commodity was known which could quickly and easily replace slaves as the staple of British trade with West Africa. This was palm oil, which could be bought in large quantities in the regions near the coast in which the oil palm grows, and which was in increasing demand in Europe as an ingredient in the manufacture of soap, candles and lubricants. A British trade in palm oil was soon prospering, particularly on the coasts east of the Gold Coast.

But more generally the positive policy was at first advocated by the abolitionists principally because they wanted to right the wrong which had been done to West Africa by the European trade in slaves to America. It was argued that West Africans had hitherto seen only the worst sides of European civilisation, its most acquisitive and destructive aspects. They should now be given the opportunity to acquire some of its moral and material benefits. With this end in view, the British abolitionists were active on the committees of the new Protestant missionary societies founded at the end of the eighteenth century—the Baptist Missionary Society (1792), the London Missionary Society (1798), the Church Missionary Society (1799), and the British and Foreign Bible Society (1803). They sponsored the establishment of the colony of Sierra Leone, and, since it was futile to plan for the material and moral development of West Africa while its vast interior and its possibilities for the development of trade in commodities other than slaves were almost entirely unknown to Europeans, they also supported the African Association, a body of leading British scientists which, from its foundation in 1788, was specifically devoted to 'promoting the discovery of the interior parts of Africa', and which stimulated a great revival of interest in African exploration and geography among western Europeans.[1]

When it became evident that, despite the anti-slave-trade treaties and naval patrols, slaves were still being exported from the African coasts in considerable numbers, the leaders of the British anti-slave-trade campaign began to think that the positive policy was the only sure means of finally bringing the slave trade to an end. The habit of trading in slaves had become such an accepted feature of West African society that they could see no way of preventing slaves being offered for sale on the coast unless the Africans were shown that there were other less destructive and equally profitable trades. It was argued that agriculture, industry and legitimate trade must be fostered and developed specifically so that they would drive out the slave trade. This idea was forcefully placed before the British public in 1839–40 in a book, *The African Slave Trade and its Remedy*, written by Sir Thomas Fowell Buxton, who in 1822 had succeeded Wilberforce as the parliamentary leader of the anti-slave-trade movement.

The positive policy of the British anti-slave-trade movement explains why, at a time when other European nations which had been engaged in the slave trade were losing interest in West Africa, a new and very different British interest began to grow. This new interest in West Africa was far deeper and more genuine than the old. When Europeans had been drawn to West Africa by the slave trade, they were concerned with that trade rather than with the country or its peoples. All that had mattered to them was that sufficient slaves should be available for sale in the coastal slave markets. What went on in the interior, what the people were like, what they did, was no concern of theirs. But during the nineteenth century the British began to take an increasing interest in the whole of the territory and its peoples. They wanted to stop the slave trade and to substitute stable conditions in which peaceful trade and orderly development could take place. It was therefore necessary to find out what the country and its people were like; to discover what useful commodities were produced, how they could best be transported and what improvements in methods of production might be made; and to ascertain what the social and political conditions were in which European missionaries and traders would have to work.

If it be asked why the rapidly expanding palm oil trade (worth nearly

[1] The African Association was later absorbed into the Royal Geographical Society, founded in 1830.

£1,000,000 ($4,000,000) a year to British merchants by the 1840s) did not serve to drive out the slave trade without further interference by the abolitionists, the answer seems to be that palm oil was exclusively a product of districts near the coast. The business of the slave trade continued in the interior, and slaves were still sent down to the coast for sale and export. The African coastal merchants who dealt in palm oil often sold slaves as well. They did their utmost to preserve their role as middlemen in the trade and to prevent Europeans making direct contact with the interior, whether for trade or any other purpose. In addition, the methods employed by both Europeans and Africans engaged in the oil trade often appeared closer to the methods of the slave trade than of legitimate trade. There thus seemed little prospect of the palm oil trade leading to the peaceful development even of the areas most affected by it, the Oil Rivers (the Niger delta) in particular.

In the remainder of this chapter, some of the effects in West Africa of the new positive British policy will be examined. But it is as well to emphasise from the outset that the new British interest in West Africa which developed out of the anti-slave-trade movement was not at first a *colonial* interest. Not until the last quarter of the nineteenth century was Britain really prepared to accept the notion that the fulfilment of her aims in West Africa might involve the establishment there of new British colonies. Until that time she tried to stick to her belief that colonies involved an unnecessary and unrewarding expenditure of money and effort, and indeed, as will be seen, on a number of occasions endeavoured to reduce her political commitments in West Africa, leaving her traders and missionaries to do their work unsupported by government.

The establishment of the colony of Sierra Leone

Following Lord Mansfield's judgement ending slavery in 1772, about 15,000 slaves who had been brought to England by their masters became free men. Many of them were unable or unwilling to settle down in a strange country to which they had been brought against their will, and it soon became a problem for the English authorities to know what should be done with them. A similar problem arose in America after the end of the War of American Independence in 1783. A considerable number of American Negroes had fought on the British side in the war, and could not be returned to the new United States. Attempts were made to settle them in Nova Scotia and in the Bahamas, but were not very successful.

At length Granville Sharp and some of his colleagues in the anti-slavery movement decided that the best thing to be done with these unwanted Negroes was to settle them in Africa, and they accepted a suggestion that Sierra Leone would be suitable for such a settlement. It was decided to make a beginning by sending out 450 Negroes and 60 white prostitutes (the latter apparently no more wanted in England than the ex-slaves). The British government provided free transport and stores for the expedition, which was placed in the charge of a naval officer, Captain Thompson.

The expedition was ill conceived and sadly mishandled. There were delays before the ships could sail, disease broke out on board, and only 430 passengers were alive when Sierra Leone was reached in May 1787. Captain Thompson set the survivors ashore with six months' provisions on twenty square miles of land which he had purchased from a local king, known as King Tom. Neither the place nor the time for the settlement were well chosen. The site was unhealthy and the rainy season made it impossible to build houses or start farming. When Thompson left after four months, a further 86 settlers had died. Granville Sharp sent out more stores in 1788 at his own expense, but the colony did not flourish. The settlers were not accustomed to working for themselves or to self-government, and although they were Negroes, life in Africa was entirely new and strange to them. Some even drifted away to work for slave-traders, and the settlement was already moribund when in 1790 it was attacked by local Africans and the settlers dispersed.

Sharp now realised that if his scheme for the settlement of ex-slaves in Africa were to stand any chance of success, he must make provision for its organisation and government. Since the British government was unwilling to spend money on establishing new colonies, Sharp and his abolitionist friends decided to call business to the aid of their philanthropy. They proposed to float a company which would develop legitimate trade with the interior of West Africa and use its trading profits to pay for the administration of the colony of ex-slaves. After some delay caused by the opposition of the Company of Merchants, which still possessed the legal right to control British trade with West Africa, the Sierra Leone Company was incorporated by Act of Parliament in 1791. The Company was not allowed to trade in slaves or to establish a monopoly of trade in its territories, the nucleus of which was to be the land which Thompson had bought in 1787. A European establishment was sent out, comprising a governor and council, traders and artificers; sixty-four of the original colonists were found and re-settled on a new and better site which became known as Freetown; and 1,200 new Negro settlers were brought from Nova Scotia.

The early years of the new colony were not happy. The governor and the members of the first council rarely agreed, and at first the former had no power to act without the consent of the latter. The competence of the Company's law courts was challenged, and it possessed no military or police force to enforce its laws. The settlers, the Nova Scotians in particular, objected to paying rent for the plots of land allocated to them by the Company, and demanded a share in the government. Trade with the interior did not develop as had been hoped: the only flourishing trade was the slave trade, in which the Company could not engage and which it lacked the power to stop. In 1794 the settlement was attacked and burnt by the French. That the colony survived at all was due largely to the good sense and strength of character of Zachary Macaulay (governor, 1794–9), who won the settlers' confidence and allowed them a share in making the colony's laws. The last serious trouble was a revolt organised in 1800 by the minority of malcontents who had not been won over by Macaulay. But this, and the risk of serious troubles with the local Temne people, was ended by the arrival of newcomers from Nova Scotia, who sided with the government. These were the Maroons (former slaves who had escaped from plantations in Jamaica and had lived in independence in its mountains until, in 1795, they had reached an agreement with the government to transport them out of the island) and an escort of soldiers. In the same year the Company's remaining constitutional difficulties were removed by a royal charter, and thereafter the Company received an annual subsidy from the British government to help towards the expenses of the administration.

Nevertheless, the ill success of the Company's commercial plans made it unwilling to continue to bear responsibility for the administration of Sierra Leone. The British government, which wanted a naval base in West Africa for the protection of British shipping (and later for its anti-slave-trade patrols), eventually agreed that from the beginning of 1808 Sierra Leone should be taken over as a crown colony. The period of Company rule had shown that liberated slaves could successfully be settled in Africa, and that they could play a reasonable part in the government of the settlement on European lines, and during the years of the anti-slave-trade patrol from 1808 onwards, the size of the colony and the number of its inhabitants began to grow as more and more slaves were liberated and landed from captured slave-ships.

Liberia

Sierra Leone is not the only modern West African state which began as a settlement for freed slaves. The French settlement of Libreville on the Gabon river is outside the scope of this book, but this is perhaps the place to say something about Liberia. The Republic of Liberia owes its origin to the American Colonization Society, founded in 1816. This private organisation proposed to solve the awkward social problems involved in the presence of numbers of free Negroes among the slave-owning communities of the southern states of the U.S.A. by sponsoring a scheme of emigration to Africa similar to that organised in Britain by Granville Sharp.

The United States government, like the British government before it, agreed to provide transport to take the free Negroes to West Africa. The earliest Negro colonists were, in fact, settled for a time in Sierra Leone, but in 1821 the American Colonization Society secured land at Cape Mesurado, which became the site of Monrovia, the Liberian capital. Various local branches of the Society established separate settlements on the coast, for the most part to the south-east of Monrovia, but by 1837 all these settlements except Maryland, in the extreme south-east, by Cape Palmas, had been brought under the control of the government at Monrovia. Until 1841 the American Colonisation Society provided white governors for these settlements; the first Negro governor was J. J. Roberts, a settler who had arrived in Liberia in 1829.

European traders refused to recognise the authority of the Society's officials, and insisted that the latter had no right to prevent them dealing directly with the indigenous peoples of the Liberian coast, who in fact resisted the attempts of the government at Monrovia to control them. European slave-traders were sometimes in open conflict with the Society's officials, but those engaged in more legitimate business, principally British and French merchants, for the most part contented themselves with protests to their governments. In 1843 the British government asked the government of the United States formally to state what the status of Liberia was and whether it was under United States protection. The American government refused to commit itself in precise legal terms, so the American Colonisation Society and the settlers in Liberia decided that it would be in the best interests of all concerned if the latter declared themselves a sovereign and independent republic. The Republic of Liberia was accordingly constituted in 1847 with a form of government closely modelled on that of the United States. Its independence was recognised by Britain in 1848 and shortly afterwards by a number of other European states, including France. The United States, however, did not grant recognition to Liberia until 1862, during the Civil War, when it was possible to ignore the opinion of her slave-owning states.

However, Liberia's problems were by no means over. By the 1860s, nearly 19,000 American Negroes had been transported to Liberia, and although they were united among themselves (Maryland was incorporated in the republic in 1857), their relations with the native Africans were by no means settled and friendly. The government at Monrovia claimed to rule all the people along the coast and for a considerable distance inland. Inland frontiers with the adjacent French and English territories were not agreed until the end of the nineteenth century, and then not without difficulty and friction. For nearly a century, effective government in the republic was limited to the coastal regions where lived the settlers and their descendants. They alone had any share in the government at

Monrovia and secured any benefit from it. Their government entirely lacked the funds and the means to open up and develop the interior, or to control its peoples, except in the most haphazard and arbitrary fashion.

The European exploration of West Africa

The commercial failure of the Sierra Leone Company was in part due to the fact that, although the wide estuaries of the Sierra Leone rivers provided good anchorages for shipping, the rivers themselves were of little use as commercial highways to the interior, since their sources lay only a short distance from the coast, in the Futa Jalon uplands and the Nimba mountains. The European explorers who went into West Africa from the time of the foundation of the African Association in 1788 onwards were at first principally concerned with the discovery and exploration of the greatest of the rivers of West Africa, the Niger.

It may seem odd to refer to the 'discovery' of the Niger, but at this time European knowledge of the interior of West Africa was extremely vague and scanty. It was based for the most part on some, but not always the best, of the Arabic accounts of the early Sudanic states in the time of their greatest prosperity, and Europeans really had little means of knowing the subsequent history of the land and its great trading cities. Thus they were led to believe that Timbuctu, in particular, was a much more splendid and wealthy city than it actually was in the eighteenth and nineteenth centuries, and to reach it became a romantic ambition of the European explorers.[1] It was known that Timbuctu and the other cities were situated on or close to a great river which the Arabs compared in size and importance to the Nile. But Europeans did not know where the Niger rose, which way it flowed, or where it flowed to. In the middle of the eighteenth century it was often supposed that the Niger rose in the east, and flowed westwards, branching into three and emerging into the Atlantic as the rivers known to Europeans as the Senegal, Gambia, and Rio Grande (the modern Jeba river). No one had realised that the Oil Rivers, to which Europeans had been trading ever since the fifteenth century, were in fact the delta of the Niger.

At a time when Europeans were rapidly acquiring first-hand knowledge of the geography of all other parts of the world, the lack of accurate information about the interior of Africa was a pressing challenge to their spirit of scientific enquiry. Explorers were attracted to West Africa first because Europeans had been visiting its coast for centuries. In particular it was hoped that the discovery and exploration of the Niger would reveal a practical means by which European enterprise could reach the interior,

[1] The first published work of the great English poet, Alfred Tennyson, in 1829, was a prize-winning undergraduate exercise on the subject 'Timbuctoo'.

drive out the slave trade, and bring Africans into the van of human progress.

Between 1788 and 1793, the African Association sent three expeditions inland, two starting from North Africa and one from the Gambia, to discover the truth about the Niger, but none of these was successful. For its fourth attempt the Association chose a young Scottish doctor, Mungo Park. Park started inland from the Gambia at the end of 1795, and in July of the following year reached the Niger at Segu, about 400 miles from the sources of the river. He was unable to travel any farther,[1] and so when, after some difficulty, he returned to the Gambia and thence to Europe, he could report little more than that the Niger was a great river flowing from the west towards the east. European geographers then concluded that it must flow into some Central African lake or swamp.

In 1805 Park undertook a second expedition, this time sponsored by the Colonial Office, which was beginning to be interested in the West African interior. Park's instructions were to follow the course of the Niger as far as he could, and to discover what prospects of trade there might be between Britain and the inhabitants of the country through which it flowed. Park's second expedition was on a much more ambitious scale than his first. He left the Gambia with thirty-nine other Europeans—carpenters, sailors and soldiers—with whom he planned to build a boat and sail down the Niger to its outlet. The expedition began its journey in the rainy season, and by the time it had reached the Niger at Bamako all but ten of Park's companions were dead from fever. Eventually Park and four survivors started down the Niger in canoes. No European ever saw them again, but one of Park's African guides was subsequently commissioned to find out what had happened, and established the fact that Park and his companions had got as far as the rapids near Bussa, in which they had all been drowned.

A great deal more was known in Europe about the Niger after Park's two journeys than had been the case before, but the great length of the river was not appreciated and its final outlet was still unknown. The next advance in European knowledge resulted from the expedition of Dr Walter Oudney, Major Dixon Denham, and Lieutenant Hugh Clapperton, R.N., who were sent out by the British government in 1822. They approached the Niger by the well-established Arab trade route across the Sahara from Tripoli. While Denham explored Bornu and the country round Lake Chad, Oudney and Clapperton set out south-westwards towards the Niger. Oudney soon died, but Clapperton reached first the great trading city of Kano, and then Sokoto, then at the peak of its power as the capital of the Fulani empire. Sultan Bello (the son and successor of Usuman dan Fodio[2]) received Clapperton kindly, but refused him

[1] Because of the war between Segu and Kaarta, see chapter 9, p. 155.

[2] For the Fulani empire and Usuman dan Fodio, see chapter 9, pp. 149–51.

permission to proceed to the Niger, less than 200 miles away. Clapperton then rejoined Denham and the two retraced their steps to Tripoli, arriving back in England in the middle of 1825.

Clapperton had failed to reach the Niger, but his and Denham's journeys had shown that the river could not continue eastwards to some central swamp, but that it must turn south and come out into the Gulf of Guinea. In addition, Clapperton and Denham had brought back to Europe the first really accurate account of the caravan route from Tripoli to Bornu, and of the country and peoples of the western Sudan from the eastern shores of Lake Chad to as far west as Sokoto.

Clapperton was at once sent out on a second expedition. His instructions were to check the course of the lower Niger and to secure the Sultan of Sokoto's signature to a treaty binding him to stop the slave trade. He landed at Badagri at the end of 1825 and made his way northwards with four companions, only one of whom, his servant, Richard Lander, a young man of twenty-one, was still with him when he reached the Niger at Bussa. Having crossed the river, Clapperton and Lander went via Kano to Sokoto, where they found that Bello was not in the least inclined to agree to stop the trade in slaves which was an integral part of the economic life of the Fulani empire.

The failure of his mission to Sokoto was a bitter disappointment to Clapperton, and his low spirits were undoubtedly a contributory cause of his death in April 1826. Although Lander's role in the expedition had been no more than that of personal servant to Clapperton, he determined to try and complete the other half of its work by travelling to the mouth of the Niger. But the Fulani emirs, by now thoroughly suspicious of Englishmen exploring their country and trying to stop the slave trade, prevented him from achieving this aim.

After Lander had returned to England via Badagri, he eventually persuaded the Colonial Office to send him and his brother, John Lander, on a further expedition to trace the course of the Niger from Bussa to the sea. In June 1830 the two brothers reached Bussa and set off down the river in canoes. Their journey proved relatively easy and uneventful until they arrived in the delta country, where the commercial competition between the African towns at the mouths of the various outlets of the Niger was extremely bitter, and the methods of the European traders, whether trading for slaves or for palm oil, were often extremely unscrupulous. After losing almost all their possessions and suffering indignities alike from African and European traders, both of whom were hostile to the European travellers coming from the interior, the Landers eventually reached Fernando Po and found a ship to take them to England.

The combined efforts of Mungo Park, Clapperton and Denham, and the Landers had solved the problem of the Niger and provided a broad

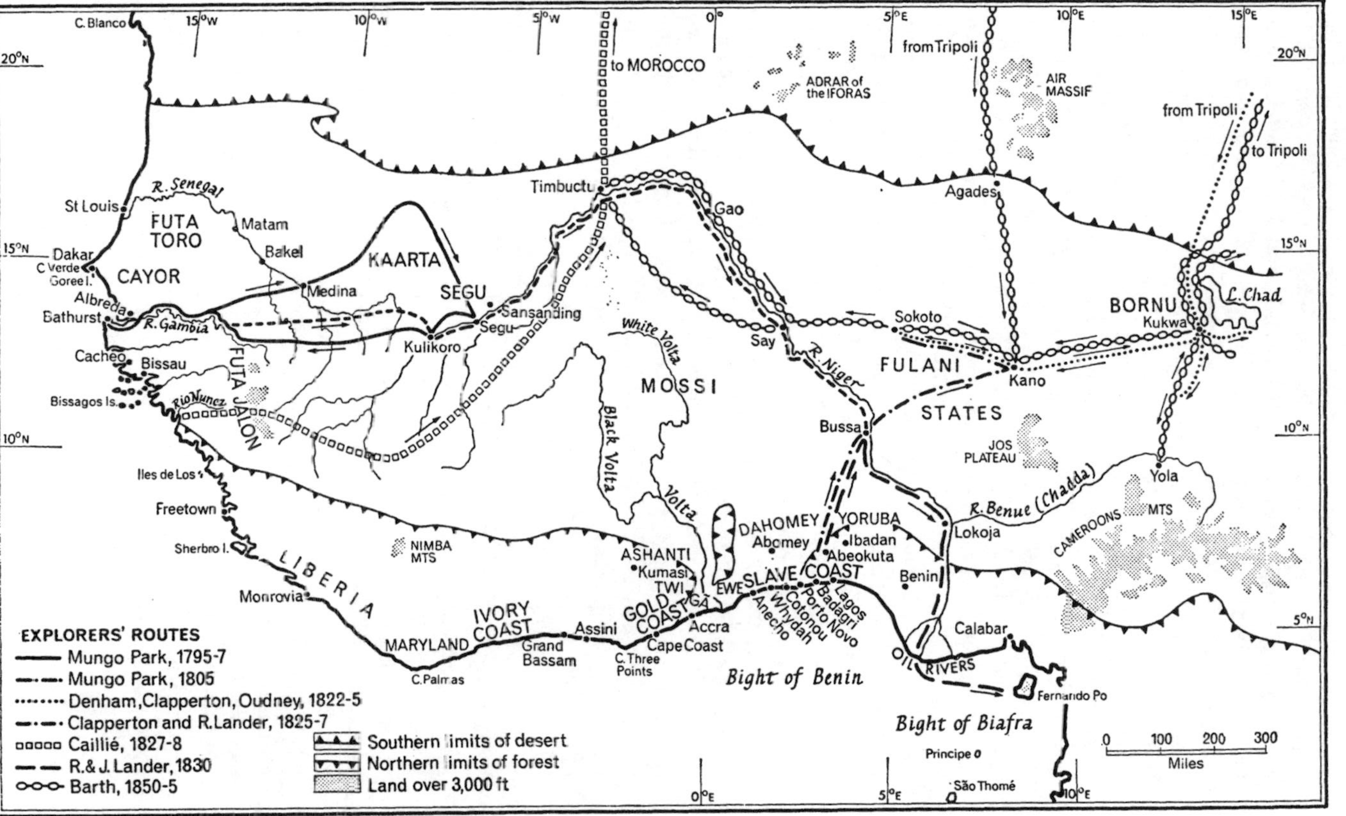

10 West Africa, 1788–1800

outline for the geography of West Africa. Their work was rounded off by men like the Frenchmen, Gaspard Mollien, who in 1818 discovered the sources of the Senegal, Gambia and Rio Grande, and René Caillié, who in 1827–9 was the first European to visit Timbuctu and to return to tell the story; the Englishman, Major Laing, who located the sources of the Niger in 1822; and the German, Dr Heinrich Barth. Barth must unquestionably be ranked among the greatest of the European explorers of Africa. He left Tripoli and crossed the Sahara to Agades in 1850 as a member of an English expedition to the western Sudan. Its commander, Richardson, soon died, but Barth and another German, A. Overweg, visited Katsina and Kano, travelled through Bornu and explored Lake Chad, and thus turned south and reached the Benue. After Overweg's death in 1852, Barth continued alone via Sokoto and Say to Timbuctu. He then returned to Bornu and travelled back across the Sahara to Tripoli, eventually reaching England towards the end of 1855. Barth covered an immense amount of ground and his observations on all he saw were extremely accurate and penetrating, so that his book *Travels and Discoveries in North and Central Africa* became for many years a standard work on the western and central Sudan, and one which may still be read with profit. After Barth's time, the remaining gaps in the outside world's knowledge of West Africa were for the most part filled in by explorers who, unlike their predecessors, were deliberately preparing the way for the European occupation of territory that began to be effective on a large scale at the end of the 1870s. The most notable of these was perhaps the French official, Captain L. G. Binger, who explored the Mossi country and the hinterland of the Ivory Coast in 1887–9.

Early attempts to trade up the Niger

After the explorers had done their work, it remained to be seen whether it was practicable to trade directly with the interior of West Africa. The first two British attempts in this direction were complete failures. The explorers had shown that only two rivers, the Niger and the Senegal, were at all suitable for the transport of goods in bulk to and from the interior. The mouth of the Senegal was in French hands, and so the British concentrated on the Niger. During 1832–4, a Liverpool merchant and shipowner, Macgregor Laird, sponsored an expedition in two specially built steamships, with Richard Lander as guide, which attempted to trade directly with the country to the north of the Niger delta. A larger and more ambitious expedition, inspired by Buxton's *African Slave Trade and its Remedy*, was sent out by the British government in three steamships during 1841–2. In addition to trading, it was planned that the expedition should establish a missionary station and a model farm at Lokoja, where the Benue (then known as the Chadda) joins the Niger. The causes of these expeditions' failures were identical. In the first place, they incurred the hostility of the established merchants of the delta, even the British merchants opposing the 1841–2 expedition because they objected to their government interfering in their trade. A more serious difficulty, however, was the high mortality among the expeditions' members, due principally to the fevers of the delta. Out of 48 Europeans in Laird's expedition, 38, including Lander, died. The government expedition of 1841 comprised 145 Europeans, of whom 48 died within the space of two months.

British traders and missionaries and the British government all decided that such high mortality rates made it futile to mount more large-scale attempts to penetrate up the Niger. Further work was left to individuals, the most outstanding of whom was John Beecroft.

Beecroft was a former merchant seaman who had found himself at Fernando Po during a brief period (1827–34) when the British navy was using the island as a base for its anti-slavery patrol, and who, after the navy had left, remained in the island to trade and to look after the interests of the liberated slaves settled there. Between 1835 and 1842 Beecroft explored the Benin and Old Calabar rivers and travelled up the Niger to Lokoja and Bussa. In 1843, the Spanish government, which in 1778 had taken over Portugal's rights in Fernando Po and Annobon, but which was not effectively occupying the islands at the time, appointed Beecroft as governor of Fernando Po. In 1848 he was given a further appointment as British consul for the Bights of Benin and Biafra, his duties being to watch over the interests of the growing number of British merchants trading between Dahomey and the Cameroons.

In 1852 the British government learnt that Barth had reached the upper Benue. Desiring to prove that this was the same river that since the Landers' time had been known as the Chadda, and also if possible to make contact with, and lend assistance to Barth, the British government collaborated with Macgregor Laird in a third attempt to penetrate the Niger from the sea. Laird provided the steamships and trading representatives, and the Admiralty provided navigating and surveying officers. Beecroft was to have commanded the expedition, but he died before it started, and it was in fact commanded by Dr Baikie, a naval surgeon. Baikie's expedition explored the Niger and Benue during 1854, and although nothing was seen of Barth, the Chadda and Benue were proved to be the same river and some successful trading was done. But the most remarkable fact about Baikie's expedition was that none of its members lost their lives; it had been shown that the proper use of quinine could overcome the fever which had defeated the earlier expeditions. Henceforward the way was clear for the use of the Niger as a commercial highway to the interior, and a number of merchants, with Laird in the lead, began to venture up it.

The missionary advance in West Africa

The earlier Christian missionaries in West Africa were of course Roman Catholics, but little of their influence survived by the beginning of the nineteenth century. A few Portuguese priests still worked around Cacheu and Bissau under the direction of the bishop in the Cape Verde Islands. The French posts on the Senegal had priests who ministered to the French Catholics there, but early French missions to the Ivory and Slave Coasts had faded out. Indeed, neither France nor Portugal were actively conducting missions to the Africans (the same was true of the Protestant Dutch, who went no further than to provide chaplains to minister to the traders in their larger forts), and the great revival of Catholic missions in West Africa dates from the period after 1860 when France undertook her great colonial expansion there.

The revolution in the Protestant countries of western Europe in men's attitude towards religion and morality, a revolution which had already produced the anti-slave-trade movement, also begot a new and active desire to preach the Gospel to the non-Christians of Asia and Africa. Britain, which had taken the lead in the movement against the slave trade, was also most active in sending missionaries out into the world, but German and American Protestant missionary societies as well became markedly active in Africa during the nineteenth century. Each country naturally tended at first to send missionaries to those parts of Africa with which its people were already concerned for other reasons. Thus in West Africa many American missionary societies sent missions to Liberia from 1821 onwards, while the earliest British missionaries went out to Sierra Leone, the Gold Coast, and Nigeria. Germany had little interest in West African trade until the latter half of the nineteenth century, and no political interest until after 1880. Just as the early German explorers had sometimes been sent out by Britain (e.g. Barth and Overweg), so we find the first German missionaries often serving with British societies.

The first British missionary society to concern itself with West Africa was the Church of England Society for the Propagation of the Gospel, which had been founded as early as 1701. Between 1752 and 1816 the S.P.G. maintained a chaplain at Cape Coast Castle. From 1765 to 1816, the post was filled by an African, the Rev. Philip Quaque, a Fante who had been educated and ordained in England.[1] However, apart from super-

[1] Quaque was by no means the first Ghanaian to receive an academic training in Europe. The outstanding early example is A. W. Amo, who, taken to Europe as a child, in the 1720s and 1730s studied philosophy and became a teacher in German universities. However, he was even less influential than Quaque after his return to his native land.

vising a school for African boys, the chaplains made little attempt to convert the people of the Gold Coast. The real beginning of the British missionary effort in West Africa was the mission sent to Sierra Leone by the Church Missionary Society (also Church of England) in 1806. The initial purpose of this mission was to minister to the needs of the liberated African community in and around Freetown. But soon the spreading of the liberated Africans in Sierra Leone and elsewhere in West Africa led it to embrace the idea of converting the African heathen generally. Its goal became the establishment of an African church, within the Anglican communion, but not dependent on England either for clergy or for funds. Fourah Bay College was founded in 1827 to train African clergy, and in 1852 a diocese of Sierra Leone was established. The Wesleyan Methodist Missionary Society was also prominent in Sierra Leone, where it began work in 1811.

Two C.M.S. missionaries accompanied the ill-fated Niger expedition of 1841, one of whom was an African, the Rev. Samuel Adjai Crowther. Crowther was a Yoruba, who had been liberated from a slave-ship and educated in Sierra Leone and England. But the effective beginning of missionary activity in what is now Nigeria dates from 1844. Between 1839 and 1842, several hundred Yorubas who had lived in Sierra Leone after their liberation from slave-ships returned to their own country and settled at Abeokuta. Some of them had been in contact with C.M.S. missionaries in Sierra Leone, and others with the Wesleyans. In 1844 the C.M.S. established a resident mission at Abeokuta, and the Wesleyans followed shortly afterwards. Crowther was a member of the C.M.S. mission, which in 1851 extended its activities to Lagos and in 1853 to Ibadan, the greatest of the Yoruba cities. After accompanying the 1854 Niger mission, Crowther was in 1864 consecrated as the first Bishop of the Niger Territories.

The British use of Fernando Po as a base for the anti-slavery patrol and for the settlement of liberated slaves led in 1841 to the establishment of a Baptist mission on the island. The Baptists extended their activities to the Cameroons, where British traders were active. In 1858, after the Spanish government, with its strong Catholic affinities, had taken active control of Fernando Po, the Baptists were forced to transfer from the island to the mainland. Another British missionary society which followed British traders in this part of the world was the Church of Scotland mission, which was established on the Old Calabar river in 1846.

The first active mission to the Gold Coast was that of the Basel Missionary Society, which began work in the Danish sphere in 1828 and steadily penetrated inland in the Gã and Twi country. In 1847, another German-speaking mission, that of the Bremen Society, began to work east of the Volta in the Ewe country. In 1835, following an interest in

Christianity resulting from Bibles sent to schoolchildren at Cape Coast by the British and Foreign Bible Society, the Wesleyan Missionary Society began to work in the Fante states under British influence. Its most outstanding figure was the Rev. Thomas Birch Freeman, son of a West Indian father and an English mother, born and educated in England. Freeman arrived at Cape Coast in 1837, and, until his death in 1890, was tireless in expanding the Wesleyan effort. He founded a mission at Kumasi in 1839; he was the pioneer of the Wesleyan mission to Abeokuta; and in 1843 and 1854 he visited the Slave Coast, though no permanent Wesleyan mission took root there until 1880.

The missions could make little headway in the interior until the coming of European rule in the last quarter of the century. Even in the coastal areas the number of active converts to Christianity was small compared with the total population. The only parts of West Africa which might reasonably be considered Christian countries during the nineteenth century were the small areas of Sierra Leone and Liberia inhabited by freed slaves and their dependants. But these people were English-speaking Negro settlers rather than native Africans, and their numbers in the middle of the century did not exceed 50,000 in Sierra Leone and 20,000 in Liberia.

Nevertheless, the influence of the early Protestant missionaries was of great importance. Almost without exception the other Europeans who had been seen in West Africa were concerned with the advancement of the material interests of themselves, their employers, or their countries. The missionaries, on the other hand, had gone to Africa to help the Africans. The missionaries thought that they could best help Africa by teaching the love of Christ, but they realised that Africans were in need of material as well as spiritual assistance. It was in the missionaries' interest to improve the material knowledge and skills of the Africans, for in this way they would be made more useful and happier members of Christian society. The missionaries were able to teach Africans, not only to read and write, and how to use such skills for their own benefit and that of their fellows, but also such things as how to build better houses, to improve their farming, to improve their standard of health. It was in the educational field that the success of the missions was perhaps greatest. The Africans were quick to realise the advantage to themselves of acquiring the material knowledge and skills of the Europeans, and soon began to ask for more schools, more hospitals, more technical training than the missions could easily provide.

In the areas where European influence was strongest, a class of Africans educated not only in European techniques, but also in European ways of thought began to emerge. At first this class was of service to the European governments and merchants as they expanded their activities in West

Africa. Its members served usefully as clerks, teachers, priests, doctors, lawyers, administrators. Britain, for example, was able to recruit Sierra Leonians to help staff the administration she began to create after 1843 in the Gold Coast, and later to recruit Gold Coasters as well as Sierra Leonians to help establish her new administrations in Lagos and Nigeria. But inevitably this educated class became dissatisfied with merely serving Europeans and, with the consolidation of European rule, a breach began to open between the educated Africans and the Europeans. By the end of the century, some of the latter were already organising political societies to defend African rights and to work for the government of Africa by Africans. The breach was regrettably not limited to politics. As European control over West Africa became more effective, so it tended to become more rigid. Europeans became less tolerant of African ways and beliefs, and more sceptical of African abilities and purposes. Many of the missions, notably the Church Missionary Society, began to think it advisable to seek to maintain European control over the churches in Africa. One consequence of this was to encourage considerable numbers of African believers and clergy to break away from the established Christian missions, and to establish independent churches of their own which they thought to be better adapted to African needs.

9

The British West African Settlements, 1808–74

When the British slave trade was abolished in 1807, there were three British settlements on the coast of West Africa, the new crown colony of Sierra Leone, with a population of perhaps four thousand, mainly former slaves, and the forts on the Gambia and the Gold Coast, the combined population of which must have been much smaller, and which were the responsibility of the Company of Merchants. For the next seventy years these settlements were the subject of continual debate.

On the one hand, the British statesmen of the time were keenly aware of their responsibilities towards the taxpayers who elected them, and so desired to keep Britain's colonial expenditure as small as they could. In general it was thought that the British West African settlements cost more to govern and to defend than was warranted by their value as trading-posts. There was therefore a strong tendency to keep the settlements as small as possible, or even, with the exception of Sierra Leone, which was valued because of the usefulness of Freetown as a naval base, to abandon them altogether.

On the other hand, the campaigners against the slave trade, and sometimes the traders and missionaries actually working in West Africa, argued that their various activities would not prosper unless the British government afforded them greater support and protection and intervened to produce more peaceful conditions in West Africa. But the British government could not give them these things unless it increased and extended its activities and responsibilities in West Africa.

Numerous commissions and committees of enquiry into British West African policy and the affairs of the British settlements between 1811 and 1865 show how this conflict of opinion continued, and, needless to say, Britain's policy towards her West African settlements was apt to change quite violently from time to time as first one, then the other, view was adopted.

British affairs in West Africa, 1808–21

The state of affairs surveyed by the 1811 Commission of Enquiry and a Parliamentary Select Committee in 1816 was not very satisfactory. The

British merchants who had been forced to leave the Senegal when that colony was returned to the French early in 1817 had established a new settlement at Bathurst at the mouth of the Gambia, but there was still friction with the French at Albreda, and the boundaries of British influence were still extremely vague.

On the Gold Coast, the Ashanti invasion of the coastal states had interrupted trade and seriously threatened the security of the European forts, none of which were strong enough to withstand an Ashanti attack. The British, Dutch and Danish authorities were all forced to come to terms with the Ashanti, recognising their claim to suzerainty over the coastal peoples and even to ownership of the land on which the forts were built. Conditions did not, however, improve. The Danish, British and Dutch abolitions of the slave trade and the desire of the coastal peoples for revenge on the Ashanti prevented the normal resumption of trade. There was continual friction between Ashanti and the coastal states. The Europeans were involved in this, since the Ashanti held them responsible for the actions of the peoples living under the influence of their forts. Although in 1817 the British Company of Merchants sent an agent, T. E. Bowdich, to Kumasi to conclude a treaty to improve relations between the Company and Ashanti, the treaty actually signed created as many new difficulties as it solved old ones.

However, because the Company's forts were proving useless as a means for stopping illegal trading in slaves, its days were numbered. In 1819 the British government sent its own representative, Joseph Dupuis, to negotiate directly with Ashanti, and then in 1821 it abolished the Company altogether, and assumed control of its forts and settlements, on the Gambia as well as on the Gold Coast.

Sir Charles Macarthy

In the meantime the colony of Sierra Leone had been growing steadily in size and importance. After the establishment there of courts for the trial of arrested slave-ships, the liberated African population of the colony steadily increased until by 1822 it numbered about 22,000. In 1814 (Sir) Charles Macarthy, an extremely active man devoted to the anti-slavery cause, was appointed governor. Under his administration, the area of territory under British control was rapidly enlarged, in part to provide room for the new settlers, but also because Macarthy believed that only the extension of British rule could effectively check the activities of the slave-traders. However, Macarthy's activities provoked criticism in Britain, not because their purpose was disapproved, but because they were expensive. In 1814 the administration of Sierra Leone had cost £24,000; ten years later it cost £95,000. Such a sum was much greater than the colony's revenue, and the difference had to be met by the English taxpayer. Thus although Macarthy was permitted in 1818 to occupy the Iles de Los to stop them being used as slaving-bases, the Colonial Office forbade him to annex Sherbro Island and the Bissagos Islands which were being used for the same purpose.

When the Company of Merchants was dissolved in 1821, Macarthy became responsible for the government of the British settlements on the Gambia and the Gold Coast as well as for Sierra Leone. His solution for the troubles of the Gold Coast was to join the coastal states into an alliance with the British and Danes to resist and defeat Ashanti. But this plan completely miscarried. When the Ashantis invaded the coastal districts in 1824, Macarthy split his forces, and his own body of Fante levies and some 250 European troops was overwhelmed and he himself killed at a battle at Bonsaso.

Although the military fortunes of the allies were redeemed in 1826, when another Ashanti invasion was decisively defeated at Katamanso, near Dodowah, Macarthy's defeat and death were fatal to his policy of furthering the cause of civilisation and legitimate trade in West Africa by extending the British government's responsibilities there. In 1827 the British government instructed Sir Neil Campbell, the governor of Sierra Leone, that British territory in West Africa should not be extended, and that alliances should not be made with African peoples who might expect the British government to protect and defend them from their enemies (a clear reference to recent events on the Gold Coast), and ordered him to withdraw the British officials and garrisons from the Gold Coast forts. This latter decision proved unpopular with the British merchants. Three of the London merchants trading to West Africa formed themselves into a committee which, in 1828, was entrusted with the management of British affairs on the Gold Coast. The British forts there were to remain British territory, and the resident British merchants were authorised to elect seven of their number as a council to govern the affairs of the forts at Cape Coast and Accra, subject to the general supervision of the London Committee. The government agreed to give the latter an annual subsidy (which varied between £4,000 and £3,000 a year) for the upkeep of the forts.

George Maclean

In 1830 the London Committee sent out as president of the council a young army officer, Captain George Maclean, who had commended himself to the merchants' attention during a brief period of service in Sierra Leone and the Gold Coast in 1826–8. The situation which Maclean found on his arrival at Cape Coast was not encouraging. Negotiations for a peace with Ashanti had not been successful, and while the state of war continued, trade was virtually at a standstill. The peoples of the coastal states had lost all confidence in the power and good faith of the British, who had at first failed to contest the Ashanti claims to suzerainty over the coastal peoples and who had then, after the battle of Katamanso, completely deserted them. Maclean did not possess the full powers of a governor of a British colony; he was merely president of a council of British merchants, some of whom proved to be critical of his policy and methods. Except for a small and not very efficient local militia, Maclean had no police force with which to back his authority. Legally the authority of his government was confined to the British subjects and protected persons living actually inside the British forts. Although one of the results of the defeat of the Ashantis at Katamanso had been the destruction of their title to the land on which the British forts were built,[1] it was not clear whether Maclean's council was authorised to administer more than the forts at Cape Coast and Accra, even though British merchants were still living in the forts at places like Anomabu and Dixcove. British relations with the other Europeans on the coast were not very good. The Danes at Osu were apt to act as though they controlled all Accra, and were intriguing to establish an inland protectorate over Akwapim, Akim and Krobo. The Dutch at Elmina were on friendly terms with the Ashantis, were supplying them with arms, and were suspected of conspiring with them to resume the slave trade.

Maclean dealt firmly and tactfully with all his problems. In 1831 he negotiated peace treaties between the coastal states, the Danes and the British on the one hand, and Ashanti on the other. The Ashantis renounced their claim to suzerainty over the coastal states and pledged themselves to keep the peace and to allow freedom of trade with the interior. Maclean then set himself to the task of restoring stability and good order to the coastal states, whose social and political organisation had been badly damaged by the slave trade and thirty years of Ashanti invasions. He adjudicated in disputes between chiefs, sat with chiefs and elders in courts to secure the humane but just punishment of murderers and thieves, pressed them to stop customs such as human sacrifice and 'panyarring'[2] which he considered obstacles to social progress, and was ready to send punitive expeditions against chiefs who continued to permit such customs when they had pledged themselves not to, or who had dealt unjustly with peaceful traders.

In this way Maclean extended British ideas of justice over an area

[1] Since the Danes had also fought on the winning side at Katamanso, they too secured the freehold of their forts. But the Dutch did not go to war with Ashanti, and continued to pay rent to Kumasi for their forts.

[2] 'Panyarring'—the forcible seizure of a person or property in order to secure redress or restitution for a grievance or a debt.

extending from the Pra in the west to the Volta in the east, and for about forty miles inland. As a result, trade prospered and the value of exports through the British forts increased from £70,000 in 1831 to £325,000 in 1840, and of imports during the same period from £131,000 to £423,000.

However, Maclean's activities on the Gold Coast did not go uncriticised. It was said that he was extending British jurisdiction over the peoples of the Gold Coast without their consent solely so that the British merchants could make larger profits; that this jurisdiction was illegal; that he was not active in suppressing slavery and the slave trade, and that the increasing imports of British goods into the Gold Coast only went to pay for the illegal export of slaves; and finally, that he was a man of unsound moral character.

Much of this criticism resulted from the way in which Maclean worked, and from inadequate knowledge of what he was doing and of the difficulties he had to surmount. Maclean was the kind of man who rarely acted without slow and deliberate reflection, but who, once he had come to a decision, was absolutely sure that it was right, and who would then act upon it firmly and swiftly. So certain was he that his decisions were right, that he did not always trouble to explain the reasons for them, and was apt to despise anyone who did not understand and agree with him. Inevitably such a man made enemies, though more among Europeans—the lesser men who were his colleagues on the coast—than among Africans, and these enemies did not hesitate to misinterpret his motives and to attack his character. Although we may still not be completely informed about some aspects of Maclean's private life, there seems little doubt of his complete integrity in matters of public policy. His motives in extending British jurisdiction were not inspired purely by the idea of increasing British merchants' profits; much of what he did went far beyond what the London Committee of Merchants was prepared to authorise. Maclean had simply realised that the peoples of the Gold Coast were in sore need of peace, prosperity and good government, and thought that they could best get these things if he helped them to administer justice and maintain order. Naturally trade increased as a result, but the African merchants and people benefited from the increase together with the British. It was true that he had no legal authority for exercising jurisdiction over Africans who were not British subjects, but he did so with their consent, and in ways which he thought were to their ultimate benefit. The charge that Maclean countenanced slavery and the slave trade arose solely because he was well aware of the limits of his authority. He refused to interfere in the customs of Africans who were not British subjects unless he thought that such customs were dangerous social evils. Human sacrifices and 'panyarring' came into this category; the forms of household slavery practised on the Gold Coast did not. Few people were

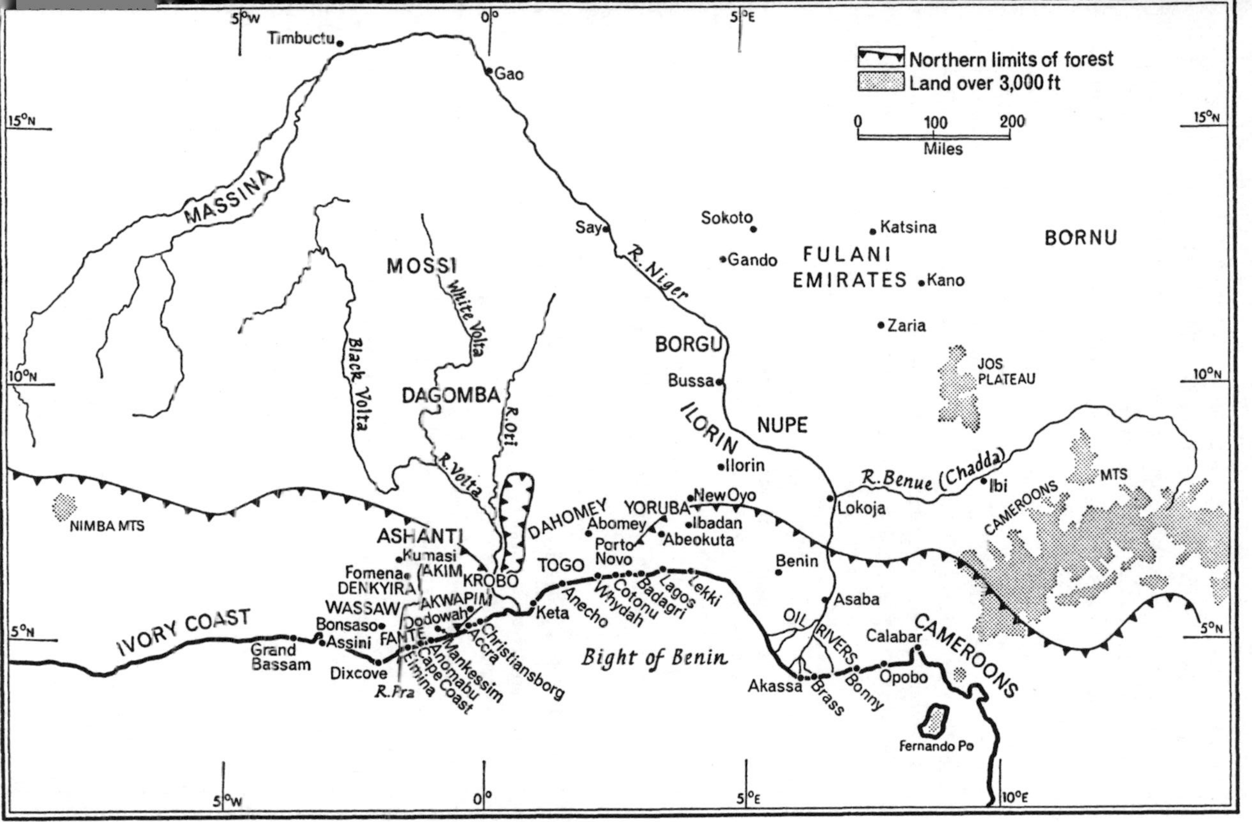

11 The Gold Coast and Nigeria, 1821–74

more hostile to the slave trade than Maclean, but he did not see that he had any authority to arrest slave-traders who were not British subjects.

In 1841 the Colonial Office sent out Dr R. R. Madden, a staunch anti-slaver, as a commissioner to inspect the affairs of the Gold Coast and the Gambia. Madden, who saw very little of the Gold Coast, wrote a report which was sadly biased against Maclean. However, the disastrous failure of the 1841 Niger expedition made it seem desirable that the whole of British policy in West Africa should be reviewed, and a Parliamentary Select Committee was set up in 1842. The Committee's report exonerated Maclean from the charges made against him by Madden and others, and indeed praised him for the way in which, with few resources of money and men, he had spread a peaceful British influence over so large an extent of territory. It recommended that Maclean's work should be continued with more adequate resources, and that the British government should re-occupy the Gold Coast forts and provide sufficient men and money for good administration. Nevertheless, the Committee could not but agree that, however beneficial it might have been, the jurisdiction which Maclean had exercised outside the British forts and over people who were not British subjects, was technically an illegal one. It therefore recommended that the British government should negotiate formal treaties with the coastal tribes which would properly define its relationship to them.

The Gold Coast, 1843–63

The British government acted on the advice of the 1842 Committee. In 1843 it resumed direct control of the British forts on the Gold Coast, placing them under a lieutenant-governor responsible to the governor of Sierra Leone. Maclean was given the post of Judicial Assessor (i.e. Chief Justice with a special responsibility for the administration of justice among the coastal states). The British Foreign Jurisdiction Act of 1843 had empowered the British government to exercise jurisdiction in non-British territories provided that such jurisdiction was authorised by treaty between Britain and the foreign state concerned. In 1844, under this Act, the new British administration on the Gold Coast induced the rulers of a number of the coastal states to sign declarations regularising the unofficial jurisdiction established by Maclean. Such a declaration was known as a 'bond' because it bound an African ruler to protect the rights of individuals and of property; to abolish such barbarous customs as human sacrifices and 'panyarring'; and to authorise British judges to help him try crimes such as murder and robbery, so that the customs of the country would become moulded to the general principles of British law. From 1844 to 1874 the Gold Coast states which entered into bonds were often loosely referred to as a British protectorate (as distinct from the British forts which constituted a crown colony), though it should be noted that the bonds did not give Britain the right to intervene in the *government* of the states, but only in their administration of justice.

With the resumption of direct control of the Gold Coast forts by the British government, there began a period in which relations between Britain and the Gold Coast peoples were neither satisfactory nor happy. When Maclean had had the direction of British affairs on the Gold Coast, he was to a great extent able to make his own policy and to act consistently on it. But the British officials who followed him were required to follow the changing policies of successive governments in Britain. Even if these officials had all possessed the same remarkable talent for inspiring the trust of Africans that Maclean (who died on the Gold Coast in 1847) had had, they would still have found it difficult to interpret this policy consistently in a manner which would have secured African confidence in them. As it was, the British governors and their aides were rarely on the coast for periods longer than a year or two, and in general lacked both the time and the incentive to get to know the country and its peoples properly.

Maclean's successors were almost as short of money for their administration as he had been, and, because they were lesser men with a poorer understanding of the Gold Coast, this was a greater handicap for them than it had been for him. British governments were unwilling that their taxpayers should have to find more money for the Gold Coast administration than the minimum needed for the salaries of its officials. There were not funds enough even to repair the British forts, most of which were falling down through sheer neglect. There were difficulties in the way of raising adequate revenue locally. The Africans could not be taxed, because they were not British subjects. Any attempt to increase the small duties levied on trade passing through the British forts would merely have meant that the trade of the British forts would have declined and that of the Dutch and Danish forts would have increased.

Yet there were good reasons why a larger revenue was desirable. A result of the growth of British influence and of the work of the missionaries was that the peoples of the coastal states were beginning to look to the British administration to provide roads, schools, hospitals and other amenities which there were no funds to pay for.

In 1850 it seemed as though the situation might improve. In the first place the British forts on the Gold Coast were made independent of Sierra Leone, whose governor was too remote to take much interest in Gold Coast affairs, and were given a governor, an executive council and a nominated legislative council of their own. Secondly, Britain was able to purchase the Danish forts, so that it was possible to hope that additional revenue might be raised from duties on trade. When, however, the continued lack of cooperation by the Dutch prevented this, in 1852 the

British authorities attempted to induce the rulers of the coastal states themselves to raise the revenue needed for public works, education and other desired improvements. A meeting of the local kings was constituted into a 'Legislative Assembly' which agreed that their peoples should pay a poll-tax. But this venture was not a success. The people objected to the methods used to collect the tax, and asserted with some justice that their kings had no authority to allow them to be taxed in this way. Resistance to the tax was so great that, instead of an expected £20,000, only £7,500 was collected in the first year, and almost all the proceeds were spent, not on the desired improvements, but to defray the costs of collection and to pay salaries. In the following years receipts declined still further, and after 1861 the tax was abandoned.

In the meantime relations between Ashanti and Britain and the coastal states were rapidly deteriorating, with the result that the trade and prosperity of the 'protectorate' declined. The growth of British influence in the Gold Coast had frustrated the ambitions of the Ashanti, denying them control of the coastal states and freedom to trade as they liked. It was still possible for the Ashanti to import arms through the Dutch forts, but it was no longer possible for them to export slaves through the Gold Coast. Some Ashanti slaves could be exported through the Ivory Coast and others through the Slave Coast, but in general it was possible for Ashanti to capture more slaves than could be exported, with the result that this most powerful of Gold Coast kingdoms was being submitted by British action to an economic squeeze.[1]

Dahomey and Lagos, 1850–61

The purchase of the Danish forts on the Gold Coast took the British as far east as Keta and brought them into closer contact with affairs on the Slave Coast. It seemed to the British government that their success in stopping the export of slaves from the Gold Coast had merely resulted in an increase in the export of slaves from the Slave Coast. A number of missions were therefore sent to Dahomey to try and persuade its rulers to stop the slave trade. Consul Beecroft went on one of these missions in 1850, but concluded that it was futile to try and stop the Dahoman slave trade while the export of slaves through Lagos continued unchecked. In fact the human spoil of the Yoruba civil wars had enabled Lagos to surpass Whydah as the principal slave port of West Africa.

Dahomey seemed so powerful a military state that if she were deter-

[1] The British also argued that, with the increasing restriction on the export of slaves, a surplus of captives was occasioning an increase in the numbers of sacrifices made on great national festivals in both Ashanti and Dahomey. Though it is difficult to know whether in fact this was really the case, this argument certainly provided a powerful humanitarian motive for Britain to take a tougher line towards both kingdoms.

mined to continue capturing and dealing in slaves, the only thing likely to make her change her mind was a full-scale military invasion. This the British governments of the time would not contemplate, so it was left to the naval patrols to continue their efforts to stop slaves being exported from Whydah. Lagos, on the other hand, was a much smaller and weaker power, and it appeared to Beecroft that Britain might intervene to stop the slave trade there without a great expenditure of effort.

The kingship of Lagos at this time was in dispute between two members of the royal family, Akitoye, and his nephew, Kosoko. Akitoye had succeeded to office in 1841, but in 1845 he was driven out by Kosoko with the support of Brazilian slave-traders whose business at Whydah was being hampered by British naval action and who, therefore, were keen to develop their trade at Lagos. Akitoye first fled to Abeokuta, where British missionaries had been established since 1844. The Abeokutans protected him from Kosoko, but were not strong enough to help him to recover Lagos. Akitoye then moved to Badagri, a town of some strategic importance, since it was the channel of communication between Abeokuta and the outside world and also between the two slaving states of Dahomey and Lagos. At Badagri a number of British merchants were endeavouring to establish legitimate trade, and Akitoye was able to get into touch with Beecroft at Fernando Po. Akitoye wanted to recover his kingdom; Beecroft wanted to stop the slave trade at Lagos. Kosoko realised the danger to himself that would result from an alliance between Akitoye and Beecroft. He induced Dahomey to attack Abeokuta and instigated an armed demonstration in Badagri against Akitoye and the British. But Akitoye had already left for Fernando Po, where he promised Beecroft that if the British would recover Lagos for him, he would outlaw the slave trade.

In 1851, at the second attempt, a British naval force captured Lagos. Kosoko fled and Akitoye reigned in his stead. He kept his word about the slave trade, and soon British merchants were settling in Lagos to engage in legitimate trade. In 1853 a British consul was appointed to Lagos to represent their interests. But Akitoye and his son Dosumu, who succeeded him in 1853, clearly owed their position to British intervention, and they failed to command the obedience of those of their subjects who wished to continue trading in slaves. The latter continued to regard Kosoko as their rightful ruler and to trade in slaves. Although in 1854 the British consul at Lagos concluded an agreement with Kosoko by which the latter relinquished his claims to Lagos in return for British recognition of him as ruler of the neighbouring territories of Palma and Lekki, some slave-trading still continued at Lagos. In 1861, therefore, the British decided that they must do themselves what Dosumu lacked the power to do, and the island of Lagos was annexed to the British Crown.

The 1865 Committee

In 1863 the Ashantis invaded the British 'protectorate' on the Gold Coast. The immediate occasion was the refusal of the British governor, Richard Pine, to send back to Kumasi refugees from Ashanti justice, who, in his opinion, would be unjustly condemned to death. The Ashanti invasion met with no serious opposition, and when Pine proposed to organise a counter-attack and to carry it into Ashanti territory, the British government, unwilling to face the extension of its responsibilities that would result were Ashanti defeated, refused to allow it. British prestige on the Gold Coast slumped disastrously. The coastal peoples no longer believed in the power of Britain to defend them, and the undefeated Ashanti armies began to raid with impunity, bringing trade to a standstill.

The consequences of doing nothing in face of the Ashanti invasion revealed to responsible people in Britain how deeply involved in the political affairs of West Africa their country had become. In 1864 a commissioner, Colonel Ord, was sent out to report on the administration of the four British colonies, and in the following year a Select Committee of the House of Commons was appointed to consider his report, and to make recommendations as to future British policy in West Africa. The general feeling of the Committee was that Britain had drifted into more obligations in West Africa than could be justified on the grounds of her own interests, which at this time were considered to be primarily commercial. It recommended that the British government should abandon all its settlements except Sierra Leone. But the Committee realised that the obligations incurred by the government to protect British traders and certain African states made an immediate withdrawal impossible. It was therefore recommended that, while these obligations continued, the most that could be done was to economise by uniting the administrations of the Gold Coast, Lagos and the Gambia under the governor of Sierra Leone; for the British government to refuse to extend its rule or protection over further African territories; and to urge the Africans already under its rule or protection to prepare for their own self-government. These recommendations were adopted by the British government.

The Gold Coast, 1865–74

The most striking consequences of the new British policy were seen on the Gold Coast. It was declared that British territory there was limited to the forts at Dixcove, Anomabu, Accra and Christiansborg (Osu), and to within a radius of five miles from the castle at Cape Coast. European-educated Fante began to persuade the kings and peoples of the Fante states to think of organising a national government which would be able to take over from the British when they departed. But before a Fante Confederation constitution and government could be formally established, the political situation on the Gold Coast changed so radically that the British officials began to have second thoughts about leaving the country.

In 1867, Britain was able to conclude a treaty with the Netherlands by which the Dutch forts lying to the east of Elmina were to be exchanged for the British forts to the west of Cape Coast. In this way the whole coast from Cape Coast to Keta came under British control, and it seemed possible, therefore, to raise sufficient revenue from duties on trade to make the British administration financially strong and independent of help from the British taxpayer. However, states like Denkyira and Wassaw did not wish to be transferred from the protection of the British, who, whatever their failings as allies, were hostile to Ashanti, to that of the Dutch, who were friendly towards Ashanti and had even supplied the latter with arms for the 1863 invasion. The people of Komenda refused to allow the Dutch to occupy the British fort there, and even began to attack the people of Elmina, who, as well as being under Dutch influence, were traditionally allies of Ashanti. Representatives from Wassaw, Denkyira, Assin, and most of the Fante states met at Mankessim and organised help for Komenda in its war against Elmina. In 1868 the Ashanti determined to come to the aid of Elmina by renewing the war of 1863 against the British, with whom no peace had been signed. However, their main armies did not advance directly against the Fante states under British protection, but began with wide outflanking movements through the Ivory Coast and Togo.

The Dutch reaction to these troubles was to decide to quit the Gold Coast for good, and in 1869 they began negotiations for Britain to take over their forts. This the British government was willing to do provided that it was satisfied that the Dutch had a valid right to Elmina which they could transfer. When the Dutch were asked whether they had not been paying ground-rent to Ashanti for Elmina Castle, they stated categorically that although they had been making regular payments to Ashanti, these were merely a continuation of the ancient practice of making presents to facilitate trade. This was not the view taken either by Kofi Karikari, the *Asantehene*, or by the people of Elmina, but in September 1871 a British messenger returned from Kumasi with a document which seemed to be a renunciation by Kofi Karikari of Ashanti claims to Elmina. It seems that this document cannot have been genuine, but it was accepted as such by both the British and the Dutch, and in April 1872, Elmina and the other Dutch forts were taken over by the British, and the Dutch severed a connection with the Gold Coast which had lasted for nearly 300 years. The people of Elmina seemed to take the transfer fairly quietly; in reality they were waiting for the Ashanti army to arrive and help them expel the British.

In the meantime the Ashanti had captured a party of German missionaries in Togo. The fact that the British administration preferred to negotiate with Ashanti, both for the release of the missionaries and over the transfer of Elmina, rather than to prepare to fight, spurred on the Fante efforts to organise a united government of their own. In October 1871, an assembly at Mankessim agreed to a constitution for the Fante Confederation which had been effectively in existence ever since the war between Komenda and Elmina. The purpose of the Confederation was stated to be to provide an administration which would serve to unite the coastal states to fight Ashanti, and which could improve the country by providing roads and schools and developing its agricultural and mineral resources. Each of the thirty-three member states was to send two members to a central Assembly, one a chief and the other an educated man. The king of one of the states was to be elected president, and, under a permanent central executive, there was to be a system of salaried magistrates and government agents in the provinces of the Confederation.

This Mankessim constitution, the work of a group of educated Africans, was a laudable attempt to combine traditional African with European ideas of government. Although it was occasioned by the reluctance of the British authorities to provide the amenities which the coastal states desired and to defend them against Ashanti, it was not anti-British in spirit. In fact the makers of the constitution requested the recognition, advice and support of the British government in order to make it work successfully. Instead they received a rude shock. The harassed British officials on the Gold Coast viewed the Confederation as a conspiracy against the British government, and arrested those of its officers on whom they could lay hands. The prisoners were soon released on instructions from the Colonial Office, but the hasty action of the British officials had necessarily estranged relations with the Confederation leaders.

By the time when it was possible to consider the Confederation in a calmer light, the attention of the British government was fully occupied with other matters. First there was the affair of Elmina to be settled, and then in January 1873 the main Ashanti army crossed the Pra river and advanced into the 'protectorate'. Only the coming of the rains and an outbreak of dysentry and smallpox in their army stopped the Ashanti from the complete conquest of the coastal districts.

The British government was at last forced to agree with Pine's conclusion of 1863 that it must try and deal with Ashanti once and for all by invading that country with a sizeable military force. In October 1873, one of Britain's leading soldiers, Major-General Sir Garnet Wolseley, arrived on the Gold Coast as administrator and commander-in-chief. A force of 2,500 British soldiers and large numbers of African auxiliaries was carefully prepared. By the time Wolseley was ready to advance, the Ashanti army had withdrawn across the Pra, and the main battles of the campaign were fought in Ashanti between 31 January and 4 February 1874. The Ashanti fought well but unavailingly against the superior weapons of the British, and on 5 February Wolseley entered Kumasi. The *Asantehene* and other leaders had fled, so that there was no one with whom a peace could be signed. Wolseley's troops were not equipped for an occupation or for further fighting, and so on the following day, after setting fire to the city, the British began to withdraw to the coast. However, envoys from Kofi Karikari caught up with Wolseley at Fomena, and a peace was agreed on terms dictated by the latter, namely that Ashanti should pay an indemnity of 50,000 oz. of gold (about £200,000 or $800,000); should renounce all claims to suzerainty over Denkyira, Assin, Akim, Adansi and Elmina; should promise to keep the roads to Kumasi open to traders from the coast; and should abolish the practice of human sacrifice.

Since the time of Maclean, British responsibility for the defence and for the administration of some of the internal affairs of the coastal states had been increasing in fact if not in law. The 1865 Committee had recognised this, and had recommended that an unsatisfactory state of affairs could best be ended by the withdrawal of Britain from the Gold Coast. But the events of 1867–74 had not only shown the dangers of Britain's half-and-half policy towards the Gold Coast; they had also suggested that Britain's difficulties might be solved in another way.

The transfer of the former Dutch forts meant that Britain could at last hope to raise sufficient revenue locally to provide adequately for the defence of the 'protected' states and to give them some of the amenities they wanted. By refusing to recognise the Fante Confederation, Britain had stopped the states from organising to provide for these things themselves. Britain's defeat of Ashanti meant not only that the trade (and therefore the revenue) of the Gold Coast could increase, but also a clear acceptance of British responsibility for dealing directly with the Ashanti threat to the 'protectorate' and for maintaining the peace of the latter.

Opinion on colonial matters in Britain had also changed between 1865 and 1874. In the latter year, Disraeli took office with a Conservative government which was much less committed than any of its nineteenth-century predecessors to the view that colonies were expensive responsibilities which Britain could best do without. In July 1874, Disraeli's government decided that the 'protected' states should be annexed and that, together with Lagos, they should be constituted into a new crown colony independent of Sierra Leone.

This decision was not welcomed by the Gold Coast peoples, particularly by those men who had organised and supported the Fante Confederation, who could not see why the bonds of 1844–5 should be set aside and their states treated arbitrarily as though they were a conquered territory. On the British side, however, two things may be said. First, that the British Crown claimed no rights to the land in the new colony, as it would have done in a conquered colony. Secondly, that it was possible for Britain to solve the problems resulting from her ill-defined but growing relationship to the Gold Coast peoples satisfactorily only by getting out altogether, or by assuming legally the responsibility for their defence and government which was already hers in fact. The events of 1867–74 had so deeply involved Britain in Gold Coast affairs that it seemed no longer possible for her to evacuate.

10

The Islamic revolution, and political developments in the interior, *c.* 1770–*c.* 1890

The beginnings of the Islamic revolution

By about the middle of the eighteenth century, the religion of Islam was widely spread throughout the western and central Sudan, and its adherents had also appeared in some parts of Guinea. There was, for example, a significant Muslim minority at Kumasi, the capital of Ashanti, by the end of the century. But in general Islam had as yet been accepted in West Africa only superficially. Almost everywhere, Muslims were a minority of the population. They were found in towns rather than in villages and the countryside, and Islam was a religion of kings and courts, and of merchant communities, rather than of whole peoples. It had spread, in fact, largely through the activities of the specialised long-distance traders such as the Dyula and the Hausa merchants. Only in the Sudan had kings so far been converted, and not all of these, and they were involved in a constant tug-of-war between their duties as Muslims and their obligations as the traditional heads of animist communities. Unless they were very strong and successful, the pull of the latter was likely to take precedence, for in the last resort they owed their positions as kings to their role as descendants of the founders of those communities, and were required to intercede with, and to make the traditional oblations and sacrifices to, their ancestors and their gods. Thus in a crisis, their Islam was unlikely to be little more than a public veneer. It is notable, for example, that when the great empire of Mali, encompassing several ethnic groups, collapsed and gave way to the smaller Bambara kingdoms of Segu and Kaarta, which essentially had only Mande subjects, the pagan aspects of Mande kingship became so strengthened that for the orthodox Muslims of Timbuctu and Jenne, the word 'Bambara' became equivalent to 'pagan Mande'. Only perhaps in Bornu after Idris Alawma, did Muslim law and practice come to challenge traditional pagan laws and customs on any scale in a major kingdom.

During the eighteenth century, however, a revolution began. In large areas of the Sudan, Islam began to become the religion of ordinary men and women, and whole states began to be governed in accordance with its precepts. In the following century, Islam also began to make much more positive progress in some parts of the coastlands.

This Islamic revolution began in the far west. It was here that Islam had first arrived in West Africa, and that the first Negro kings to be converted, those of Takrur, had ruled. The successes of the Almoravids in the latter part of the eleventh century further encouraged the expansion of Islam in the western Sudan, and also provided a bridge of Muslim peoples tying this part of West Africa to the Muslim kingdoms of North West Africa. This bridge was further strengthened after the fifteenth century, when the Sanhaja Berbers, who had constituted the Almoravids, were conquered and overrun by Arab tribes, so that the population of the western Sahara became Arabised as well as Islamised. Then, beginning in the sixteenth century with the Qadiriyya, the brotherhoods which had developed out of the Muslim mystical movement called Sufism, which was strongly established in North West Africa, began to penetrate across the Sahara into the westernmost Sudan.

These Muslim brotherhoods, in which chains of disciples were trained to propagate pure and rigorous concepts of Islam derived from the teachings of a saintly founder, were of particular importance in a religion which possessed little in the way of a formal priesthood. The Qadiriyya established themselves smoothly and peacefully in the towns and along the trade routes of the Western Sudan. The results were the spread of Koranic schools, the development of an organised proselytising movement, and, in the westernmost Sudan, the conversion of whole peoples to the Muslim way of life. By the eighteenth century, one of these peoples, the Tukolor, had developed a significant clerical class, the *torodbe*. The second brotherhood, or *tariqa*, to play an important role in West Africa was the Tijaniyya, a much later order, founded in Morocco in 1781. The Tijaniyya tended to be more militant in outlook, more willing to expand the world of Islam by force, and from the middle of the nineteenth century their influence spread rapidly along paths already prepared by the Qadiriyya and largely at their expense.

The revolution sponsored by the *torodbe* and the brotherhoods achieved its first political successes in the Futa region. Here, by the 1770s, after half a century of warfare, the *torodbe* succeeded in replacing the animist rulers with Muslim *almamis*, clerical kings who ruled as the agents on earth of the will of God, and who, for this reason, demanded an absolute allegiance, both spiritual and political, from all their subjects. It proved impossible in practice to maintain this theocratic view of the state, but the experiments had very wide and significant consequences, for the people who were for the most part involved in them were Fulani, and as a result of the expansion of the latter (chapter 3), the *torodbe* of Futa Jalon had important connections throughout the western and central Sudan.

The Fulani empire of Sokoto and Gwandu

Fulani had been settled in Hausaland for some four centuries. In addition to the pagan pastoralists, there were Muslim Fulani in the towns, and their *mallams* had inherited the scholarly traditions of the urban Muslim communities of the Niger bend during the great period of the Mali and Songhai empires. As such, they became leaders of the Muslim communities in the Hausa states. Their relations with the Hausa kings varied according to the latter's varying degrees of attachment to Islam, but there was an inherent risk of strain due to the fact that the constituents and government of the kingdoms were still essentially animist at base.

About 1775, a leading Fulani *mallam* in Gobir, Usuman dan Fodio, influenced by the *torodbe* revolution in and around Futa Jalon, began to preach that the Islam of the Hausa kings and their states was not the true and pure Islam, and that reforms were urgently needed to bring the Hausa kingdoms into line with Islamic law. As he began to acquire a considerable following, this teaching was eventually recognised by successive kings of Gobir as a direct challenge to their traditional pattern of government and power. An open breach developed which, from 1795 onwards, led the kings to take active measures to try and check the growth of Dan Fodio's movement. The result was to convert a movement of reform into an open revolt. In 1804, Dan Fodio fled from Gobir, and declared a *jihad* (holy war) against the Hausa kings.

It then became apparent that it was not only a small minority of devout Muslim Fulani who had grievances in the existing state of affairs in the Hausa states. There were also the very much greater numbers of pagan Fulani cattle-herders, who had few rights in the Hausa states, but who were subject to taxes and exploitation by their rulers. The peasant farmers among the Hausa themselves could also often see in the *jihad* a means to ridding themselves of oppressive taxation. The king of Gobir's failure to suppress or to contain Dan Fodio's movement in its early stages led to a great snowballing of organised revolt against the Hausa kings and aristocracies throughout the country. The latter were unable to cooperate against it, and by 1809 the territory of all the Hausa states was under Fulani control.

Usuman dan Fodio was a scholar and a divine who was not particularly concerned with practical politics, and he left the direction of the *jihad* and of the empire that resulted from it to his son, Muhammad Bello, and his brother, Abdullahi. Bello oversaw the eastern half of the empire from a new capital city built at Sokoto, in the borderland between Gobir, Katsina and Zamfara, where Usuman dan Fodio had made his headquarters during the *jihad*; while Abdullahi, residing at Gwandu, a few miles to the west in Kebbi, was responsible for the western half. Usuman himself continued to live at Sokoto until his death in 1817, and it was Bello and his successors at Sokoto who succeeded to the title of *Amir al-Mu'minin* (Arabic) or *Sarkin Musulmi* (Hausa), i.e. 'commander of the faithful', which had been assumed by Usuman when he had proclaimed his *jihad*. Under Sokoto and Gwandu, the old Hausa kingdoms became emirates ruled by the Fulani who had raised the flag of revolt in them, or who had been sent out as flag-bearers by Usuman to conquer them. The succession to these emirates lay in the gift of either Sokoto or Gwandu, though, provided that they remained loyal, it was likely to remain in the families of the original emirs.

To a considerable degree, the administrations of the emirates were the old Hausa administrations, but these were now subject to overhaul and reform. For about fifty years, they were also subject to very real supervision from Sokoto and Gwandu, with the aim of securing not only an efficient flow of tribute, but also a uniform and fair system of taxation, law and administration for the whole empire. This, together with the ending of the constant disputes and quarrels between the old independent Hausa kingdoms, was greatly to the advantage of Hausa trade and industry, which flourished as never before, confirming the supremacy of the Hausa market cities in the trade both across the Sahara and in the eastern half of West Africa. Partly for the same reasons, but also because the *jihad* was fought to establish sound principles of religion, ethics and government, and its leaders, Bello and Abdullahi as well as Usuman dan Fodio, were learned and scholarly men, there was also a great renaissance of scholarship and literature, most obviously perhaps in Arabic, but also extending into the vernaculars. The three leading members of the Dan Fodio family are themselves known each to have been responsible for something like a hundred literary works—treatises on religion, morals, government, and many other subjects—for the most part inspired by the need to make the beliefs, principles and laws of Islam better and more widely known among a hitherto largely animist population, and to interpret them in relation to the many problems of conscience and practice that were bound to arise when extending Islamic civilisation and law over such a population.

One particular aspect of this literary output is of particular interest, namely the effort made to justify the Fulani *jihad*, and especially in relation to the Muslims of Bornu. The *jihad* did not stop at the frontiers of Hausaland. Bornu had been invaded in 1808, and the resources, moral as well as material, of this most ancient of West African monarchies proved powerless in face of the Fulani drive. That Bornu was not incorporated into the Fulani empire was basically due to the leadership of a Muslim cleric, a Kanembu from Kanem, Muhammad al-Kanemi, who was able to inspire a new resistance through his assertion that the Fulani clerics had no monopoly of Islamic rectitude. By 1812 the invaders had been repelled, and in the next dozen years, al-Kanemi, as well as engaging in a lively epistolary debate with Bello, established his authority throughout Bornu and Kanem. The ineffective palace regime of the Sefawa *Mais* was replaced by a new, efficient Muslim administration parallel in many respects to that established by the Fulani in Hausaland. The *Mais* remained as titular rulers until 1846, when the *Mai* of the time unsuccessfully tried to rebel against al-Kanemi's son and successor, 'Umar, who henceforth ruled both in fact and in name, though not as *Mai*, but as *Shehu* (sheikh).

Though repulsed in Bornu, the Fulani *jihad* achieved great success further to the south-east, in what is now northern Cameroon, where there had been considerable Fulani settlement. Here, under the leadership of a local Fulani, by *c.* 1840 there had been built up one of the most extensive Fulani spheres of influence, the emirate of Adamawa, so named after its founder. To the south of the old Hausa states, although the new kingdom of Abuja was built up by the Hausa king and aristocracy who had been ousted by the Fulani from Zaria, pagan peoples were subject to continual attack, and many were forced to become tribute-paying vassals in new emirates. In Nupe, the Fulani were able to intervene with ever more decisive effects in a civil war between two branches of the royal family, with the result that by about 1850 the whole kingdom was under their control. To the south-west, a similar opportunity for the expansion of Muslim Fulani rule was presented by the break-up of the Oyo empire. This is thus perhaps a suitable point at which to turn aside from the Islamic revolution to consider political developments in what is today southern Nigeria.

Political developments in southern Nigeria

The *Alafins* of Oyo, unlike the kings of Ashanti and Dahomey, did not succeed in creating under their direct control an administration with which to maintain their hold over their empire. Perhaps the *Alafins* assumed that, as descendants of Oduduwa, they could rely on the allegiance of subject kings who were Yoruba themselves. Such imperial administration as they had was basically an extension of that of Oyo itself, and depended on the cooperation of its traditional chiefs, and, as has been seen (chapter 7), the second half of the eighteenth century was not a harmonious period in Oyo politics. With the concurrent growth of trade on the coast, the southern Yoruba communities were becoming richer, and had every incentive to make themselves independent of controls from Oyo, in the far north, which were alternately too harsh or little effective.

The final blow to the imperial pretensions of the *Alafins* of Oyo came about 1817, with the revolt of the commander-in-chief of the Oyo army, Afonja. Afonja apparently thought he might strengthen his position with Fulani assistance. In this he was greatly mistaken; he was quickly thrust aside and his town, Ilorin, became the capital of a new Fulani emirate. The whole of northern Yorubaland was now open to Fulani pressure and to conversion to Islam. When *c.* 1835, *Alafin* Oluewu was defeated and killed in battle, his capital was abandoned and its people forced to take refuge in the south, where his successor established a new Oyo. This disaster might conceivably have been avoided if the other Yoruba had supported Oyo against the Fulani, but this they were in no position to do, for they were engaged in bitter fratricidal wars of their own.

These began in 1821 with a quarrel between Owu and Ife, in which Ife was supported by Ijebu and by Oyo refugees from the Fulani. The town of Owu was destroyed and its people driven west into Egba country, which was subsequently ravaged by competing armies of freebooters who, whatever their ostensible motives, were largely sustained by the fact that there was a flourishing market for their captives at nearby ports like Lagos and Badagri. Many of the invaders of Egbaland settled, *c.* 1829, at a war camp at Ibadan, out of which developed the greatest of the Yoruba cities. Many groups of Egba, on the other hand, together with the Owu survivors, came together for self-defence in another great settlement at Abeokuta. Oyo men dominated the council at Ibadan, and this made possible a pact with the New Oyo, by which Ibadan became responsible for stemming further Fulani advances.

By the beginning of the 1840s this end had been achieved, but the very power and success of Ibadan occasioned further troubles. Ibadan in effect was aspiring to replace Oyo as the centre of Yoruba empire, and this was resented by other Yoruba cities, chief among them Ijaye. In the ensuing warfare, Ibadan at one stage actually sought help from the Fulani of Ilorin. The political rivalry was intensified by commercial competition for the trade routes which ran south to the coast from Ibadan and Abeokuta through Ijebu and Egba country. By the 1850s the divisions among the Yoruba had become so acute that it was open to question whether they could ever achieve harmony through their own efforts. It was a critical situation for them. In the east lay the military state of Dahomey, which attacked Abeokuta in 1851, and thereafter presented a constant threat to Yorubaland. The military and political advance of the Fulani had been checked, but Islam continued to make inroads into traditional Yoruba society. In and around Abeokuta, a new spiritual and, perhaps also, a political solution to the problems facing this society seemed to some to lie in the Christianity and the western education implanted by the liberated Africans from Sierra Leone and by the European missionaries. Finally, yet another external political factor

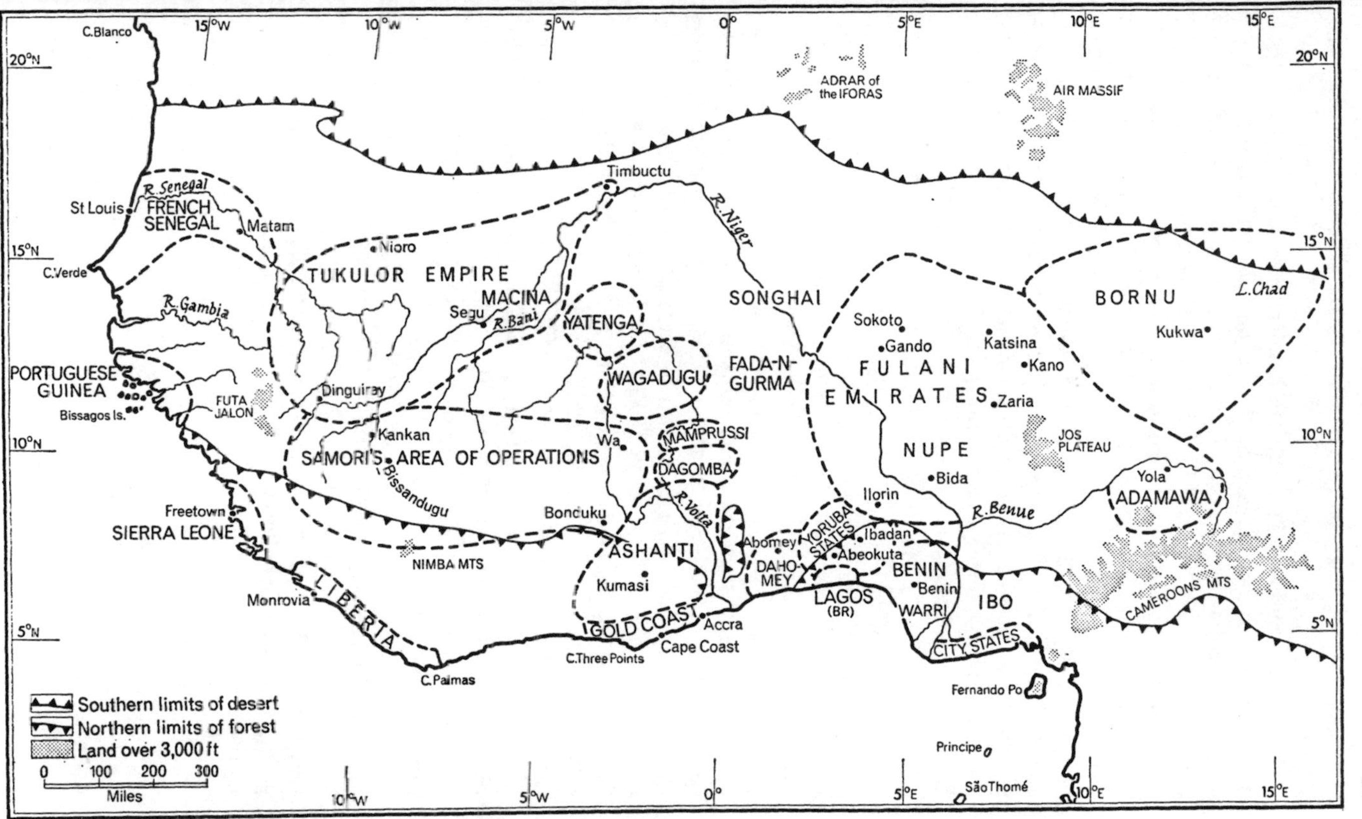

12 The political situation in the 1860s and 1870s

entered the scene when in 1851 the British established themselves at Lagos.

The decay of authority in Yorubaland under the strains imposed by the pull of trade with the coast and by the Fulani invasion contrasts sharply with the situation on the coast further east. Here, by the eighteenth century, in Warri, in the small Ijo fishing villages at the mouths of the Oil Rivers, and among the Efik of Old Calabar, new political structures had been evolved specifically to deal with the growth of trade caused by the European demand first for slaves and then for palm oil. Not all the slaves obtained from the Ibo traders of the hinterland were exported. An appreciable number were retained by the principal African traders and incorporated, together with their kinsmen, into corporations called 'houses', to serve their needs for transport, defence and general labour. Even a small house might number as many as a thousand persons; larger ones might be very much bigger—in the mid-nineteenth century one Old Calabar house had the capacity to man 400 canoes.

The heads of houses would meet together to settle disputes between them, the chairmanship of the meeting being either with a king (as at Warri, New Calabar and Bonny) who would usually head the most powerful house, or open to competition. But, either way, this was a system by which those who had economic power also had political authority, and in which the way to the top was defined by ability and not by a man's traditional status. A man who had started as a slave could, if able enough, become the accepted head of a house. In one outstanding case, in 1869–70, the ex-slave head of one of the houses at Bonny, Jaja, following a dispute with the king, established a new city-state of his own, Opobo, which succeeded in taking much of Bonny's trade. All in all, the houses and the city-state governments of the Niger delta were a remarkably successful African adaptation to the new economic forces engendered by the presence of European traders on the coast. Since the system produced the goods which the latter required, by and large they were prepared to operate within it. The British merchants who had followed their government to Lagos, on the other hand, felt increasingly frustrated by the disruption of trade occasioned by the wars in Yorubaland, and so, together with the missionaries, became a force tending to pull the British government towards political intervention in the hinterland.

The Fulani kingdom of Macina

The Fulani seizure of power under the banner of Islam in Hausaland was a powerful example to Fulani elsewhere: their success in Adamawa, for example, was essentially due to the initiative of local Fulani. Another area in which considerable numbers of Fulani had settled was Macina, the area of the Niger valley between about Jenne and Lake Debo. Political authority here had been weak ever since the fall of the Songhai empire. At first the area had been at least nominally subject to the *Arma* of Jenne and Timbuctu, but by the eighteenth century these had become tributary to the Bambara kingdom of Segu. During the first half of the eighteenth century, however, the Bambara monarchy split into two halves, and the kings at Segu became involved in continual warfare with the rival kings who had established themselves in Kaarta, to the north-west. As a consequence, their power in the east declined: Timbuctu was lost to the Tuareg in 1787, and the Fulani in Macina under their traditional *ardo* were left very much to themselves.

One of their clerics, *Seku* Ahmadu Lobo, who may have assisted in the early stages of Usuman dan Fodio's *jihad*, soon began to propagate the cause of Muslim renewal in his own homeland. This provoked from the *Arma* of Jenne and from the king of Segu much the same reaction as Dan Fodio had met with from the Hausa kings, and occasioned a similar Fulani uprising with a similar dramatic success. Between 1810 and 1815, the whole-hearted support of the Fulani enabled Ahmadu Lobo to establish his control throughout Macina, and to establish a centralised Islamic monarchy which he ruled from a new capital, Hamdallahi. By 1827 his power had reached as far as Timbuctu.

The empire of al Hajj 'Umar

Yet a third major Muslim state arose from the activities of al-Hajj 'Umar. 'Umar was a Tukolor cleric from Futa Toro who in 1825 set out on the pilgrimage to Mecca, where he was appointed to be the Tijaniyya leader for the Sudan. His return home was a leisurely one in which he spent some time at al-Azhar in Cairo, in Bornu, and at Sokoto and at Hamdallahi. By the time, *c.* 1845, he had finally settled down on the borders of Fulani-held Futa Jalon at Dinguiray, he was a man of notable learning and authority, very well acquainted with the political achievements of the Muslim revival in the western and central Sudan (he had married daughters both of al-Kanemi and of Bello).

At Dinguiray, 'Umar began to build up the Tijaniyya order with recruits from the Fulani and Tukolor *torodbe*. He was not successful, however, in securing the position of influence which he sought among the Muslim clerics of his own homeland of Futa Toro. Consequently 'Umar's movement began to develop in its more political and military aspects. He attracted a growing following of able and ambitious men from many ethnic groups and many walks of life, whom he was able to arm with modern weapons obtained from trade at the coast. By the beginning of the 1850s, 'Umar had sufficient power at his command, material as well as spiritual, to launch a *jihad*. This swept northwards through the petty Mande principalities of Bambuk and Boure (the ancient Wangara), until in 1854 his army entered Nyoro, the capital of the major Bambara state of Kaarta. Progress down the Senegal valley proved to be blocked by the French advance in the opposite direction (see chapter 11), and after 1857 'Umar turned east, against the Bambara kingdom of Segu.

So far 'Umar's victories had been against animist or quasi-animist peoples, Mande for the most part, whom he and his clerics were remarkably successful in converting, and in forming into an organised state under a central Muslim government. But his attack on Segu brought him into conflict with a major Muslim power not unlike his own, namely Macina. Originally, 'Umar had hoped that Macina would join with him against the Bambara of Segu. But Ahmadu Lobo's grandson, Ahmadu III (1852–62), refused to do this. He argued that the Segu kingdom lay within the sphere of influence of the Macina Muslims, and that the responsibility for converting it to a true Islamic way of life lay with them alone. As well as this fundamentally political dispute, there was also a doctrinal element in the argument, for 'Umar, representing the Tijaniyya, could retort that the Macina Muslims, who were Qadiri, were not taking the cause of Muslim revival sufficiently far. 'Umar's invasion of Segu therefore provoked a fierce reaction from the Macina Fulani, who joined forces with the Bambara and with the Kunta Arabised Berbers of the southern Sahara against him.

Nevertheless, in 1861 'Umar gained possession of Segu, and in the following year he had no alternative but to march against Macina. Hamdallahi was destroyed, and in 1863 Timbuctu was reached and taken. 'Umar's army had thus proved its military superiority, but its advance occasioned bitter resistance among the Fulani of Macina and among the clerics and adherents of the Qadiriyya. He was unable to hold and to organise his new conquests as he had his old ones. In 1864 'Umar was killed during a Fulani revolt, and his chosen successor, his son Ahmad bin Shaikh (Ahmadu Seku), received a very disturbed inheritance. Much of his thirty-year reign was spent in trying to establish his authority, not only over the Fulani of Macina, but also against other sons and kinsmen of 'Umar's whom the latter had appointed to provincial governorships, who were jealous of his power, and who could often command enough local support to enable them to be virtually independent of the central Muslim monarchy. Ahmad had hardly had time to establish his authority before it was threatened by the advance of the French from the Senegal into the Niger valley which began in 1879.

The empire of Samori

This advance also brought the French into contact and conflict with yet another new Muslim power, but of a different type from the other new Muslim states of the nineteenth century. These, as has been seen, were established primarily by Fulani or Tukolor clerics who had been affected by the Islamic revival symbolised by the *tariqas*. The empire of Samori, on the other hand, was a Mande empire based on the commercial expansion of the Dyula. Samori was born about 1830 in a village in what is now the Republic of Guinea, but within a few miles of the frontiers of both Sierra Leone and Liberia. He was no cleric, indeed he may possibly have been illiterate, and many of the Toure family to which he belonged had reverted to animism. However his early travels as a Dyula trader must have brought him to places influenced by the contemporary Muslim revival. He also gained early experience as a soldier in the service of the local petty Mande king. The two experiences together seem to have suggested to him the idea of developing by conquest a new Muslim state from among the petty Mande chieftaincies to the south of al-Hajj 'Umar's domains.

By the mid-1860s, the nucleus of this state was in being, with its capital at Bissandugu, close by Samori's birthplace. Samori and his lieutenants were efficient, if ruthless, soldiers. They sold the booty and slaves they captured, and used the proceeds to buy horses and modern weapons, and so to equip themselves for further conquests. The conquered villages were organised into provinces whose governors collected tribute in gold and agricultural produce. The greater Samori's success, the more Muslim he became. He took the title *almami* (*c.* 1874), built mosques, and enforced the practices of Islam upon his subjects. Left to himself, Samori, controlling the gold resources of Boure and keen to extend his conquests to the Niger (he was at war with Ahmadu Seku in 1884), might have created a new empire of Mali. As it was, he had to face the equally imperialistic French, who could call on much greater resources. Early brushes with them (1882–7), however, were by no means one-sided, and led to a treaty defining a common boundary. But from the French point of view, this was but a temporary expedient. In 1891 the French occupied Bissandugu, and Samori had to move east into what is now the northern Ivory Coast and north-western Ghana, where, until the French finally caught up with him again and captured him in 1898, he was busy building his empire anew.

West Africa on the eve of European expansion

The West Africa into which by the 1870s and 1880s the French, British and Germans were poised to advance, was very far from being the land of ignorant savages imagined by many of its European conquerors. The western Sudan had seen a remarkable revival of, and advance by Islam, and under Ahmadu Lobo and al-Hajj 'Umar and their successors, and also under Samori, was struggling to overcome the political and social disruption resulting from the consequences of the defeat of the Songhai empire by the Moroccans three hundred years earlier. In the central Sudan, the ancient kingdom of Bornu had been thoroughly revived under al-Kanemi, and the Fulani *jihad* had brought a new purpose and organisation to the manufacturing, trading and cultural centres of Hausaland which afforded the foundations for a vast new empire.

It is not clear whether the heirs to al-Kanemi, Dan Fodio, al-Hajj 'Umar or Samori could have maintained their achievements, and in the event they were not given the chance to do so. Obviously al-Hajj 'Umar's successor, Ahmadu Seku, faced formidable problems in his Tukolor empire. There were signs, too, of a falling-off of the quality and efficiency of the administrative supervision exercised over the Fulani emirates from Sokoto and Gwandu, so that by the 1880s Europeans felt able to stigmatise at least the southern emirates of Nupe and Ilorin as slave-raiding tyrannies. But the history of the western and central Sudan —and, indeed, of mankind generally—affords many examples of great political achievements being followed by periods of reaction without forfeiting the chance of making further advances later. The effective advance of a restored Islam in conjunction with the growth of the new states, and the concomitant growth of literacy and scholarship, could well have provided a new platform from which very considerable further advances would have been possible.

However, the Sudan no longer possessed the economic strength it once had as West Africa's gateway to the trade of the rest of the world. There is no evidence that the trans-Saharan trade was declining in volume or value before the last quarter of the nineteenth century. Indeed it may have reached its peak *c.* 1875, when one estimate puts the value of the two-way flow of goods across the Sahara at about £1,500,000 or $3,600,000. But this was now small compared with the trade flowing to and from West Africa by sea. Already a single port like Lagos could be dealing with almost as much trade as all the trans-Saharan routes combined. The maritime traders, and this means Europeans on one side and coastal Africans on the other, were probably already by the mid-1870s handling five or six times as much trade as the trans-Saharan merchants, and the disproportion was increasing. After the European conquest, the trans-Saharan trade shrank to a trickle, and the maritime trade grew out of all proportion. It is apparent that both al-Hajj 'Umar and Samori knew the value to their empires of maintaining trade with the coast; perhaps the Fulani drive into Yorubaland was in part motivated by a similar interest.

Economically, then, it was the Africans of Guinea who were in the stronger position on the eve of the European expansion. They profited not only from acting as intermediaries in trade between the coast and the hinterland, but also from their commercial production of crops for export: first and foremost, palm oil and kernels, but also groundnuts, forest rubber and cotton, and soon, on the basis of the commercial and agricultural experience they had gained, totally new and potentially very valuable crops like cocoa and coffee.

Politically, however, the Guinea Africans were less secure. They had not been backward in evolving new political organisations to meet the new situations facing them: the kingdoms of Ashanti and Dahomey, the Oil Rivers city-states, the Fante Confederation—all were in different ways examples of intelligent development to meet changing circumstances. Their problem was rather that they were directly face to face with the Europeans, who during the course of the nineteenth century had made considerable inroads. Some of these were political or military: Britain had established her colonies in Sierra Leone, the Gold Coast and Lagos, and had sacked the Ashanti capital; and France had conquered the lower Senegal valley during 1854–65. It was becoming clear in fact that, in any direct clash of interests with Africans, the Europeans could, *if they wished*, bring vastly superior forces to bear. It was also becoming clear by the 1870s that the confrontation with Europeans, with traders and with missionaries as much or more as with officials of European governments, was producing more and more situations in which the Europeans *would* wish to take positive and aggressive action. The seizure of Lagos and the outlawing of the Fante Confederation are but two early examples. With the growing power of European traders and the growing hostility of Christian missionaries to the African way of life, the chances of further positive European intervention were becoming steadily greater. It would, in fact, make little difference to the Europeans whether their action was against kingdoms which had shrunk from former glories, like those of Oyo or Benin, against thriving new entities like the Oil Rivers states, or, ultimately, against the revived Muslim empires of the Sudan.

11

The renewal of French activity, and the European scramble for colonies

The revival of French interest in West Africa

In the early years of the nineteenth century, Britain was almost alone among the nations of Europe in wishing to extend her commercial, missionary, and sometimes her political influence in West Africa. Britain's interest in the country and its peoples remained, and indeed increased, at first because she alone took really active measures against the West African trade in slaves, and later because of her development of legitimate trade, in part as a weapon against the slave trade. On the other hand, as the slave trade declined, Britain's former competitors in it tended to lose interest in West Africa. Portugal had lost her Brazilian empire in 1822, and the active Portuguese-speaking merchants on the coast of West Africa thereafter were increasingly Brazilian, and their desire to continue the slave trade was ever more frustrated by British naval action. Dutch and Danish interests both declined because their governments, though opposed to the slave trade, were less concerned than the British government with the need to suppress it in West Africa, and so gave less support to those of their merchants who remained on the coast.

In 1815, however, when the Napoleonic wars were over, French merchants were able and anxious to resume their activities in West Africa. As a result of more than a century of conflict with Britain, France had lost the greater part of her once extensive empire in America and Asia, and Africa was one of the relatively few overseas areas which offered opportunities for French enterprise. But at first her progress was slow. After the excesses of the French Revolution and Napoleon, Frenchmen did not find it easy to achieve a stable form of government, and so to secure consistent support for a policy of colonial expansion. For some sixty years they wavered between republican and monarchical or imperial constitutions, each of which involved a different attitude to overseas empire. The first, stressing the liberty, equality and fraternity of mankind, denied that France had any right to force her rule on other peoples. The second, looking back to the glories of the time of Louis XIV or of Napoleon I, believed French civilisation to be so excellent that it should be imposed on less fortunate peoples for their benefit.

The military conquest of Algeria was begun in 1830, but at first was neither very successful nor very popular. Some progress in empire-building was made during the time of Napoleon III (1848–70), but in West Africa France did not emerge as a serious rival to Britain until after about 1879, by which time other European nations, notably Germany, were also embarking on schemes of territorial aggrandisement in Africa, and the general European scramble for African colonies had commenced. Until then Britain's influence among the peoples of West Africa from Sierra Leone to the Cameroons had been virtually unchallenged by any other European power.

But in 1817 France was able to re-establish her domination north of Sierra Leone. During the Napoleonic wars, the French posts on and near the Senegal had been cut off from France, first by the British control of the sea, and then, after 1809, by the British occupation of St Louis and Goree. As a consequence their trade with the interior had greatly deteriorated. In 1817 France was able to re-occupy, besides St Louis and Goree, only two up-river trading posts on the Senegal, and Albreda on the Gambia. Instead of trying to rebuild their trade, the French at first concentrated on trying to establish cotton and other plantations on the lower Senegal and in the neighbourhood of Cape Verde. By 1826 these ventures had failed, and the French were forced back to trade as a means of deriving some advantage from their connection with West Africa.

There were broadly two ways in which the French could develop their trade with West Africa. They could endeavour to extend their influence over the peoples of the interior, so that the Senegal would become a highway of commerce under their exclusive control. Secondly, they could follow the example of the British merchants by establishing trading-posts at intervals along the coast. Exploratory journeys up the Senegal soon revealed that the peoples of the Sudan were for the most part organised in comparatively strong states, much of whose external trade was with North Africa and was controlled by Muslim merchants. Only military conquest was likely to bring these states under French influence and to turn their trade towards the Senegal. On the other hand, there were a number of parts of the Guinea coast where British merchants were not already in possession, or were not so firmly established that French merchants would have no chance in competition with them. French trading firms accordingly pressed their government to establish French influence at points on the Guinea coast, at some of which French merchants had been active in the seventeenth and eighteenth centuries.

French activity on the Guinea coast, 1838–65

Between 1838 and 1842 a French naval officer, Bouët-Willaumez, secured treaties with African rulers near Cape Palmas, at Grand Bassam and Assini on the Ivory Coast, at Bonny in the Oil Rivers, and also on the Gaboon river. Cape Palmas was on the coast of what was to become the Republic of Liberia, and although the French disputed the sovereignty of the government at Monrovia, they did not establish a firm footing there. However, in 1843 fortified trading posts were built at Assini and Grand Bassam, and the French fort at Whydah was reoccupied and relations established with the king of Dahomey. During the next twenty years, French influence was extended, not altogether peacefully, to other points on the Ivory Coast, while on the Slave Coast a French protectorate was established over Porto Novo and Cotonu, and Anecho was also occupied.

But Porto Novo was under the suzerainty of Dahomey, and although French relations with Gelele, the king of Dahomey, were not unfriendly, the ruler of Porto Novo, becoming uneasy at the growth of French influence, appealed for support to the authorities of the newly established British colony of Lagos. The latter, besides extending their control westwards along the coast to Badagri and beyond, were keenly interested in the disturbed affairs of Yorubaland, where British missionaries and traders were active. Gelele's armies were raiding into Yorubaland, and the French thought it advisable to evacuate Anecho and to abandon their protectorate over Porto Novo and Cotonu.

Although French political ambitions on the Slave Coast were thus checked for a time, their traders rapidly gained ground both there and on the Ivory Coast. North of Sierra Leone they operated to the exclusion of British merchants. In 1857, by agreement with Britain, the French evacuated their post at Albreda, but they did so only so as to secure the abandonment by Britain of her trading rights on the coast near Goree. The exclusive control of the trade of the Gambia which the British secured as a result was of little value, since French traders were reaching to the interior not only to the north of the river, in Senegal, but also south of it, along the River Casamance.

The French advance on the Senegal, 1854–*c.* 1865

After Napoleon III's accession to power in France in 1848, his government proclaimed its intention of pursuing an active policy of developing the trade of the Senegal and of extending French influence up that river into the interior. In 1854, the government of Goree was separated from that of the Senegal, and Goree, in addition to its role as a naval base, became responsible for the affairs of the French trading-posts on the

Guinea Coast. A new governor was appointed to the Senegal, Captain (later General) Louis Faideherbe, who was free to concentrate on the extension of French power up the river into the interior. During his ten years' governorship, Faideherbe established French forts at Matam and Bakel in Galam, and at Medina in Khasso, which served, as has been seen, to check and repel the westwards advance of al-Hajj 'Umar. In addition, Futa Toro was occupied, and, after the French occupation of Dakar in 1857, the conquest of Cayor was begun, while official French missions were sent to spy out the land in Futa Jalon and to as far east as Segu.

Faideherbe was a good deal more than a mere military conqueror. Indeed his conquests were inspired principally by the economic purpose of extending his administration over a sufficiently large area of territory to secure prosperity for the French traders based at St Louis. In addition to his military work, Faideherbe sponsored the development of groundnuts as a crop which the Senegalese could grow for export, and he did much to provide a good administration and a good educational system (secular as well as missionary) for the lands he had brought under French rule or protection.

After Faideherbe's departure from the Senegal in 1865, there was a period of about fifteen years in which the French made little or no further advance in West Africa. Napoleon III's government was becoming increasingly bankrupt and insecure, and then in 1870–1 it was overthrown and France herself disastrously defeated by Bismarck's Germany. France did not sufficiently regain confidence in herself to embark on further colonial expansion until after about 1879. But in the last twenty-one years of the nineteenth century, the French swept swiftly across the whole Sudan from the Senegal almost to the Nile, engaged in the conquest of the Sahara from Algeria to Lake Chad, and linked up these new conquests with their trading-posts on the coasts of Guinea. Since, during the same period, the Germans were establishing their colonies of Togo and the Cameroons, the once extensive British influence in West Africa was rapidly confined within precise political boundaries, which, with the exception of Nigeria, enclosed comparatively small areas of territory.

The origins of the European scramble for African colonies

The motives behind the French and German acquisition of extensive new colonies in Africa during the last twenty years of the nineteenth century were complex, and are not very easy to understand without a very full study of political and economic conditions at the time in western Europe, a study which is hardly possible within a book of this size and scope. However, in general it may be said that the struggle for power that was going on within Europe between 1870 and 1914 produced diplomatic and economic rivalries which were forcefully projected outside Europe itself, and particularly into Africa. Few European statesmen of the first rank were as yet convinced that their countries actually needed African colonies. However, the work of the explorers and of the anti-slave-trade campaign had brought Africa to the notice of Europe as never before. With its own society disrupted by the slave trade, Africa generally seemed ripe for European intervention and development. More particularly, however, European statesmen had become aware of the paramount position on the coasts of Africa, especially of West Africa, that had been achieved by British traders.

With the decline of the slave trade, British merchants had tended to be more successful in the development of alternative trades than merchants of other European countries, partly because theirs was then the strongest and wealthiest industrial nation in Europe, but also because, thanks to the support given by their government to the anti-slave-trade campaign, they had been able to secure better footholds in Africa than most of their competitors. In these circumstances, Britain had had little cause to establish *colonies* in Africa, that is, areas with precise boundaries that were under her direct control. What she had done, rather, was to bring about *spheres of influence* over areas in which for the most part political authority still remained with the African rulers. The existence of these British spheres of influence in Africa presented a useful opportunity to German and French statesmen to bring pressures to bear on Britain to help achieve their own diplomatic or strategic ends in Europe or elsewhere (for example in Egypt, where Britain and France were bitter rivals). The creation of extensive colonies under direct French or German control, where British (or other European) merchants and missionaries and others were either not allowed to operate at all, or only on terms which placed them at a disadvantage compared with Frenchmen or Germans, would, it was hoped, have worthwhile effects on the general course of British foreign policy.

As it happened, the European partition of Africa was actually set off less by direct action by the French or German governments than by the doings of an individual, King Leopold II of the Belgians. His desire to carve out a private empire for himself in the Congo conflicted with the existing interests there of Britain, France and Portugal, with the result that in 1884 Germany and France acted together to call a conference in Berlin of all the European powers concerned with Africa to consider the Congo and other problems of mutual interest. In 1885 the representatives of the powers at the Berlin Conference signed an agreement declaring that, in the best interests of Africa and the world as a whole, traders and missionaries and other agents of all countries should have free access to the interior of Africa, so that its slave trade would be finally crushed, and the material and moral benefits of European civilisation made freely available to all its peoples. In particular, it was stipulated that the navigation of the Congo and Niger rivers should be open to the people of all nations alike. However, few practical steps were ever taken by the signatories of the Berlin agreement to make this freedom of access to the interior of Africa a genuine fact in their colonies. In practice most of them limited it to their own subjects. A much more significant section of the agreement was that stipulating that no new European annexations or protectorates on the African coastline would be recognised as valid unless they were accompanied by *effective occupation*, that is to say, unless the European power concerned sent officials to make its power effective along the whole of the coastline annexed or under its protection. In 1890 another international African conference, meeting at Brussels, decided that this effective occupation rule should apply to the interior of Africa as well as to its coasts.

French and German advance in West Africa, *c.* 1879–*c.* 1896

One result of the Berlin and Brussels Conferences, then, was that the spheres of influence which British merchants and missionaries had built up on the West African coast and its immediate hinterland had no significance in international law unless the British government had also established administrations there, as it had, for example, on the Gold Coast and at Lagos. Before the signatories to the Berlin agreement had left Berlin, German officials had arrived in the Cameroons and on the short stretch of coast between the Gold Coast and the French stations on the Slave Coast, and had hastily negotiated treaties with their rulers by which the latter placed themselves and their territories under German protection. German missionaries and merchants had been active for some years in the coastal districts of what soon became the German colony of Togo, but the Cameroons coast had long been dominated by British merchants and missionaries, who, after 1885, found their activities so restricted by the German authorities that most of them decided to leave. Britain hastened to prevent similar action in the Niger delta, and quickly placed the coast between Lagos and the Cameroons under a protectorate, the Oil Rivers Protectorate. Control was exercised by the Foreign Office through the Consul for the Bights of Benin and Biafra, who had in 1882 moved his headquarters from the island of Fernando Po to the mainland at Old Calabar.

In similar fashion the French took steps to consolidate their position on the West African coast. In 1871 the garrisons had been withdrawn from the French posts on the Ivory Coast, which had been left to the care of the French merchants residing there. In 1886, however, direct control of the posts was resumed by the French government, and its officials hastened to negotiate protectorate treaties giving France control of the whole coast between Liberia and the Gold Coast. In 1887 Conakry was occupied, and French rights made effective on the coast between Sierra Leone and Portuguese Guinea. This progress was completed in 1893 by the constitution of the new colonies of the Ivory Coast and French Guinea.

On the Slave Coast, the cession of Cotonu to France had been confirmed in 1878, and the French protectorate over Porto Novo had been re-established in 1882. In 1885 these points were effectively occupied, and further treaties of protection extended French control of the coast to as far west as Anecho, on the border of German Togo. This extension of French power was not undertaken without protest from the kings of Dahomey—Gelele (1858–89) and Behanzin (1889–93)—who asserted that the coastal states were not independent and could not be placed under French protection or rule without their permission. War between France and Dahomey inevitably followed, and in 1893 the French entered Abomey, deposed Behanzin, installed a nominee of their own in his place, and placed the whole country under their protection. Seven years later Dahomey was constituted into a French colony.

But the most striking French advance was in the interior, the rapid extension of their power through the military conquest of the Sudan from the Senegal to Lake Chad. Captain J. S. Gallieni occupied Bamako on the upper Niger in 1883, and in the following years treaties were made with Samori by which the latter agreed to keep south of the Niger and Tinkisso rivers. Henceforward, whatever Samori may have thought, the French regarded his territory as being under their protection. In 1890, on his own initiative, Colonel Archinard invaded the Tukolor empire subject to Ahmadu Seku. A series of campaigns forced Ahmadu eastwards, from Segu and Kaarta to Macina. All these territories had fallen to the French by 1893. Ultimately Ahmadu fled into Sokoto territory, dying there in 1898.

Meanwhile the French and Samori had been accusing each other of breaking the treaties between them. In 1891 the French occupied Samori's home country around Bissandugu, but Samori continued his resistance further east until his final capture by the French in 1898 (he died in exile in 1900). In the Niger valley, Timbuctu was occupied early in 1894, and by 1896 the French had got as far east as Say. By this time, too, Futa Jalon had been conquered, and Binger and others had secured treaties placing the Mossi lands of the upper Volta, and the lands between them and the Ivory Coast, under French protection.

In this way it was possible for the French to confine the commercial and other activities of the Liberians, of the Portuguese at Bissau, Cacheu and Bulama, and of the British on the Gambia and at Sierra Leone,

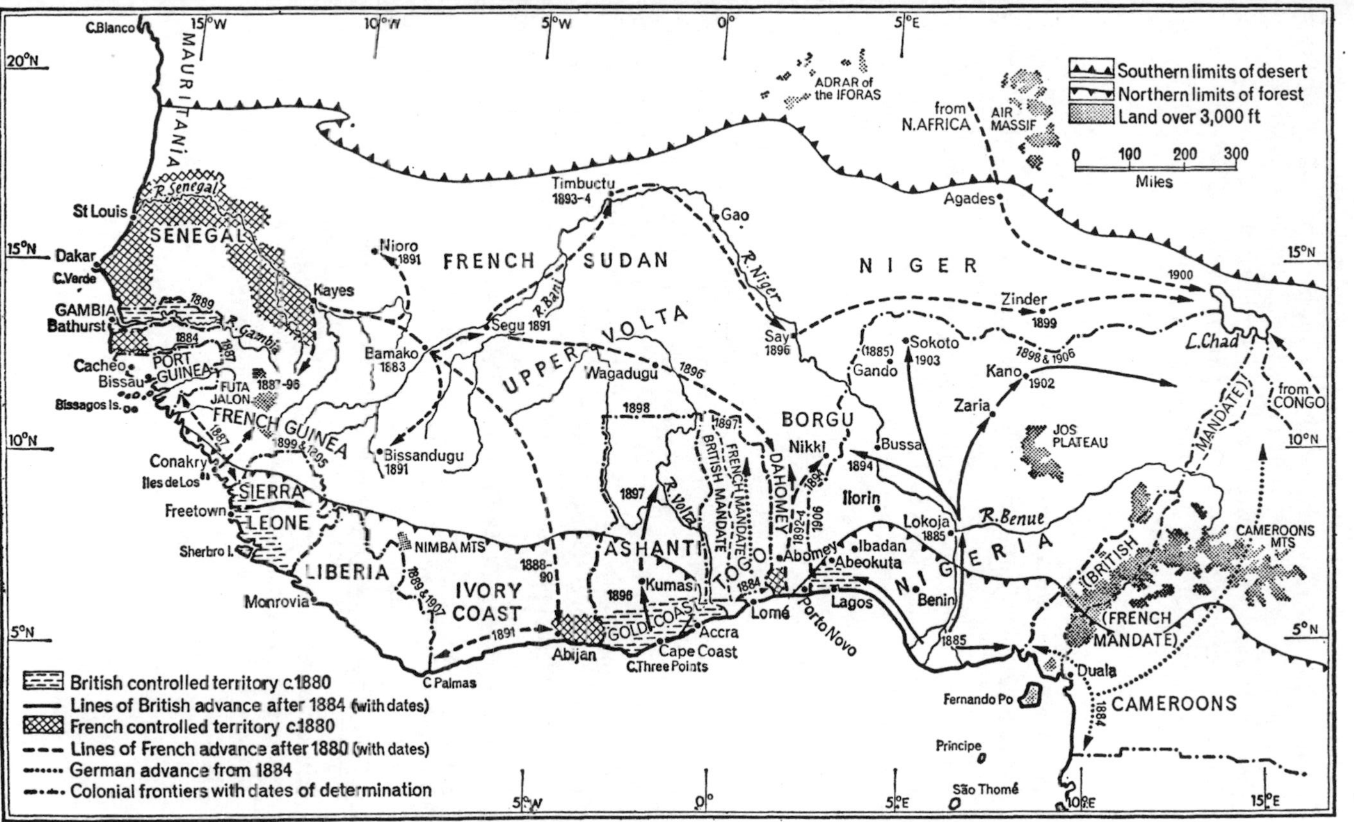

13 The European advance into West Africa

within political frontiers (for the most part agreed with France in treaties between 1884 and 1895) which enclosed comparatively small areas. The Liberian coastal settlements were allowed a hinterland of about 40,000 square miles, and Britain was able to add a protectorate of some 27,700 square miles to her tiny crown colony of Sierra Leone (256 square miles) but the French frontiers were drawn so closely around the Gambia that it became quite useless to the British or to anyone else as a navigable waterway into the interior.[1]

British advance into Ashanti and beyond, 1874–98

By the time (*c*. 1888–9) that the French began to be active in the hinterland of the Gold Coast, the British had advanced some distance inland themselves. They had hoped that the defeat inflicted on Ashanti in 1874 would be sufficient to prevent the kingdom causing any further trouble to their Gold Coast colony, and for twenty years they left the Ashanti more or less to their own devices. This policy, or rather lack of policy, proved short-sighted. The events of 1874 had indeed destroyed the authority of the ruling *Asantehene* and brought the union of states to the verge of collapse. But Kofi Karikari was destooled, and a new *Asantehene*, Mensa Bonsu, soon regained the allegiance and confidence of the Ashanti states proper. A movement rapidly gained ground for the reconquest of the states nearer the coast which had been subject to Ashanti but which had secured their independence since 1874. When Mẹnsa Bonsu seemed unwilling to run the risk which this involved of further conflict with Britain, he too was destooled (1883). After some years of uncertainty and civil strife, the forward party gained the day, and their nominee, Prempeh, was accepted as *Asantehene*.

At length, with both the French and the Germans active in the hinterland, the British realised the danger of leaving Ashanti alone. In 1895 an ultimatum was sent to Kumasi charging the Ashanti with failure to keep the Treaty of Fomena, and requiring them to accept a British protectorate. When the Ashanti tried to negotiate, a British expeditionary force marched to Kumasi for the second time, and early in 1896 Ashanti gave in without fighting. Prempeh and his chief supporters were exiled, Ashanti's constituent states were each separately required to accept treaties recognising a British protectorate, and a British Resident was installed at Kumasi.

For the next four years there was an uneasy calm in Ashanti. The Ashantis felt that they had been tricked. They had not been conquered,

[1] It is interesting to note that between 1866 and 1876 France and Britain had engaged in negotiations for the exchange of the Gambia for Assini and Grand Bassam. The scheme failed because of objections to it by the merchants and people of the Gambia.

yet their leaders had been deported, and, although they still had their Golden Stool, their Union was treated as though it had been dissolved. The British made little effort to understand the situation, and when in 1900 their governor on the Gold Coast, Sir Frederick Hodgson, tactlessly demanded the surrender of the Golden Stool, the Ashanti rose in a bitter rising against the British, which was quelled only after nine months' hard fighting. The British then realised that they would have to rule Ashanti themselves, and in 1901 they decided to annex the country as a crown colony.

After 1896 it was possible to extend British protection over the country to the north of Ashanti whose trade with the coast was controlled by Ashanti merchants. Indeed it was necessary to do this to forestall the French advance from the Niger and the German expansion in Togo, and also to check the raids of Samori's armies. British officials had first penetrated to the north of Ashanti in the 1880s, since when much of the country had been explored and mapped by an able and courageous African surveyor, G. E. Ferguson. Ferguson, who was eventually killed by Samori's soldiers, joined with other British agents in negotiating treaties of protection with the northern chiefs, with the result that by 1898 a British protectorate had been extended to 8° N. latitude. The boundaries of this protectorate and of the Gold Coast as a whole, as agreed with the French to the west and north and with the Germans in Togo to the east, took no account of the African racial and political groupings. Thus, for example, some Ewe found themselves in the Gold Coast while the majority were in Togo; the Dagomba state was divided between Togo and the Gold Coast; and parts of some of the Akan states found themselves in the French colony of the Ivory Coast, while other parts were in British territory.

The extension of British power in the Oil Rivers and Yorubaland

Although by 1902 the acquisition of Ashanti and the Northern Territories had extended the British control of the Gold Coast into a colony stretching 400 miles into the interior and containing more than two million inhabitants, it was only in what is now Nigeria that the British acted sufficiently positively and swiftly to preserve a really large area of West Africa for their traders free from French or German control. It was British merchants rather than the British government that took the initiative which led to the British occupation of Hausaland, but they would hardly have been able to do this had British officials in the Oil Rivers and at Lagos not earlier embarked on the business of securing control of the coastlands.

Something has already been said of the foundation of the Colony of Lagos in 1861[1] and of the establishment in 1885 of a British protectorate

[1] Chapter 9, p. 141.

over the Oil Rivers,[1] which in 1893 became known as the Niger Coast Protectorate. On paper this protectorate reached as far north as the Benue, but a generation was to pass before an effective British administration was established over the whole of this area. The first problem was the trading states of the Niger delta, each of which was anxious to preserve a monopoly of the commerce to and from the country behind it. Some of their leaders, such as Jaja at Opobo and the Itsekiri (Jekri) chief, Nana, were highly capable and very independently minded men who were not going to give up their positions until forced to do so by British gunboats. Having forced their will on the Delta states, the British were then faced with the difficult task of asserting their authority over the innumerable independent groups of Ibo villages in the hinterland. This they did not do quickly, and a number of military expeditions were necessary, including one in 1902 to destroy the Aro-Chukwu oracle. Effective British administration in Iboland hardly began before 1906, and was not established over all parts of the country until about a decade later. Benin also resisted British control, being reluctant to open its territory to British traders and to cease the practice of making human sacrifices. Following the massacre of a British mission, a strong military and naval force was sent against Benin City in 1897. Many of the art treasures of its palace were seized, and the *Oba* was sent into exile, as Jaja and Nana had been before him.

After the occupation of Lagos Island in 1861, British authority had quickly been extended along the coast both to west and east, but trade and other relations between Lagos and the interior remained very uncertain because of the constant warfare in Yorubaland. A principal theme was the rivalry between Ibadan and Abeokuta. This came to centre more and more on Ibadan's desire to use its military strength to establish trade roads to the coast free from Egba or Ijebu control and taxation, and on the attempts of Abeokuta and other more southerly states to preserve their role as intermediaries in the trade with the interior. After 1864, Dahomey was no longer a serious threat to Yorubaland, but all sorts of other factors were involved in this competition for power. Thus at one stage Abeokuta enlisted the help of the Muslim Fulani from Ilorin; at another the British sent soldiers to clear Abeokutan forces from Ikorodu, a trade route terminus on the Lagos lagoon. There were the British missionaries and the Christian Yoruba repatriates from Sierra Leone at Abeokuta, on whom the Egba could bring pressure, and who had their own independent ideas on policy which were by no means identical with those of the British officials at Lagos. There were attempts by the *Alafin* of Oyo to use his traditional position to mediate in the disputes, and there was growing pressure from the British palm-oil merchants at Lagos for British government intervention.

[1] p. 165.

The situation began to be resolved in and after 1886, when the wars had brought trade between Lagos and the interior practically to a standstill. Since this was also a period of low prices in the world markets for palm oil and other tropical produce, the British traders at Lagos became convinced that only the extension of British control over Yorubaland would save the situation. The British authorities were as yet still unwilling to incur the expense of a military occupation of the Yoruba states, but unless they took some action there was now a real risk of French intervention from nearby Porto Novo. Lagos was given a governor and an administration of its own distinct from that of the Gold Coast Colony, and British mediators negotiated a general peace settlement embracing all the Yoruba states (though not Ilorin). In 1888, the *Alafin* of Oyo was induced to declare that all Yorubaland was under British protection. In 1890, the British began to station troops in the interior; in 1892, Ijebu-Ode was decisively attacked; in 1893, both Ibadan and Abeokuta were brought to accept British Residents. By 1896 all Yorubaland south of Ilorin was under the effective control of the Lagos government; only the Fulani emirate barred further access to the interior for British trade.

The Royal Niger Company

Ilorin and the other Fulani emirates came within the sphere of operation of the Royal Niger Company. This was the creation of Sir George Goldie. Goldie was a former officer of the British army who held an interest in one of the British companies trading on the lower Niger. In 1877 he visited the river and came to the conclusion that unless the British companies trading there were amalgamated, they would not be strong enough to withstand the competition of their French and German rivals or to stand up to the multitude of African rulers who levied duties on the trade passing through the various outlets of the river. By 1879 Goldie had persuaded the principal British companies to join together in a company known at first as the United African Company, but after 1882 as the National African Company.

At this time two French trading companies, the Compagnie Française de l'Afrique Equatoriale and the Compagnie du Sénégal, were very active in establishing trading posts on the Niger and Benue. The trade done through these posts was considerable, and the French companies also endeavoured to use them as bases for the extension of French political influence. However, the French companies were not supported by their government, and the National African Company was financially strong enough to buy them out, in 1884 and 1885 respectively.

Goldie's company was now in a sufficiently powerful position to prevent German and other European traders making any headway on the lower Niger, but he was seriously worried lest the advance of France from the

Senegal and of Germany from the Cameroons might place political barriers in the way of the extension of British trade north of Lokoja. In 1885 an agent of the Company forestalled a German expedition, and secured from the sultans of Sokoto and Gwandu treaties by which these rulers promised that their peoples would trade only with the National African Company. The activities of the Company formed the basis of the British claim at the Berlin Conference that the Fulani emirates were under British protection. But clearly the British government had done nothing to make this protection effective, and it was as yet unwilling to extend its responsibilities so far into the interior. From 1881 onwards Goldie began to press the British government to grant his company a charter authorising it to act as the government's agent in the administration of justice and the maintenance of law and order in areas into which it had extended its influence by treaty with African rulers.

The idea of a chartered company exercising powers of government was a very old one in the British empire (e.g. the East India Company), but it had fallen out of use largely because the early chartered companies had possessed monopolies of trade in the areas under their control, which conflicted with the free trade principle which became established in Britain during the nineteenth century. But the Conservatives were more inclined than the Liberals to afford government recognition and support for merchants seeking to preserve parts of Africa for British influence, and in 1886 the Conservative government which took office shortly after the Berlin Conference granted Goldie the charter he wanted. In the same year the name of the company was changed from the National African Company to the Royal Niger Company.

By its charter, the Royal Niger Company was empowered to administer justice and to maintain order in areas where it was authorised to do so by treaties between it and African rulers. It was to do its utmost to discourage and to secure the abolition of slavery, but otherwise it was enjoined not to interfere with the laws, customs and religions of African peoples except in so far as these were contrary to humanity. The Company was expressly forbidden to set up any trading monopoly. In accordance with the Berlin Act, the trade of the Niger was to be open to the subjects of all nations without distinction, and the Company was to levy only such duties on it as were necessary to provide a revenue for its government. In 1887 a British protectorate was formally proclaimed over those territories whose rulers had signed treaties with the Company's agents.

Although the Company maintained an advanced base at Lokoja, its administrative and commercial headquarters were set up at Asaba, in the Niger Coast Protectorate. In 1891 a strip of the protectorate between Asaba and the Company's coastal port of Akassa, on the Nun entrance to the Niger delta, was handed over to the administration of the Company.

The greater part of the trade done by the Company was in the south, and it cannot be said that it honoured its obligation to maintain free trade. It obstructed German and French attempts to penetrate the delta, and it seriously interfered with the trade of the African merchants established there. Its insistence that all trade with the territory under its control should pass through Akassa dealt a severe blow to the income of the African kings and merchants who controlled the trade of the other outlets of the Niger. In addition, since these Africans lived for the most part not in territories under the Company's control, but in the Niger Coast Protectorate, they were required to pay duties on their trade passing through Akassa. Consequently, the Company incurred the hostility of most of the delta Africans, and in 1895 the men of Brass attacked and destroyed the Company's post at Akassa.

However, the Company succeeded in its political purpose of keeping the French and Germans out of northern Nigeria. The Royal Niger Company's agreements with Sokoto and with other northern states were the foundation for an Anglo-French agreement of 1890, by which the French agreed that the Fulani emirates south of a line between Say, on the Niger, and Barruwa, on Lake Chad, were reserved to the Company. But the French did not accept the British view that, as a consequence of this agreement, they (the French) should not penetrate to the east of a line drawn southwards from Say to the sea. In 1894, the French began to advance from Dahomey into Borgu, with the result that the Company had hurriedly to send Captain (later Sir) Frederick Lugard on a treaty-making race.

In 1897 the Company embarked on war with the Fulani emirs of Nupe and Ilorin, who persisted in raiding into territory on the banks of the Niger which the Company claimed to be under its protection. Following the conquest of these two emirates, the Company was brought into dangerously close contact with the French, who on the one hand were pressing north-eastwards from Dahomey and on the other had advanced down the Niger beyond Say to as far as Bussa. The British government decided that the Company could not be left to face the military forces of the French government unaided, and in 1897 it agreed to provide money and officers for a West African Frontier Force, command of which was entrusted to Lugard. Thus strengthened, the Company was able to hold its own against the French, and in 1898 the present western and northern boundaries of Nigeria were determined by agreement between the British and French governments. In the west, the French were brought to accept a boundary drawn halfway between Say and Bussa. In the north, although the French were able to reach Lake Chad, they were only able to do so through the southern fringes of the Sahara; the greater part of the agricultural land of the Fulani emirates was recognised as British territory.

In 1899 the British government decided that the Royal Niger Company had outlived its usefulness as its agent for the extension of British influence in Northern Nigeria. In the first place, the British government was already paying for the defence of Northern Nigeria, and it was thought undesirable that control of the West African Frontier Force should remain in the hands of the Company. Secondly, the Anglo-French agreement of 1898 gave the French the right to navigate the Niger between Bussa and the sea,[1] and with the Company's past record in mind, it was thought undesirable that control of this navigation should remain with the Company. Accordingly, the Charter of 1886 was revoked, and, on payment of compensation, the British government took over the administrative and military assets of the Company at the beginning of 1900, though the Company continued in existence as a commercial corporation.[2] Sir Frederick Lugard was entrusted with the work of establishing a British administration for the Protectorate of Northern Nigeria, which he accomplished through a series of military expeditions extending up to 1906. Also in 1900, the Colonial Office took over from the Foreign Office responsibility for the administration of the Niger Coast Protectorate, which was renamed the Protectorate of Southern Nigeria. Since the Colonial Office was already administering the Colony of Protectorate of Lagos, it was henceforward responsible for the government of all three British territories in Nigeria.

[1] In practice the French found the commercial transport of goods up and down the lower Niger to be uneconomic and they soon ceased to exercise this right.
[2] Now part of the United Africa Company.

12

West Africa under European rule

The extension of European authority

Maps published at the beginning of the twentieth century showed the whole of West Africa except Liberia as being under the rule or protection of European powers. France was shown as the mistress of a vast empire of some 1,800,000 square miles (about nine times the area of France herself). The next largest area of territory, about 480,000 square miles, had been secured by Britain, not in one continuous block like French West Africa, but in four separate colonies cut off from each other by intervening French territory. Germany possessed the 33,000 square miles of her colony of Togo, and, on the fringe of West Africa proper and more a part of equatorial Africa, the very much larger Cameroon colony of about 200,000 square miles. Portugal's once extensive influence in West Africa was now confined within the 14,000 square miles of Portuguese Guinea.

But in reality European power and influence in West Africa in 1900 were nothing like as extensive or as effective as the maps seemed to indicate. European claims to the greater part of the territory shown as being under their rule or protection had been asserted only within the previous twenty years. The steps taken by France, Britain or Germany to convince other European powers that they were in effective occupation of the areas claimed by them were not always sufficient to secure the submission to their authority of the inhabitants of the territories in question. In 1900 the maps showed large areas of West Africa as being under French or British or German rule or protection where in fact no European had ever been, or where none had been seen since the first European military conquest, or where the African rulers were unaware of the implications or even of the meaning of the protectorate treaties they had signed.

Thus the first problem facing France, Britain and Germany, after their scramble for colonies in West Africa had been completed, was to secure African recognition of their authority throughout their territories. Most rulers in the interior were unwilling to allow real power in their states to pass from their hands to the Europeans without a struggle, and many too were unwilling to stop the trade in slaves on which they depended for much of their wealth. After 1900 the French were obliged to secure the submission of some of the forest peoples of French Guinea and the Ivory Coast by a series of military operations which in some cases continued until 1915. Active resistance to French authority by the nomadic tribes of the desert north and north-east of the Niger lasted even longer: the colony of the Niger, which lay to the north of the British colony of Nigeria, remained in military hands until 1922, when it was at last handed over to the civil administration. In similar fashion, Lugard and the West African Frontier Force were fully engaged until 1906 in the conquest and subjugation of Bornu and the Fulani emirates of Northern Nigeria. Even as late as 1914, German administration was still hardly effective in the northern districts of Togo and Cameroon.

The difficulties of the new European rulers of West Africa were by no means over when they had secured the submission or defeat of all the traditional rulers. The European powers had claimed at the Berlin and Brussels Conferences that they had a twofold duty, or 'dual mandate' (as it came to be called), to extend their rule in Africa: on the one hand, to stop the slave trade and to bring in its stead the material and moral benefits of European civilisation; and, on the other hand, to make the trade and resources of Africa available to the rest of the world, perhaps for the benefit of their own nations in particular. But the slave trade could not be stopped, and orderly conditions for the development of peaceful trade and material and moral progress could not be secured, unless the Europeans established administrative officers and police forces throughout the vast areas in which their coming had upset the authority of the native rulers.

French administration, 1854–1945

Although the French had been active on the West African coast since the seventeenth century, they had had little experience of governing Africans before Faideherbe's conquest of the Senegal. Before 1854, France had actually ruled in West Africa only in St Louis and Goree, small urban areas (*communes*) in which European influence had been paramount for a long time, and where in consequence the character of society had become as much European as it was African. Laws for these French trading settlements were generally made by decrees issued in Paris, but it was possible for the French to accept their inhabitants, black as well as white, as French citizens. This meant, among other things, that they were subject to the ordinary law of France, and that they had the possibility of electing a deputy to represent them in the National Assembly at Paris which made the French laws. At a later stage, the natives of Dakar and Rufisque were likewise admitted as French citizens.

The first expansion of the French empire in West Africa, the conquest of the Senegal between 1854 and 1865, took place during the time of the Second Empire of Napoleon III, when France herself was subject to the autocratic rule of the emperor and his government. It was logical, therefore, that from the beginning the newly conquered territories should be governed autocratically by French officials responsible, through the governor at St Louis, to the government in Paris. But these territories, unlike the older coastal settlements, had not previously been subject to any great degree of European political or social influence, and their inhabitants could not be expected to observe French law and to fulfil the responsibilities of French citizens. They were therefore allowed to retain their own traditional laws and customs for the regulation of their own affairs, so long as these traditional laws and customs did not conflict with the demands of the French government upon them. French law was imposed on them principally to regulate their duties and responsibilities towards the French government. They did not therefore become French citizens, but they began to be treated as French *subjects*, possessing the same duties as citizens but a different set of rights. Nevertheless, it was supposed that, in course of time, the growth of French influence—French education, French methods of doing business, Christian marriage laws etc.—would cause the people of the Senegal to think and act in the French manner, so that they too would eventually be able to foreswear their traditional way of life and join the inhabitants of the coastal towns as French citizens.

Although the greater subsequent expansion of the French empire in West Africa between 1879 and 1900 took place when France had a republican constitution, the principles of colonial administration already established in the Senegal were adhered to, and they were extended to the new French West African colonies. But the expansion occurred so rapidly over so vast an area of territory (about thirty times as big as Faideherbe's Senegal) that at first the French were unable to find enough administrative officials to rule the newly conquered peoples. For a time they were forced to use the native governments as their agents, confirming the authority of chiefs who had submitted to them, and creating new chiefs to replace those they had deposed or exiled. But this was only a temporary measure. As soon as they were able to do so, the French established administrations of French officials for the colonies of French Guinea, the Ivory Coast, the Sudan and Dahomey.

The only African authorities who were allowed any power were the headmen of villages. But these were subordinate to French district officers and provincial commissioners, who were responsible to the French governors of the various colonies. In 1895 the colonial governors were made subordinate to the governor of the Senegal, who thus became in addition governor-general, the delegate and representative of the president of France for all the French colonies in West Africa. In 1902 a separate office of governor-general, with headquarters at Dakar, was set up, to whom the governor of the Senegal at St Louis was responsible just as the other colonial governors were. By 1922 three new colonial governments, each with its own governor and hierarchy of French officials, had been created and placed under the governor-general at Dakar: the governments of the Upper Volta (formed principally from the eastern districts of the French Sudan), the Niger, and Mauritania (the coastal zone to the north of the Senegal).

The system of government thus evolved for the French territories in West Africa can be likened to a pyramid. At the top was the minister for the colonies, a member of the French government of the day and, like his colleagues, responsible to the National Assembly in Paris. Under the minister for the colonies came the governor-general of French West Africa at Dakar, and under him were the governors of the various colonies and their subordinates, the provincial and district officers. Under the latter came the African village headmen. French West Africa was governed, then, by an authoritarian hierarchy of French officials subordinate to the French government in Paris. The average African had no say in the way in which he was governed except in the purely local affairs of his village, and even the village headmen, although Africans, were appointed by, and were subordinate to, the French district officers.

At first the French assumed, as they had done in the Senegal, that their West African subjects would eventually become French citizens, whereupon they would secure, at least in theory, a much larger say in the way they were governed. Africans who were French citizens could be appointed to posts in the colonial administration equally with citizens of French parentage—they might even rise to be governors of colonies. They could elect deputies to represent them in the French Assembly, and so help to make the laws under which they were governed.

But in practice the scheme of converting the inhabitants of French West Africa into French citizens, and in this way giving them a share in their own government, did not work well. In the first place, the colonial representatives in the National Assembly were always a small minority. The Assembly itself was not much interested in colonial affairs, and it left the making of laws for the colonies mainly to the minister for the colonies. The latter, and also the governor-general and the governor of each colony, possessed colonial advisory councils, but most of the members of these councils were nominated, many of them were French officials, and it was obligatory for them to be consulted only on financial matters. But, above all, the difficulty was that the influence of French ideas and civilisation did not succeed in converting many Africans to French ways of life and thought. The country was too vast, and its peoples were too thoroughly convinced of the value of their own traditions and customs. Africans born in the communes of St Louis, Goree, Rufisque and Dakar became French citizens automatically, and so, after 1916, did their descendants. Other Africans could qualify for French citizenship only if they were prepared to surrender their rights under native law, if they had reached the age of eighteen, were monogamous, had been educated in the French language, had done the military service required of French citizens, and had been in French employment for at least ten years. In 1937, out of some 15,000,000 Africans in French West Africa, only 80,500 were French citizens, and all but 2,500 of these had acquired citizenship by the accident of birth in one of the communes of the Senegalese colony.

By about 1920, the French had been forced to realise the failure of their plan to convert Africans into Frenchmen and to govern French West Africa as though it were part of France. But although it was declared that the policy would henceforward be to preserve African institutions and to encourage local self-government in native districts and in the larger towns, the conduct of affairs in the colonies still remained in the hands of French officials who were reluctant to change their autocratic and bureaucratic methods. Consequently there was little noticeable change in the practice of French colonial administration until the events of the war of 1939–45 caused the French drastically to reconsider their policy towards their colonial subjects in West Africa and elsewhere.

British administration to 1945: the legislative council

Before about 1870 the British had had little more experience of governing Africans than the French. The early British possessions in West Africa—Sierra Leone, Bathurst, the Gold Coast forts and Lagos—were, like the early French colonies, small trading settlements whose inhabitants had become relatively assimilated to European ways. On the Gold Coast, between 1830 and 1843, Maclean had developed a scheme of adapting British ideas of justice and administration to suit Africans living in traditional societies, through cooperation with their natural rulers. But much of Maclean's work had been undone by subsequent mistakes of British policy, and in any case the area in which he had worked had been for some time under the strong and increasing influence of European merchants, missionaries and officials. When the Gold Coast colony was established in 1874, little difficulty was experienced in administering it directly through British district officers. Similar systems of administration were extended to the protectorate territories of the Gambia, Sierra Leone, Lagos and the Oil Rivers when these were created after 1884.

Whereas the French from the first had a definite idea as to the manner in which their West African colonies should be governed, and developed a highly centralised system of administration which was the same in each colony, taking little or no account of the various native systems of government already in existence, the British had no such preconceived notions. Although in most cases they began to govern their new territories through the direct rule of British officials, it soon became clear: first, that each colonial government was to have a considerable degree of autonomy, in that most administrative decisions and most laws were to be made within the colony itself rather than by the Colonial Office and Parliament in London; and, secondly, that the system of administration in each colony could be varied to make use of the systems of government already developed by its African inhabitants. The first of these ideas is revealed by the importance and the development of the legislative councils in the British colonies; the second in the application of the system of indirect rule first developed in British West Africa by Sir Frederick Lugard in Northern Nigeria.

In addition to executive councils of officials to advise the governor in the conduct of his administration, each of the British colonies was from an early date given a *legislative council.* The legislative council possessed the power, with the assent of the governor, and provided the secretary of state for the colonies in London did not disapprove, to make the laws of the colony. A legislative council was established in the Gambia in 1843, in the Gold Coast in 1850, and in Lagos in 1862. At first the crown colony of Sierra Leone made do with a dual-purpose council which it had inherited from the days of company rule, but in 1863 it too received separate executive and legislative councils.

The idea that each colony should as far as possible make its own laws, and manage its own administrative and financial affairs, originated with the earliest English colonies, those established in America in the seventeenth century. Most of the inhabitants of these colonies had been settlers from Britain. They had asserted their right as British subjects to govern themselves through their own elected assemblies, and these assemblies had claimed similar powers and privileges to those of the English Parliament of the time. The experience of the American Revolution had further convinced British nineteenth-century statesmen of the importance of taking account of colonial opinion, and of allowing the colonies a considerable say in managing their own affairs.

But the inhabitants of the new British colonies in Africa were for the most part Africans unaccustomed to English legislative and administrative methods, and to begin with they were not given the power of electing the members of their legislative councils. At first the majority of the members were British officials, who were normally also members of the executive council, but from an early stage inhabitants of the colonies who were not officials were nominated to the legislative councils by the governors as representatives of colonial opinion. To begin with, these unofficial members were usually British residents in the colonies, mainly merchants and missionaries, but before 1890 some educated Africans were also being nominated to the legislative councils. The next stage in the development of the legislative council in British West Africa occurred when it was provided that some or all of the African unofficial members should be elected to the legislative councils by African voters. Between 1922 and 1925, Nigeria, Sierra Leone and the Gold Coast all received constitutions which provided for the election of African legislative councillors; in the larger coastal towns, such as Lagos and Accra, which already possessed partly elective town councils, usually by systems of direct election, and in the provinces usually by councils of chiefs.

A further advance came when the number of unofficial members in the legislative councils was made greater than the number of official members. This stage was reached in the Gold Coast, Nigeria and Gambia in 1945, and in Sierra Leone in 1948. However, the fact that the elected members were in a majority in the legislative councils did not mean that these colonies were self-governing. They had *representative* but not *responsible* government. The colonial legislature was representative of the inhabitants of the colony, but the colonial government was not responsible to the legislature. If the elected members defeated the official members in a division in the legislative council, the latter did not resign, as would a British government defeated in Parliament by the opposition, because the elected members had no right to form a government to replace them. Responsibility for the government of the colony rested with the governor and his subordinate officials, and the governor was responsible not to the legislative council, but to the colonial secretary in London, who in his turn was responsible for his actions to Parliament. In addition, the governor retained the power to veto legislation and even, in emergency, to legislate and to carry on the administration without the consent of the legislative council. But these were reserve powers to be used only in exceptional circumstances; the system of representative government assumed that there would normally be sufficient agreement and cooperation between the British officials and the African elected representatives to make their use unnecessary. In an attempt to improve this understanding and cooperation, the plan was adopted early in the 1940s of appointing unofficial African members to the executive councils of the Gold Coast, Nigeria and Sierra Leone.

So long as both the unofficial and official members of the legislative council were prepared in normal circumstances to make concessions to the others' point of view, the system of representative government allowed Africans some share in their own government. In particular it enabled them to exert some control over the nature and extent of the colonial government's taxation, and over the manner in which the resulting revenue was spent. Indeed, the legislative council of the Gambia did not develop as fast as those of Sierra Leone, the Gold Coast and Nigeria principally because this tiny colony experienced difficulty in finding enough revenue to pay for the educational, social and economic advancement of its people as well as for the direct costs of its administration. Not until 1946 did an elected member appear on the Gambian legislative council, and although thereafter the unofficial members outnumbered the officials in the council, the majority of them were still nominated and not elected.

British administration: indirect rule

Although Maclean's administration in the Gold Coast had the makings of a system of *indirect rule*, and systems of ruling Africans through their natural rulers were also evolved by British nineteenth-century administrators elsewhere in Africa, it was mainly the success of Sir Frederick Lugard's administration in Northern Nigeria, and his subsequent fame and influence as an expert on colonial administration, which led to the wide adoption of systems of indirect rule in British West Africa after about 1920.

In Northern Nigeria, Lugard lacked both sufficient trained administrators and sufficient funds to enable him to provide for the direct administration by British officials of the large and relatively densely populated territory which he had conquered between 1900 and 1906. Even if Lugard had had sufficient men and money to administer Northern Nigeria directly, it is doubtful whether he would have done so. He himself had already done something to start indirect rule in East Africa, in Uganda, and Sir George Goldie, under whose government Lugard had first come to Nigeria, had already planned that when the Niger Company had secured control of Northern Nigeria, it should rule it indirectly. The Fulani emirs all possessed systems of officials, for the administration of justice and for the maintenance of order and the collection of taxes, which the British could recognise, even if they might not always think them sufficiently efficient or impartial in some of their practical applications. Lugard therefore determined to rule the emirs, and to leave them and their officials to rule the people under the supervision of British Residents attached to each of their courts.

The Residents interfered in the traditional emirate governments mainly to check abuses in them. Though the status of slavery was abolished, the people of Northern Nigeria continued to be subject to Muslim law administered by the emirate courts. The Fulani system of taxation, which was complicated and liable to abuse, was replaced by a single tax levied on each village. But taxes continued to be collected by the emirs' officers and were paid into the emirs' treasuries. A fixed proportion of the emirs' revenues, at first one-quarter and then one-half, was transferred to the central British administration and used to finance the specialised services —health, agriculture, railways, etc.—which could best be provided by British experts, but the rest of the revenue remained at the disposal of the emirs' governments.

Great stress was laid on the financial aspect of this system of indirect rule. It came to be thought that the African authorities could not be expected to develop without acquiring responsibility for the collection and disbursement of increasingly large sums of money. So, provided that they paid regular salaries, prepared proper budgets, and presented their accounts for audit, the 'Native Authorities' could use their incomes more or less as they chose, subject to the guidance and the advice of the Residents.

Some difficulty was experienced in applying this principle of indirect rule in the pagan areas of Northern Nigeria which had not been fully conquered by the Fulani, but Lugard's system was remarkably successful in winning the confidence of the Fulani ruling class of the greater part of this large territory, and in enabling Britain to control it cheaply and effectively. Lugard's main difficulty was in finding enough money to enable his central administration to develop the transport and other services that the country required. There was a limit to the amount of direct taxation that could be levied without damaging the local economy, and Lugard was handicapped in that he had little or no revenue from customs duties. Since the British occupation, the bulk of Northern Nigeria's trade had passed through Lagos or the Protectorate of Southern Nigeria, and the two southern administrations retained almost all the customs revenue arising from goods passing through their territory to the north. By 1906 Lugard was convinced that the three separate British administrations in Nigeria should be amalgamated. If this were done, the revenue of Northern Nigeria would benefit from the commercial prosperity of the south, a planned railway system could be developed for the whole country, and administrative expenses could be reduced by amalgamating the separate technical services maintained by each of the three governments.

Although in 1906 the governments of Lagos and the Protectorate of Southern Nigeria were amalgamated to form the Colony and Protectorate of Southern Nigeria, the British government did not at first agree to the greater amalgamation advocated by Lugard. For a time Lugard left Nigeria and served as governor of Hong Kong. In 1912 he returned as governor of both Northern and Southern Nigeria, and was entrusted with the work of preparing the way for the amalgamation of their two administrations. This was effected in 1914, and Lugard then became governor-general[1] of all Nigeria.

It was now possible for Northern Nigeria to secure an adequate share of the revenue from customs, and for railways and other services to be planned for the territory as a whole. Although the northern and southern political administrations were not amalgamated, but were placed under separate lieutenant-governors responsible to the governor-general, Lugard set out to apply the principles of indirect rule to Southern Nigeria. But conditions there were very different from those which Lugard had experienced in the north. In the first place there were large towns, such as Lagos, Calabar and Port Harcourt, whose African inhabitants were to a great extent detribalised and could only be governed through European municipal institutions. Secondly, although in Yorubaland there were definite states whose rulers could be recognised without too much difficulty as Native Authorities, the situation in south-eastern Nigeria, with its diffuse and egalitarian society, made it virtually impossible to discern traditional rulers receiving allegiance from any significant numbers of people. An attempt by the government to create its own 'traditional' rulers, or 'warrant chiefs', had disastrous results, and ultimately it was forced to the expedient of recognising as Native Authorities a large number of more or less traditional councils.

In 1919 Lugard retired, thenceforward becoming an important influence on the shaping of colonial policy behind the scenes in Britain. He became the British member of the Permanent Mandates Commission of the League of Nations. In 1928, he became Lord Lugard, and a prominent speaker in debates on colonial matters in the House of Lords. Many of the officials who had served under Lugard in Nigeria subsequently reached high positions in the British colonial service, for example Sir Gordon Guggisberg (governor of the Gold Coast, 1919–27), Sir Donald Cameron (governor of Tanganyika, 1926–31, and of Nigeria, 1931–5), Sir Alan Burns (governor of the Gold Coast, 1941–8), and Sir Herbert Palmer (governor of the Gambia, 1930–3). It is hardly surprising that Lugard's views on native administration became widely adopted throughout the British territories in tropical Africa.

What these views were can be seen from Lugard's book *The Dual Mandate in British Tropical Africa*, first published in 1922. Lugard argued that no European power was in Africa for purely altruistic motives, and that in practice one side of the 'dual mandate' which Britain and the other colonial powers had undertaken in Africa was apt to succeed at the expense of the other. The European desire to exploit African trade and resources was apt to be a stronger force than the feeling of obligation

[1] The title of 'Governor-General' was personal to Lugard; until 1954 his successors in office in Nigeria were all styled 'Governor'.

to help the African peoples to advance. The advance of European trade and administration in Africa was destroying the old African society and doing little to help build a new one. Lugard claimed that this would be prevented if the European powers were to do what he had done in Nigeria, that is, to rule the Africans indirectly, through their traditional chiefs, and to train the latter for their new responsibilities. In fact indirect rule was the best means of achieving the dual mandate.

Steps were taken during the 1920s and 1930s to introduce indirect rule into the Gold Coast, Sierra Leone and the Gambia. While the crown colony areas of Sierra Leone and the Gambia remained under direct administration, local government in their protectorates passed increasingly into the hands of the tribal authorities, supervised by the British district officers.

The situation in the Gold Coast was more complicated. In Ashanti, British direct administration had never won the confidence of the people. During the 1920s the work of a government anthropologist, Captain R. S. Rattray, revealed that this failure could in large part be explained by the fact that the political life of the Ashanti could not be separated from their social customs and religious beliefs; the refusal of the British authorities to allow the traditional chiefs any part in the administration was in fact leading to a dangerous disintegration of the whole of Ashanti society. Accordingly, steps were taken to reconstitute the power of the chiefs. In 1924, the state chiefs were allowed a limited jurisdiction. In 1926, Prempeh, who had been brought back from exile, was recognised as *Kumasihene*. Finally, in 1935, after Prempeh's death, his successor was recognised as *Asantehene*, and a council of state chiefs under his chairmanship, the Ashanti Confederacy Council, was recognised and given definite powers. In the Northern Territories, the hierarchies of chiefs in the Dagomba, Mamprussi and lesser kingdoms lent themselves readily enough to indirect rule, but there were also acephalous societies which presented the same sort of problem as those found in eastern Nigeria or with the pagan communities in northern Nigeria. In the colony, where Native Authorities and provincial councils of chiefs were created after 1925, there was a growing and increasingly influential class of European-educated Africans who wanted democratic government on the European model, and who regarded any attempt to increase the power of the old chiefs, most of whom had had little modern education and some of whom were illiterate, as a backward step. Moreover, since the chiefs generally lacked a regular system of taxation, the amount of revenue available to the Native Authorities tended to be too small to enable them to function effectively as units of indirect rule of the kind envisaged by Lugard.

Indirect rule served a useful purpose in enabling the British to extend their influence over Northern Nigeria and in helping to win the confidence of the people of Ashanti principally because, at the time of the British occupation, both these territories had possessed efficient African forms of government which commanded the respect of their peoples. Experience in Southern Nigeria and in the Gold Coast colony, however, showed that indirect rule had its limitations as a system of administration, and that it could not be used indiscriminately throughout British West Africa. By the 1940s it was evident that indirect rule was not a universal formula for the planning of the advancement of African colonies. The very fact of colonialism was accelerating economic and social processes which were changing, even eroding, traditional African ways of behaviour, law, and government. Even in areas where indirect rule seemed to work well (that is, in areas where traditional African authority was strong and authoritative enough to have survived European infiltration and conquest more or less intact, and sufficiently conservative or isolated to survive the processes of economic and social change with little or no modification), it was no longer clear that it was the best means of fulfilling the dual mandate. A great increase of production and trade had followed upon the extension of European rule in West Africa. Africans were becoming wealthier, and were using their new wealth in new ways, especially in seeking European education. As a consequence, they were demanding, and were becoming able to pay for, much better and more extensive systems of transport and public works, and education, medical and other social services. British officials began to join with the leaders of the educated Africans in doubting whether traditional African forms of government, even when under European control or supervision, could be adapted to provide and manage such services, or whether they could be adapted quickly enough to meet the growing demand for them.

German administration: the League of Nations mandates

When Germany first acquired colonies in West Africa, her government and people possessed no previous experience of ruling African peoples, or, indeed, of colonial administration in any part of the world. Initially, power was concentrated in the hands of the officials in each colony with but little check on their use of it. By and large these officials took little account of African institutions and customs, and established a highly authoritarian form of administration. This was a system of government which was open to abuse by high-handed or unscrupulous administrators. However, abuses were less in Togo than in the other German colonies in Africa. In part this was because, under German rule, southern Togo rapidly experienced the same kind of spontaneous economic development that occurred in the southern Gold Coast. Trade and government revenue rapidly increased, and there was thus little cause for the drastic German interference with African life that was apt to occur elsewhere. However, by 1907, criticism in parliament and press of the German way of handling matters in many African territories had reached such a pitch that the German organisation for handling colonial affairs was changed, and a considerable programme of colonial reform was entered upon. More attention was given to the ways in which African societies were organised and by which they had governed themselves, and the Germans also began to take note of the methods of colonial administration adopted by other European powers, Britain in particular.

The new German colonial policy had had little time in which to produce results when, in 1914, France and Britain found themselves at war with Germany. Within a few weeks, British and French colonial troops had occupied Togo, and by 1916 they had also defeated the German forces in Cameroon. The two colonies came under temporary British and French administrations until 1919, when, as a result of the Treaty of Versailles, Germany's colonies were taken away from her, and mandates for their administration were entrusted by the League of Nations to those of Germany's vanquishers who were already colonial powers.

The mandate system of the League of Nations was an attempt to put into practice the ideas of international trusteeship for under-developed areas of the world which had already been ineffectively proclaimed for Africa at the Berlin and Brussels Conferences. The actual business of administering each of the former German colonies was entrusted to a particular power (the 'mandatory'), but it was made clear that the mandatory's first duty was to promote the material and moral well-being and the social progress of the inhabitants of the mandated territory, and the conduct of his administration was subject to the scrutiny of the League of Nations and its permanent Mandates Commission at Geneva. In particular, the mandatory was required to abolish slavery and forced labour, to respect native land rights, and to allow all members of the League free access to, and equal rights in, the territory; and he was forbidden to set up economic monopolies, or to develop the territory as a military or naval base.

The former German colonies of Togo and Cameroon were each divided into two—a larger eastern part which was placed under French mandate, and a smaller western part which was placed under British mandate. In each case the railway system built by the Germans to open up the territory came into the French sphere, and France set up separate administrations for her mandates which were independent of the governor-generals of French West Africa and French Equatorial Africa. On the other hand, Britain was allowed to administer her Togo and Cameroon mandates as though they were parts of the Gold Coast and Nigeria respectively. In this way the Gold Coast and Nigeria in effect acquired new eastern frontiers which coincided rather better than the old ones with the boundaries of the former independent African communities.

When, as a result of the 1939–45 war, the League of Nations ceased to exist, the French and British mandates in Togo and Cameroon became territories administered by France and Britain as trustees for the United Nations.

Economic development of French West Africa

With the mouth of the Niger in British territory, the French planned to open up the trade and resources of the western Sudan from the west, using the Senegal and the upper Niger as the principal means of communication. They planned to link the navigable stretches of the two rivers by a railway from Kayes to Bamako (320 miles), but this railway, though begun as early as 1882, was not completed until 1906. Before it had been finished, the French had been forced to modify their original scheme. They realised, first, that St Louis was not capable of development into a good port for modern ocean-going ships, but that Dakar was. Accordingly, in 1885, a railway was opened connecting St Louis and Dakar (165 miles). Experience then showed that the Senegal, which was navigable as far as Kayes only for less than three months each year, was not adequate as a means of communication with the Sudan, and it was decided to link Kayes with Dakar directly by rail (400 miles). But this railway, begun in 1907, was not completed until 1924.

Long before this, the French had been forced to realise that the economic exploitation of the western Sudan was neither as easy nor as profitable as they had expected. The coming of colonial rule, in North Africa and the Sahara as well as in West Africa, had completed a process begun by the development of the ocean trade routes, and the trans-Saharan trade was now relatively insignificant. Since there were few large towns or areas of dense population in the western Sudan, its peoples were not now growing foodstuffs or manufacturing goods on any very much larger scale than was needed for purely local use. The Sudan was thus poorly organised for production for export, and lacked both the earnings and the population to provide a good market for European goods.

The development of production for export was hampered by a number of factors. The Sudan was not linked to the coastlands and to the outside world by an efficient transport system until 1924. With the exception of the ancient and not now very remunerative gold-workings of the Bambuk–Boure region, the country had hardly any minerals worth exploiting. Agricultural development was handicapped by the shortage of labour and by the relative poverty of the soil. It was possible to overcome these difficulties by schemes of irrigation and mechanised cultivation, but these were expensive. France had relatively little capital available for overseas investment, and Frenchmen were reluctant to invest their savings in expensive schemes for the development of the Sudan, because they knew that a considerable time was likely to elapse before these schemes could produce results and show a profit. An ambitious scheme for controlling the flood-waters of the Niger to irrigate large areas of land, though first proposed early in the twentieth century, did not make much progress before the late 1940s.

Inevitably the French began to turn their attention away from the Sudan to the coastal regions, whose more numerous inhabitants were more accustomed to trading with Europeans. It proved comparatively easy to develop the production of groundnuts from the Senegal; of cocoa, timber, coffee and bananas from the Ivory Coast; of palm produce from Dahomey; and of bananas from French Guinea. Although coffee and bananas were first grown mainly on European-organised plantations, the African inhabitants of these colonies soon realised the profits that would come to them if they themselves cultivated cash crops for export. In some cases, for example with groundnuts in the Senegal, production for export became so profitable that farmers practically ceased to grow foodstuffs for local consumption. However, from their cash crops they earned enough money to buy foodstuffs grown in other parts of West Africa, in particular from the Sudanic interior, as well as to buy manufactured goods from Europe. The resulting increase in trade provided increased revenue which the colonial governments could use to improve transport. Modern ports were constructed to handle the growing trade, and from them railways were built into the interior. It thus became easier and cheaper to get the export crops to the world markets and also to bring foodstuffs and manufactures to the areas which concentrated on production for export. In French Guinea, the railway from the port of Conakry had by 1914 reached 410 miles inland to the Tinkisso river, one of the tributaries of the Niger. From Abidjan on the Ivory Coast, a railway begun in 1903 reached Bobo-Dioulasso, nearly 500 miles distant. In Dahomey, 360 miles of railway had been constructed by 1936.

This expansion of trade and its penetration along the railways towards the Sudan meant a considerable increase in the wealth and prosperity of French West Africa. In 1913 the value of the territory's exports and imports combined was only about £11,600,000 ($55,700,000); by 1951 it was approximately £204,000,000 ($980,000,000). The French colonial governments, which could raise only about £2,000,000 ($10,000,000) of revenue to spend in the territory in 1913, had a revenue of some £73,000,000 ($350,000,000) in 1951. But since the territory's trade was

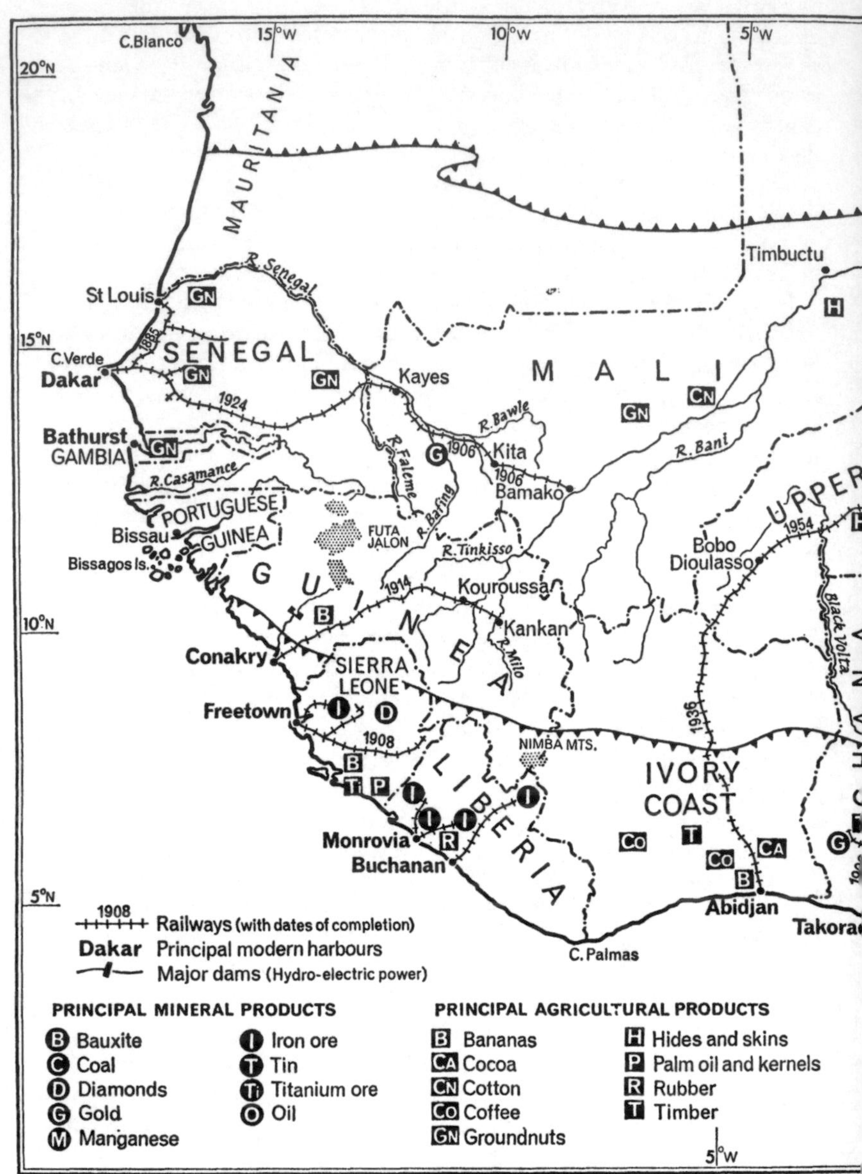

14 The economic development of

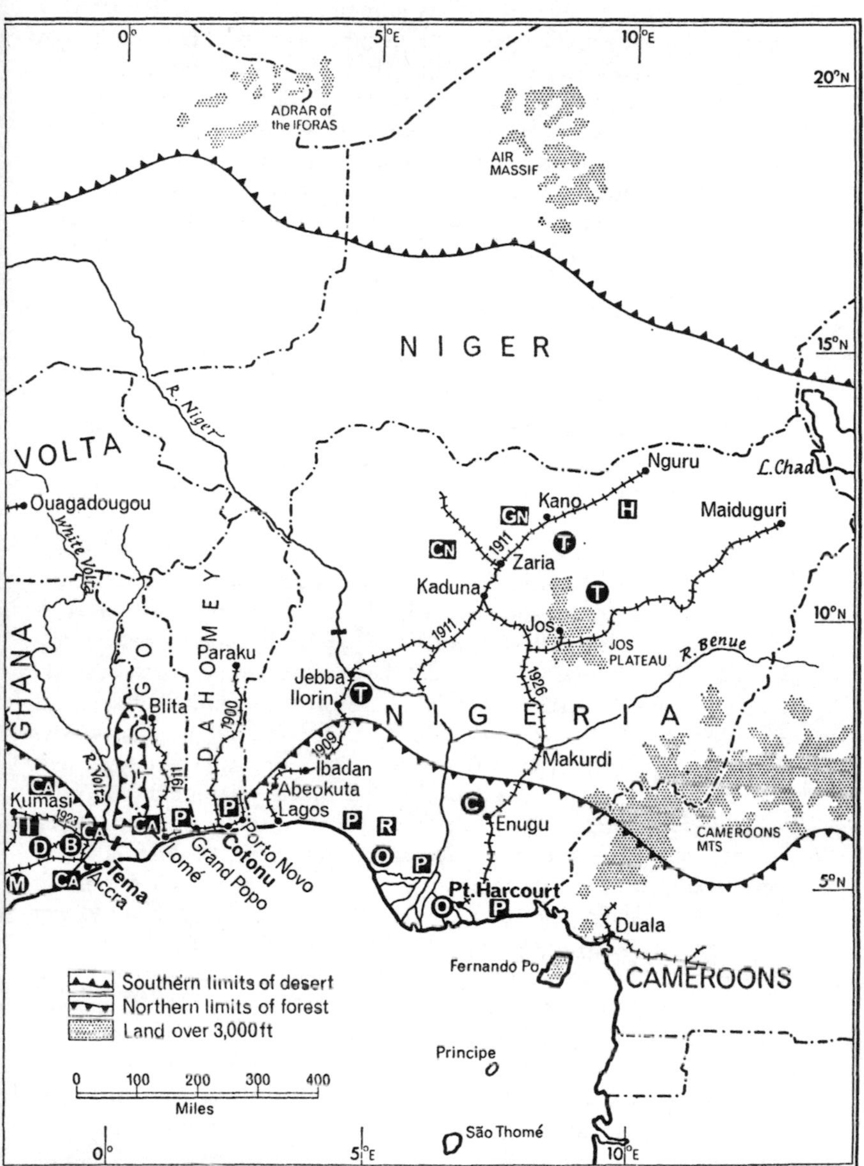

West Africa in the twentieth century

largely dependent on the export of a few agricultural products[1] grown in the more densely populated regions near the coast, its wealth was very unevenly distributed. The people in the interior, who were in most need of better transport, better education, better medical and agricultural services, etc., were least able to pay for them. Moreover, the total revenue received by the French administration was not large in relation to the problems involved in administering such a large and thinly populated territory: in 1951 something like 17,000,000 people were scattered over 4,800,000 square miles of country. It is hardly surprising then that French West Africa had less miles of railway per square mile and a smaller proportion of its children going to school than was the case in most of the neighbouring British territories.[2]

Economic development in British West Africa

The economic development of the British colonies in West Africa was in general swifter and greater than that of the French territories. In part this was due to the fact that Britain had more money available for investment in overseas colonies than was the case with France; and in part to the natural economic advantages of the British colonies in West Africa compared with the French. This, of course, made them more attractive to the European trader and investor, and in general the parts of West Africa occupied by Britain were those where European, particularly British, trade was already well established before the twentieth century. Compared with the French territories, the British territories were small in area and thickly populated. They possessed mineral as well as agricultural resources, and their inhabitants had already begun to exploit these resources themselves. It was therefore much easier for Britain, with her greater resources of capital, to develop the trade and exploit the resources of her West African colonies than it was for the financially and commercially weaker French nation to develop and exploit her much larger, more thinly populated, and relatively poor territories. It was estimated that whereas by 1936 the British West African colonies had attracted £116,730,000 of European capital, only £30,426,000 had been invested in French West Africa.

The economic development of the Gold Coast in the nineteenth century was held back by the Ashanti wars and by the difficulty of finding a commodity to take the place of slaves as the principal export. In the twentieth century, however, the Gold Coast rapidly became the richest territory in West Africa. At first her most valuable export was rubber from wild rubber trees in the forest, but the trees were over-exploited and

[1] Groundnuts alone accounted for a third of the value of the exports of French West Africa, coffee for nearly a quarter, and cocoa for about one-sixth.

[2] See Table F, p. 198.

the trade rapidly declined after 1900. However, the British occupation of Ashanti made it possible to construct a railway from Sekondi, on the coast, through the gold-bearing districts of the western part of the colony to Kumasi (1898–1903). This railway made it possible to import machinery enabling European companies to mine gold at great depths, and thus to revive the declining export trade in gold. By 1913 exports of gold from the Gold Coast were worth £1,656,000 ($8,000,000). The world demand for manganese during the war of 1914–18 and for bauxite (the ore of aluminium) during that of 1939–45 brought other European companies to the Gold Coast to mine for these metals. The Gold Coast also possessed deposits of diamonds, which were mined by African diggers as well as by European companies.

The development of gold, manganese and bauxite mines would have been impossible without railways to bring heavy machinery and stores to the mines and, in the case of manganese and bauxite, to take the bulky ores away to the ports for shipment. In the long run, however, a more valuable service rendered by the railways was to make possible the export of large quantities of cocoa and timber from the Gold Coast forest. The completion of the railway from Accra to Kumasi in 1923 and of the Huni valley line in 1927 meant that there were few parts of the forest which were not within relatively easy reach of the railway.

Commercial cocoa farming began, in the south-eastern Gold Coast, during the 1880s. The world demand for cocoa beans was great and increasing; the plant was fostered and seeds distributed by missionaries and government botanists, and soon African farmers were growing cocoa on small farms cleared from the forest. The first export of cocoa from the Gold Coast was in 1891, and in 1910 the value of exports of cocoa for the first time exceeded those of gold. By 1913, cocoa comprised half the value of the colony's total exports of £5,000,000 ($24,000,000). Thereafter ever-increasing quantities of cocoa were produced in the Gold Coast, and although during the 1930s and 1940s the cocoa trees suffered seriously from the swollen shoot disease, cocoa remained easily the most valuable of the territory's exports and the colony was the world's largest producer of the crop. In 1951, the value of cocoa exported from the Gold Coast was £60,300,000 ($169,000,000), two-thirds of the value of the colony's total exports of £91,249,000 ($255,000,000). In comparison, the value of the gold exported from the Gold Coast in 1951 was £8,500,000 ($23,800,000), of manganese ore £7,217,000 ($20,200,000), of diamonds £5,971,000 ($16,800,000), and of timber £4,976,000 ($14,000,000).

The Gold Coast's flourishing export trade made it possible for her to buy large quantities of manufactured and other goods from other countries (in 1951, her imports were worth £63,313,000 or $177,275,000), and for her government to raise a considerable revenue, principally from duties on imports and exports, and from taxes on the incomes of the people and companies in the colony (in 1951, the revenue was over £34,000,000 or $95,000,000). This enabled its government to develop education, medical and other social services, and to construct public works like railways and roads, water and electricity supplies, and modern ports like Takoradi and Tema, on a much more ambitious scale than was the case with any other West African colony. The most impressive scheme of all was the damming of the River Volta to supply electric power to convert bauxite into aluminium, but this was not proceeded with until after independence. Though its northern territories were contributing little to its wealth, the Gold Coast had more trade and revenue in proportion to its population than any other territory in West Africa.

Nigeria was also potentially rich, but its development was slower and less spectacular than that of the Gold Coast, principally because half or more of its enormous population (thought to be in excess of 30 million by about 1950) lived in the north in conditions not very different from those which had impeded the economic development of the French Sudan. At an early stage in the colony's history, the construction was begun of railway lines to make Northern Nigeria accessible from the sea, and by 1926 there were two lines to the north, one from Lagos, the chief seaport in the west of the colony, and the other from Port Harcourt, the chief port in the east. These railways were expensive to build, and at first they did not carry enough goods to enable them to make a profit. However, the people of Northern Nigeria, much thicker on the ground and, at the start of the colonial period, economically more flourishing than those of the French Sudan, soon began to produce goods for export, including hides and skins, cotton, and, most important of all, groundnuts. By 1950 groundnuts alone accounted for one-sixth of all Nigeria's exports, and so many groundnuts were being grown that the railways were finding it difficult to transport the crop to the ports. In all, the North produced about one-quarter of all Nigerian exports in 1950.

For a long time, the mainstay of the Nigerian economy was the export trade in palm oil and kernels from the coastal districts, a trade which had developed steadily throughout the nineteenth century, and which greatly increased after the extension of British rule in Southern Nigeria. Palm produce remained the principal export of the south, though cocoa became of increasing importance in the south-west. These two crops accounted respectively for one-third and one-quarter of the value of Nigeria's exports in 1950.

Although Nigeria was an important producer of tin and had, at Enugu, the only coal mines in West Africa, her trade and prosperity depended principally on the export of agricultural produce. However, she was not dependent, as was the Gold Coast, principally on one crop. In 1951,

Nigeria's exports were worth £127,000,000 ($355,000,000) and her imports £83,200,000 ($233,000,000) and the revenue of her government was £50,227,000 ($140,640,000). Impressive though these figures were, for in 1951 Nigeria's trade was greater than that of all French West Africa, and her government's revenue little smaller than that of all the French West African governments combined, it must be remembered that Nigeria had more inhabitants than all the other West African colonies, French as well as British, together. Although the progress of economic and social development was impressive during the colonial period, Nigeria still had a long way to go to catch up with the Gold Coast.

In Sierra Leone, the construction of a railway from Freetown into the Protectorate (1896–1908) made it possible to develop an export trade in agricultural produce, principally palm kernels and oil, and kola-nuts, which by 1913 was worth £1,375,000 ($6,600,000) a year. However, the colony remained comparatively poor until during the 1930s valuable deposits of iron ore and diamonds in the Protectorate began to be exploited by European mining companies. By 1951, the value of Sierra Leone's exports had risen to £10,068,0000 ($28,200,00), while her imports were worth £8,207,000 ($23,000,000). Minerals accounted for about half of the value of the exports. Sierra Leone's mineral wealth seemed to ensure her future prosperity, though it was noteworthy that a great and increasing part of her trade was due to the activities of European mining companies, whereas the trade of the Gold Coast and Nigeria was essentially based on the work of African farmers.

The Gambia was the poorest of the British colonies in West Africa. The colony's economy was entirely dependent on the production of groundnuts, which constituted over nine-tenths of its exports. Indeed more groundnuts were produced in the colony than its own people could easily cultivate, the explanation being that farmers from French territory entered the colony for a few months each year especially to grow groundnuts. Provided that the world price for groundnuts was high, the colony was just able to pay for the cost of its government, but there was very little revenue left over to pay for schemes of economic or social development.

The development of Liberia

Compared with the colonial territories in West Africa, the economic and social development of Liberia was hampered by the difficulty experienced by its independent Negro government in raising revenue or borrowing money. Until recently the government of the republic was too poor and weak even to extend its administration into the interior. The natives of the country were reluctant to take any notice of the government of immigrant Negroes at Monrovia, and in any case they possessed little or no trade or wealth which could be taxed to provide revenue. Early attempts by the Liberian government to borrow money from European investors were disastrous fiascos, little of the money ever being spent in the country.

About 1912, however, the United States began to provide increasing financial and technical assistance to its Liberian godchild. In 1925 the American Firestone Rubber Company acquired a 100-year lease of 1,000,000 acres of forest land inland from Monrovia, and began to develop a huge rubber plantation. Until recently, the economic life of Liberia was almost entirely dependent on the export of rubber from this plantation. As late as 1950, rubber constituted 90% of Liberia's exports. The Firestone Company was by far the largest employer of labour in the country and had a share in many of its financial and commercial enterprises. Until 1948, when other foreign companies began to mine ore in Liberia, Firestone's activities were practically the only source of wealth for the country and its peoples. During 1945–8, the American government built a modern harbour at Monrovia primarily for strategic purposes, but its facilities were of great value for the economic development of Liberia.

American loans and the money brought into the country by the foreign companies provided the Liberian government with sufficient funds to secure administrative control of the whole of its territory, with the incidental result that its natives were able to secure a share in the government. But comparatively little was done to stimulate the native production needed to make the country really prosperous and to give the government sufficient revenue to provide the transport, education, and other works and services so badly needed.

SOME STATISTICS OF THE COLONIAL PERIOD

The two following tables provide some data by which the development of the various West African territories during the colonial period may be compared. Unfortunately it is not always easy to separate the statistics for individual French colonies from those of the French West African federation, and figures have therefore been given for the latter only. 1912–13 has been chosen for the date of Table E, since before that time the volumes of trade, revenue, etc. were often relatively insignificant, and the statistics are neither always easy to obtain nor always very reliable. It must be remembered that the population figures given are essentially *estimates*, and also that recent research has (as stated in chapter 6) tended to show that the estimates were generally too small, perhaps by about 10 per cent on average. This has its effect on the absolute accuracy of the ratios given in columns 3, 7, 9 and 13 of the tables, but they remain useful as measures of comparison between one territory and another.

TABLE E *West Africa in 1912–13*

	(1) Area (1000 sq.m.)	(2) Population (1000's)	(3) People per square mile	(4) Imports (£1000)	(5) Exports (£1,000)	(6) Total trade (£1,000)	(7) Value of trade per head	(8) Revenue (£1,000)	(9) Revenue per head	(10) Miles of railway	(11) Ratio of miles of railway to square miles of area	(12) No. of school-children (1,000s)
Gambia	4	146	40	619	655	1,274	£8.0	125	£0.85	Nil	—	?
Gold Coast	80	1,502	19	3,510	5,014	8,524	£5.65	1,302	£0.85	222	1:380	19
Nigeria	336	17,124	51	6,324	6,779	13,103	£0.75	3,327	£0.20	912	1:350	22
Sierra Leone	28	1,502	53	1,438	1,376	2,814	£1.85	618	£0.40	271	1:100	?
All British West Africa	*448*	*20,274*	*45*	*11,891*	*13,824*	*25,715*	*£1.3*	*5,372*	*£0.25*	*1,405*	*1:320*	*?*
French West Africa	1.798	10,700?	6?	6,333	5,250	11,583	£1.1	1,723	£0.15	1,545	1:1160	11?
German Togo	33	1,000?	30?	530	455	985	£1.0	1,536	£1.50	203	1:165	15
Liberia	38?	1,750?	46?	334	224	558	£0.3	107	£0.05	Nil	—	?

TABLE F *West Africa in 1956–7*

	(1) Area (1,000 sq. m.)	(2) Population (1,000s)	(3) People per square mile	(4) Imports (£1,000)	(5) Exports (£1,000)	(6) Total trade (£1,000)	(7) Trade per head	(8) Revenue (£1,000)	(9) Revenue per head	(10) Miles of railway	(11) Ratio of miles of railway to square miles of area	(12) Number of schoool-children (1,000s)	(13) Ratio of no. of school children to total population
Gambia	4	276	69	3,729	2,552	6,281	£22.7	1,461	£5.0	—	—	6	1:36
Ghana	92	4,620	50	88,836	86,599	175,436	£30.15	45,178	£9.8	617	1:148	571	1:8
Nigeria	373	31,500	84	152,577	132,169	284,746	£9.0	62,626	£1.95	1,903	1:196	2,020	1:15
Sierra Leone	28	2,260	80	23,093	13,185	36,278	£16.5	9,586	£4.15	337	1:83	61	1:37
All British West Africa	*497*	*38,656*	*78*	*268,235*	*234,505*	*502,740*	*£13.0*	*118,851*	*£3.1*	*2,857*	*1:174*	*2,658*	*1:14*
French West Africa (excluding Togo)	1,798	18,735	10	113,102	101,737	214,839	£11.5	112,640	£6·0	2,358	1:765	288	1:65
Togo	20	1,091	55	4,525	3,960	8,485	£8.4	1,466	£1.35	294	1:70	50	1:22
Liberia	43?	1,000?	23?	9,571	15,906	25,477	£25.45?	5,643	£5.65	45	1:955?	50	1:20?

13

The regaining of independence

European attitudes to Africa, *c.* 1879–1914

The partition of West Africa (and of most of the rest of the continent also) between the European powers towards the end of the nineteenth century was in part a reflection of struggles for power in Europe itself. But it was also an expression of a contemporary belief that Europeans were better fitted than other peoples to govern the world and to develop its resources. Western Europeans of this time were supremely confident in their civilisation and its achievements. In the material sphere, certainly, the extent and the speed of the advances they had made during the previous hundred years or so seemed unparalleled in human experience. Man had become able to command the earth's resources and to convert them into wealth as never before in history. Europeans began to believe that the ever-growing progress of their power and wealth was a result of, and a just reward for, the excellence of the manner in which they ordered and managed their affairs. Consequently, not only did other parts of the world begin to seem backward and poor in comparison with the nations of western Europe, but many Europeans became convinced that they alone possessed a key to human progress denied to others.

In the case of Africa in general and West Africa in particular, a number of factors tended to strengthen these Europeans' sense of superiority. They were woefully ignorant of the achievements of Africans in the past. They then knew nothing, for example, of the great art of Ife and Benin. When this did begin to be revealed to them, they at once assumed that it could not be a purely African achievement: it must stem from some forgotten influence from the classical Mediterranean civilisation that lay behind their own culture. They knew very little of the great African empires of the past, Ghana, Mali, Songhai and the like. By the time that they were beginning to penetrate effectively into Africa, most of the greater African kingdoms they first came across, such as Benin, Dahomey and Ashanti had passed the peaks of their power. The European campaign against the slave trade, and the growth of European influence generally, had constricted their economic development, and had produced serious internal stresses and difficulties. The Europeans were especially appalled by their practice of human sacrifice, the volume of which may have been on the increase just because they had now made it impossible for surplus slaves to be exported. This, as much as any other factor, led them to dismiss African societies as barbaric, and to make it impossible for them to appreciate the well-ordered social and political thinking that made such kingdoms possible.

At the personal level, all too often the Africans with whom Europeans had dealt had been active participants in the slave trade (which Europeans now regarded as immoral), influenced by its methods, or slaves themselves. The achievements of other Africans were forgotten or misconstrued. When men like Philip Quaque, Bishop Crowther, or G. E. Ferguson were remembered, they were thought exceptional and even peculiar. Similarly, few Europeans were able to see in the activities of men like Chief Jaja, or the founders of the Fante Confederation, intelligent attempts to remould African society and thought to cope with the alien forces invading the continent from Europe. All too often the typical European view was that either Africans were incapable of entering upon the path of progress embarked on in Europe, or that they would take a very long time indeed to reach the European level. Moreover, it was felt that by the time the Africans had reached as far as Europeans had then attained, the latter, progressing with ever-increasing momentum, would have gone even further ahead. It was therefore thought to be not only for their own benefit that Europeans should colonise Africa, but for the benefit of both the Africans and of the world at large, for otherwise the resources of the continent would never be properly developed.

With such a philosophy behind them, the Europeans who colonised Africa tended to make two major assumptions. The first was that if they established in Africa the same sort of law and order which they believed themselves to have established in Europe, and which they thought had been so signally lacking in Africa, the forces of trade and industry, education and science, philosophy and religion, which had so transformed Europe, would automatically move in and transform Africa. Secondly, if African colonies were not perhaps permanent, at least their life would be a long one, measured more in centuries than in decades. As has been seen, the French theory was that the colonial period would ultimately come to an end because Africans would have become Frenchmen. The British supposed, equally vaguely, that some day their colonies might develop into self-governing dominions of their commonwealth. But at first, of course, both the French and the British concentrated on building up their colonial administrations and increasing their power, and the more established and powerful these administrations became, the more permanent they appeared. Furthermore, the more the French came to know Africa and its peoples, the greater seemed to be the difficulties in the way of making Africans into black Frenchmen. As for the British, they were inclined to think that if colonies like Canada or Australia, the vast majority of whose peoples were Europeans like themselves, had taken a century or more to reach dominion status, purely African colonies like the Gold Coast or Nigeria would of necessity take much longer.

Changing attitudes to Africa, 1918–45

In fact both these assumptions were proved false much more quickly than anyone had supposed possible. The great war of 1914–18, in which something like ten million Europeans died from direct military action alone, did more than raise the question as to whether a people who could so miserably and brutally mismanage their own affairs had any right to control those of others. It led many of them to begin to doubt the whole philosophy of the inevitability and the rightfulness of progress of the European kind. This doubt was greatly enhanced by the great depression of the 1930s, when, for instance, there was for some time no work available for one in every four of the working population of Britain.

Such great human disasters, followed shortly by the world war of 1939–45, could not but influence European attitudes to Africa. Thus, as has been seen, the German colonies conquered by Britain and France and their African soldiers during 1914–18, did not become the absolute possessions of the conquerors. Their administration became subject to the control of world opinion as expressed through the League of Nations. The great depression made both Britain and France (but especially perhaps the former) anxious to increase the volume of their overseas trade, and so to increase the opportunities for employment in their countries. They began to appreciate that only an insignificant proportion of their trade, less than 3 per cent, was with their African colonies. The idea that the simple imposition of European rule on African territories would lead to the same kind of economic and social revolution that western Europe had itself experienced was clearly invalid.

The philosophy of government which nineteenth-century Europe had brought to Africa was generally a narrow one. The duties of a government were thought to involve little more than the maintenance of internal law and order, and defence against aggression from without. Most other activities, especially those in the economic and social fields, were the responsibilities of individual citizens and corporations. As early as the 1900s, however, it was appreciated that most African colonies were, by European standards, so poor and backward that their administrations, in order to be able to operate efficiently, had to provide and maintain essential services—such as railways, water supplies and hospitals—which usually in Europe would have been left to private enterprise. Furthermore, in order to secure trained African personnel to supplement their costly European staffs, from an early stage, most colonial administrations began to subsidise the educational work of the Christian missions, and even sometimes to run schools themselves.

But for a long time colonial governments were normally expected to find the money for such developments from their own resources. They had to finance them either directly from revenue, or from such loans as they were able to raise on the security of their revenue. But in the early days of any colonial administration, its revenue was naturally small. Most African peoples could not afford to pay much in the way of taxes, and customs duties brought in little because trade was small. Consequently, the greater part of a colonial government's meagre income was swallowed up simply by the cost of administration. There was little over to invest in programmes of economic and social betterment which would equip the colonies with modern facilities and amenities and increase the efficiency of their peoples. Thus most African peoples remained poor, while at the same time their undeveloped territories could offer little attraction for the investment of private European capital. A vicious circle was set up in which, because the people's capacity to contribute revenue to the colonial governments was small, the funds available for economic and social development remained small also, with the result that the capacity of the people to gain in wealth and to provide the colonial governments with more revenue equally remained limited.

The beginnings of a colonial development policy

It was the world depression of the 1930s that first suggested that this policy of making colonies pay for their own development was wrong, for, as well as being harmful to the interests of the colonies, it was seen not to be in the interests of the colonial powers either. Thus the British government, with its Colonial Development Act of 1929, for the first time took general powers to lend or give money from its own resources for the economic development of its colonies. However, facing severe financial difficulties itself, the amounts it made available for the colonies were small. By 1938, only about £4,000,000 ($19,000,000) had been received from this source by all the British colonies in all Africa.

Not until the war of 1939–45 and the world shortages of many essential commodities that followed it, was there a real breakthrough in the approach to the problems of African development. Britain, France and their allies needed all the strategic raw materials and foodstuffs they could get. Many traditional lines of supply were disrupted, some by actual fighting, many more by difficulties and shortages of transport or by lack of foreign currencies. What the colonies could produce, and what they might be made to produce by active development programmes, suddenly became an urgent priority. The British policy, begun in 1929, of actively aiding colonial development, was greatly stepped up. In 1940 it was agreed that, instead of the previous maximum of £1,000,000, up to £5,000,000 ($20,000,000) a year could be lent or given to the colonies. In 1945 the permissible annual expenditure was raised to £12,000,000 ($48,000,000) or even more. In this year, development plans for the four British West African colonies were embarked on which envisaged the spending of at least £137,000,000 ($548,000,000) by 1955. The equivalent French post-war plans were even more ambitious. Their West African colonies, generally poorer and less attractive to private European capital, were to spend £277,000,000 ($1,108,000,000) on development during the same period.

The African contribution towards the new development plans

But not all these large sums were to come from the pockets of the tax-payers in Britain and France. The war and its consequences had brought a marked improvement in the financial situation of many of the colonies. Those of them that had already made appreciable progress as producers for the world market found that with the greatly increased demand for their exports they were appreciably better off than they were before. The prices they received for their produce had risen sharply, while the fact that they had also to pay more for the manufactures they imported was offset by the fact that these were in short supply, so that they could not get all they wanted. They therefore accumulated substantial credit balances in Europe on which their governments could draw to help finance their development plans.

This accumulation of West African credits in Europe was most marked in the case of the richer British colonies. This was in part because the areas of West Africa that became British had on the whole been more effectively penetrated by European trade than those which became French, so that their peoples had gone over to production for the world market to a more marked extent than was often the case with their neighbours in French territory. But it was also due to deliberate government policy in the British colonies.

West Africans had come to suffer from two major disadvantages in their foreign trade. The first was that they were entirely dependent on world economic conditions for the prices they got for their exports. The western world's alternations of boom and depression caused these prices to fluctuate widely, and there were consequent wide fluctuations in the incomes which Africans had available for the purchase of the goods that they wanted to import. The second disadvantage stemmed in part from the first. Whereas up to the great depression of the 1880s, African merchants had shared with Europeans in the trade of exporting African produce and importing European goods, the increasing integration of West Africa in the economy of the western world operated to force the Africans out of business. The Africans proved to have inadequate reserves of capital to continue their trading during the depressions, when the prices obtained by African produce on the world markets were often extremely low. They were either forced out of business altogether, or they decided that it was better to invest what capital they had in land or in property. On the other hand, the Europeans' response to the depressions was often to pool their resources of capital, and to combine in ever larger trading corporations. The result was that by the 1930s, both the marketing of the Africans' produce and the business of importing the goods on which much of their resultant income was spent, had become the virtual monopoly of a few large and powerful European companies whose policies and prices were determined in Europe and not in Africa.

During 1939–45, however, the major exports of British West Africa were purchased in bulk by the British government, which acted as agent for their allocation and sale to the rest of the world to ensure that their proceeds would be available for its war effort. After the war, this system of controlled marketing was continued by boards which were *responsible to the colonial governments*. This did more than help free the African producers from their dependence on foreign traders. The marketing boards set a guaranteed price in advance for each season's crop. If the world price rose above this, the board's extra income was put into a reserve which could be drawn upon to subsidise the prices paid to the farmers when world prices were low. The farmers were thus shielded from fluctuations in the world market. They were enabled to plan their production in advance, and did not run the risk of being caught with large surpluses which they could only dispose of at prices inadequate to cover their costs. In the event, world prices for West African produce remained high throughout the post-war period. The marketing board reserves became so substantial that they were able to lend or grant considerable sums to the colonial governments for development schemes which would benefit the whole community and not only the farmers. Furthermore, the high prices for West African produce enabled many West African governments to secure large new incomes from export duties.

Thus whereas the post-war development plans for French West Africa were largely financed from France, even the smaller and poorer British colonies were able to find a good proportion of the capital required for their 1946–55 development plans from their own resources—35 per cent in the case of the Gambia's £2,000,000 ($8,000,000) plan, and 45 per cent of the £5,250,000 ($21,000,000) required by Sierra Leone. Nigeria's plan envisaged the expenditure of £55,000,000 ($220,000,000), of which only £23,000,000 ($92,000,000) needed to come from Britain. The most remarkable situation was that of the Gold Coast. Its development plan was much more ambitious than that of the other colonies, envisaging the spending of about £15 ($60) per head of population (about seven times more than the Nigerian figure). The plan originally called for £75,000,000 ($300,000,000) to be spent over the ten years, and of this all but £3,000,000 ($12,000,000) was to come from its own resources. In the event, the world price for cocoa remained so high throughout 1946–55 that it was possible to spend appreciably more than this.[1]

New currents of change in West Africa, 1939–48

The war of 1939–45 and its consequences did much more than merely improve the economic situation of West Africa. It also produced important changes in the political and social climate governing the colonial situation both in Europe and in Africa. Britain and France thought of themselves as fighting a war for freedom against tyranny, and this was bound to affect their thinking about colonies. Their new colonial development plans were inspired not only by their appreciation that poor and backward colonies were of no value to them, but also because they began to feel a more positive obligation to do good to their colonial subjects. Thus a sizeable proportion of the post-war development plans was devoted to projects of social welfare, such as the development of educational and health services, in addition to schemes of economic development. It was, for example, during the war itself that the plans began to be laid in Britain for the founding of the first universities in colonial Africa.

When the United States, with its strong anti-colonial tradition, joined in the struggle, and the Atlantic Charter was proclaimed and the new United Nations was born, it became increasingly apparent that world opinion demanded that the colonial powers begin to prepare also for the political advancement of their colonial peoples. Furthermore, the war drastically demonstrated that colonies were not permanent features of the world landscape. Valuable British, French and Dutch colonies in Asia were overrun or threatened by the Japanese, and when the war ended it proved impossible to return them to their pre-war situation. Burma, India, Pakistan and Ceylon quickly became independent, to be followed eventually by French Indo-China and Dutch Indonesia.

In West Africa, the political effects of the war were more indirect. Nevertheless, the German occupation of France during 1940–4 had important repercussions in French Africa. Frenchmen became divided into supporters of the government at Vichy, which collaborated with the Germans, and into the 'Free French' of General de Gaulle who wished to continue the struggle. In West Africa, the French administrations

[1] That is, more in terms of £s, for in 1949 the £ was devalued from $4.03 to $2.80.

declared for Vichy. This lost them the sympathies of many Africans, especially since the racist policies of Nazi Germany, which had previously been well and unfavourably publicised by the French in Africa, now seemed to influence the official attitude towards coloured peoples. French Equatorial Africa on the other hand, one of whose governors, Félix Eboué, was a West Indian Negro, sided with the Free French. De Gaulle saw the need to regain African confidence, and cooperated with Eboué, who was soon governor-general, in the evolution of a completely new French colonial policy. The French Empire was to become the French Union, in which the colonies would be 'overseas territories' in partnership with France. The privileges of French citizenship, including the right to vote at elections for and to be represented in French legislatures, were to be made available to all Africans. For the first time also, elective assemblies, with some control over finance, were envisaged in each colony. This policy was first outlined at a conference at Brazzaville in 1944. By this time the British and American armies had liberated French North Africa from the Germans and were about to liberate France herself. Germany's final defeat was only a matter of time, and the French in West Africa had already changed sides (1942). In 1946 delegates from West Africa were able to share in forming a new constitution for France and the French Union which adopted some of the Brazzaville proposals.

The comparable adjustments in British West Africa were less dramatic, because at the time it was still thought that the existing legislative councils afforded a suitable and sufficient foundation for the necessary moves towards eventual colonial self-determination. During 1946–8, as has been seen, African majorities were established in each of the four legislative councils in West Africa. At the time most Britons—and indeed many Africans also—thought this was a revolutionary step forward. In fact it very soon proved to be quite inadequate to meet African political aspirations.

The rise of African political parties

At first African opposition to European rule, for example the Ashanti rising of 1900, tended to be mobilised behind or in defence of the traditional authorities whose position and power were being subverted by the growth of European administration. But later on, in both British and French territories, though in rather different ways, African rulers had tended to become associated with the European governments. Thus in the British West African legislative councils, most of the elected African members were representatives of the traditional rulers, and were not chosen directly by the people. In the circumstances, popular dissatisfaction with European rule began to seek new outlets. During the later 1940s, the West African political scene began to be revolutionised by the appearance of political parties of the kind known in Europe, which sought popular support for campaigns which aimed at gaining control of the administrative machines imposed on Africa by Europe.

European-style political agitation in West Africa had quite a long history behind it. This was especially the case in coastal regions, such as the Gold Coast colony, southern Nigeria or the Senegal, which had been early exposed to the growing influence of Europe in education and other matters, and where the growth of trade had at once tended to increase personal wealth and to disrupt the traditional organisation of society. Thus on the Gold Coast, for example, there had been the Fante Confederation movement of 1868–72, and then the Aborigines' Rights Protection Society founded in 1897. As early as 1918, a Gold Coast lawyer, J. E. Casely Hayford, had founded a National Congress of British West Africa to press for the kind of changes which in fact did not begin to appear until a generation afterwards. In the Senegal, the first political party was probably the Senegalese Socialist Party founded by Lamine Gueye in 1920.

But these early movements were rather political associations than effective political parties in the modern sense. They were the creation of a few Africans whose educational attainments, often extending to university or legal training in Europe, were very much greater than those of the mass of the people. Their modes of thought could have little general appeal, and they did not have any very wide support. In any case they faced the difficulty that the colonial administrations were ultimately responsible not to opinion in Africa, but to governments in Europe. In so far as the colonial administrations did take African opinion into account, they thought that it was better represented by the traditional rulers than by the views of the small European-educated minority. The early political associations were therefore little more than intellectual debating societies, aiming much more to influence African chiefs and European administrators in Africa, or politicians and opinion in Europe, than to appeal to and to educate the mass of their fellow Africans. Furthermore, until the 1920s at least, they were often more concerned with protecting the traditional rights of African chiefs and peoples from the encroachments of the colonial governments than they were with the object of taking over the power of those governments for themselves.

However, the war and immediate post-war years greatly changed and widened the outlook of many West Africans. There was the new promise of colonial freedom implicit in the Atlantic Charter and in the charter of the United Nations. Shortly after the war, there was the actual example of independence for many Asian colonies. During it, considerable numbers of African soldiers had served outside their own territories, and notably in Asia, as valued allies for the defence of the free world. Some had actually fought and died to help liberate Burma from the Japanese; many more had seen something of the strength and feeling of the Asian nationalist movements. Those who had stayed at home had had their traditional conception of Europeans as a privileged aristocracy—accustomed only to administer Africans or to direct their labour—exploded by the activities of numbers of ordinary British and American soldiers and airmen who had served in West Africa. War service of all kinds joined with the new social directions taken by African development plans greatly to increase African opportunities for both literary and technological education. The great stepping up of development seemed to open even wider horizons. In countless ways, growing numbers of Africans felt that a new world was being born in which their opportunities for education, for wealth, for freedom, were all expanding.

But the reality of the immediate post-war period was a severe disappointment. The new wealth gained from the high prices for West African produce proved of little value to the average man. The consumer goods he wanted were both expensive and in short supply, and the European importers were suspected of exploiting the situation to their own advantage. For lack of the capital goods required, the new development plans were slow to bring results. While the numbers of their directors, technical advisers, research workers, teachers and the like, brought out from Europe at considerable expense to earn high salaries, continually increased, the opportunities for ambitious Africans who had acquired new educational standards or technical skills did not.

A new generation of political leaders was available which was capable of harnessing and directing the growing popular unrest. Thus in 1935, Dr Nnamdi Azikiwe had returned from his university studies in the United States to launch, first in the Gold Coast, which had the widest spread of literacy, and then in his own Nigeria, the beginnings of a popular press. This sought to reach and influence not merely the well-educated Africans (to whom earlier newspapers had been largely addressed ever since their first appearance in West Africa nearly a century before), but anyone who could merely read, and who might be expected to pass on what he had read to those who could not. In 1944, Azikiwe came together with some older political leaders, such as Herbert Macaulay, to launch Nigeria's first modern political party, the National Council of Nigeria and the Cameroons[1] (N.C.N.C.). Azikiwe's influence helped send to America to follow in his footsteps a young Gold Coast teacher called Kwame Nkrumah. In the United States, and later on in Britain, Nkrumah and others like him became caught up in the excitement of Pan-Africanism. This had developed from the growing feeling among many American and West Indian Negro leaders, men like Marcus Garvey and W. E. B.

[1] Subsequently renamed the National Council of Nigerian Citizens.

DuBois and, later on, George Padmore, that their people had been too long depressed by European domination, and that they must break free and give expression to the true African personality. In 1945 Nkrumah took a prominent part in the fifth Pan-African Congress, held at Manchester in England, at which leadership of the movement passed to African Negroes determined to end the colonial status of their countries and to set up in its stead new and greater African nations. Then in 1947 he was recalled from the work of promoting the African anti-colonial movement in Britain to organise a national following for the United Gold Coast Convention (U.G.C.C.), a political party which had recently been formed in the Gold Coast by nationalists of a somewhat older school, among whom the leading spirit was Dr J. B. Danquah.

Towards self-government in British West Africa, 1948–61

In the following year (1948), the situation in the Gold Coast, where the changes and tensions of the times were perhaps most strongly in evidence, boiled over into violence. A well-organised boycott of European trading firms was followed by an ex-servicemen's demonstration which led to riots in Accra and other major towns. The U.G.C.C. made effective capital out of the unrest, claiming that British administration had broken down, and demanding immediate self-government for the colony. The official inquiry into the disturbances (Watson Commission) reported forthrightly that their underlying cause was the frustration felt by ever-increasing numbers of Africans. To prevent this, a new constitution was needed which would represent a positive step towards eventual complete self-government. African ministers responsible to an elected assembly should be given considerable control over the administration, and this itself should be Africanised as quickly as possible.

In 1949 the Gold Coast government appointed an all-African committee under Mr Justice Coussey to work out the details of such a constitution. This brought a parting of the ways between the old and new schools of African nationalists. While Danquah and the older leaders took part in the Coussey Committee and its deliberations, Nkrumah struck out on his own. He had judged, correctly, that the popular following he and the younger men had built up for the U.G.C.C. wanted 'self-government *now*', and not the compromise offered by the Coussey constitution. He and his lieutenants left the U.G.C.C., and quickly built up a much larger and more effectively mobilised mass party of their own, the Convention People's Party (C.P.P.), pledged to secure the popular will. This involved them in 'positive action', such as strikes, which soon brought about their arrest and condemnation. But this only served to make them martyrs and to increase their popular following. When in 1951 the first elections were held under the new Coussey constitution, the C.P.P. easily defeated the U.G.C.C. in contests for those seats in the Assembly which were open to direct popular election. The new governor of the Gold Coast, Sir Charles Arden-Clarke, sized up the situation, released Nkrumah and his colleagues, and appointed them to the leading ministerial posts. There then began a period of close cooperation between the British officials and the C.P.P. ministers in working out the details of the complete self-government finally won by the Gold Coast six years later when it became the new Ghana.

Once having granted the principle that the Gold Coast should advance to dominion status and freedom from British control, the British government could not deny the same opportunities to the other British colonies in West Africa. Nigeria in fact received a constitution equivalent to that of the Coussey constitution in the same year, Sierra Leone in 1954, and the Gambia in 1956. But in each of these three territories there were difficulties of a kind either not experienced in the Gold Coast at all or experienced to a much lesser degree. Consequently their attainment of complete self-government was slower. Nigerian independence was proclaimed in 1960, and that of Sierra Leone in 1961, while independence for the Gambia was delayed until 1965.

The problem with the Gambia was that it was not easy to see how such a tiny country, with a population of little more than a quarter of a million people, and with government revenue and foreign trade as little as £1,000,000 ($2,800,000) and £8,000,000 ($21,600,000) a year respectively, could really stand on its own in the harsh reality of the modern world. An obvious remedy was some kind of a union or federation with Senegal, whose territory surrounded the Gambia along its long and inconvenient land frontier, and which had achieved independence in 1960. But the constitutional, political, legal and fiscal problems involved in any sort of combination with a former French colony (especially one whose economy was still closely linked with the French economy) were not ones which could be quickly or easily solved.

Sierra Leone was also small and poor by world standards, but its population of 2,500,000, and its revenue and trade worth £14,000,000 ($39,000,000) and £45,000,000 ($126,000,000) a year respectively, placed it in a different category from the Gambia. Indeed, though small, it is both more populous and wealthier than some other independent African territories. For a long time its major problem was the political one of the competition for power between the Freetown creoles, descendants of the liberated slaves, who had hitherto had a virtual monopoly of influence and education, and the more numerous and less advanced peoples of the hinterland. Inevitably the latter eventually carried the day, but they did so under the calm leadership of Sir Milton Margai, a respected doctor who could also command confidence among the creoles, and his Sierra Leone People's Party.

Nigeria, of course, is the giant among the countries of West Africa. Indeed many of its problems stem essentially from its great size and from the resultant diversities among its enormous population. One consequence of this is that no one knows for certain just how big the population is. Attempts to take a census in 1962–3 were in effect sabotaged by politicians who, because the distribution of seats in the national Assembly was determined on a population basis, were anxious to claim as many people as they could for their own particular regions. The ultimately accepted figure of 57½ million was probably about 10 million too high. Even so, Nigeria is easily the most populous country on the African continent.

At the time of independence in 1960, its rulers also commanded economic resources (government revenues over £160,000,000 ($448,000,000) a year; foreign trade totalling some £350,000,000 ($980,000,000) a year) which in total were very much greater than those of any other West African territory. However, in relation to the size of the population, Nigeria was poorer than Ghana, which was appreciably the richest state in tropical Africa. Thus in Ghana, 6,700,000 people generated foreign trade worth about £225,000,000 ($630,000,000) a year, provided the government with revenues in excess of £100,000,000 ($280,000,000) a year, and shared a national income amounting to about £80 ($224) a head. The larger trade and government revenues of Nigeria had to be spread over a population seven times as large, and national income was probably rather less than £30 ($84) a head. Nevertheless Nigeria was not a poor country by West African standards. Higher national incomes were to be found only in Ghana, Senegal (with about £63 or $176 per head), and the Ivory Coast (with about £57 or $160 per head). Comparative figures for other territories were about £25 ($70) per head for Sierra Leone, the Gambia and Togo, and about £15 to £20 ($42 to $56) per head for the remainder.

Moreover, Nigeria's very size gave it unusual possibilities for development. It commanded a considerable range of natural resources, and its large population meant that it had sufficient consumers to provide a market large enough to encourage the establishment of many kinds of industry. But economic and social development could only proceed if constitutional and political development were sound also. Neither the British nor their Nigerian successors found it easy to evolve a satisfactory political and administrative machinery for so large and diverse a country and population. The colonial solution was regionalisation, with different policies and rates of development for the north and the south, with the poor and more populous north always lagging behind. The Nigerian politicians proved no more successful in achieving national unity. Azikiwe's N.C.N.C. came to receive most of its support from his native eastern Nigeria. This made it seem too much an Ibo party for many western Nigerians, particularly the Yoruba. A Yoruba reaction against it led to the formation of Chief Awolowo's Action Group. But neither of these parties was able to make much headway in Northern Nigeria, the most populous but least developed of the three principal regions of the country. Lagging behind the other regions, in education in particular, northerners feared domination by the more politically alive southerners. Moreover, the power of the Muslim emirs, protected by indirect rule, remained strong in a region largely sheltered from the social and economic changes taking place further south. The Northern People's Congress, which came to dominate northern politics, began life more as an association of traditional rulers desiring to preserve their interests and their country from over-rapid change (and able to instruct their subjects how they should vote) than as a nationalist political party.

By 1953 the regional and party differences in Nigeria had resulted in a virtual breakdown of effective central government. The N.C.N.C. and the Action Group vied with each other with promises of a rapid advance to self-government. But neither was able to command a majority in the Nigerian Assembly, where, on the basis of population, half the seats fell to suspicious and conservative northerners. Their leaders tended to withdraw from the national scene and to concentrate on the affairs of the regions which their parties could dominate. In 1954 it was at length agreed that if Nigeria was soon to advance to independence, it could only be as a federation in which each regional government had considerable autonomy. Full internal self-government was in fact first achieved in the regions, in the West and East in 1957, and by the North in 1959.

With each region now in command of its own destinies, there was a possibility that politics at the centre might become more harmonious, and in 1957 the deputy leader of the N.P.C., Alhaji Abubakar Tafawa Balewa, was able to take office as the first prime minister of the federation. (It is noteworthy that the leader of the N.P.C., the Sardauna of Sokoto—like both Azikiwe and Awolowo at that time—preferred office in his own region.) The two southern parties continued to compete with each other and for support in the north (both directly and by supporting democratic opposition to the aristocratic N.P.C.), and also by advocating the re-alignment of regional boundaries or the creation of completely new regions which they thought might decrease the power of the N.P.C. or increase that of their own party. But the commanding initiative was now with the N.P.C. Its leaders had been brought into touch with the intensity of nationalist feelings in the south, and intelligently appreciated the need for a truly national approach to independence. In 1960, it was

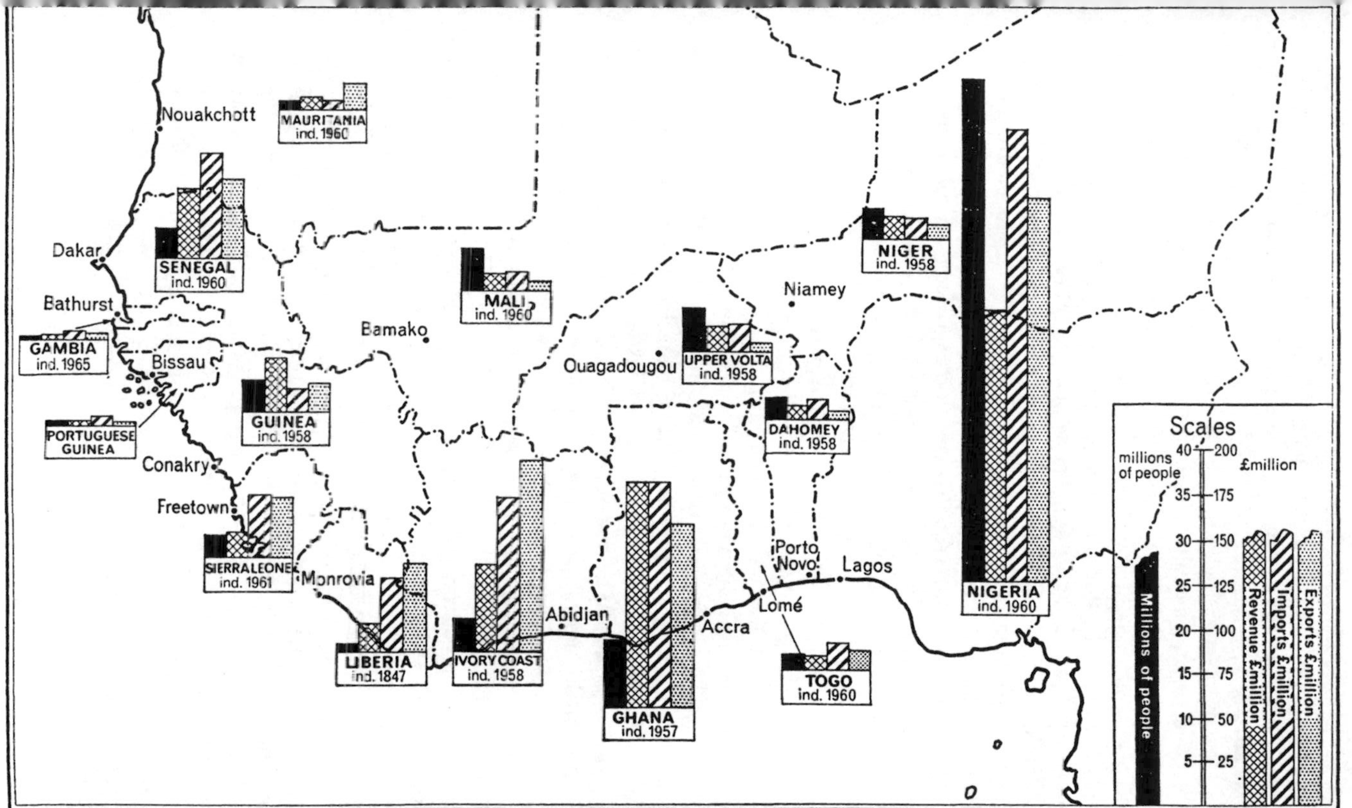

15 West Africa in the mid-1960s

Alhaji Sir Abubakar who became the first prime minister of an independent Nigeria, though his government was an N.P.C.–N.C.N.C. coalition, and Dr Azikiwe was shortly appointed to be the first African governor-general.

The controversies between the regions in Nigeria had their echoes in the Gold Coast, especially during 1954–6. There was little genuine case for federalism here; the country was too small. There was probably little deep general desire for it either. But the more conservative politicians combined with the traditional rulers in Ashanti, the Northern Territories and Togo to think that regional devolution might save something of their old influence from the ever growing power of the C.P.P. central government. But Nkrumah was determined that the Gold Coast should become independent as a single strong nation, pledged as one man to work for Pan-Africanism and the total redemption of Africa from colonialism. He would therefore tolerate no tribalism or factious opposition which would deter him from this goal. On the eve of independence, largely to placate British anxieties, a few concessions were made to the regions and to the chiefs. But with the C.P.P. consistently winning 70 per cent of the seats in the Assembly at general elections, and with the mass of the people benefiting from the continuing general prosperity of the country and the extensive development schemes undertaken by Nkrumah's government, there was no need for these concessions to be maintained after independence. The Gold Coast was now Ghana, named after the first of the great West African states of the past known to history. Between 1957 and 1960, Nkrumah completed his work of converting the former colonial possession into a single nation state totally dominated by his personality and his party. In 1960, Ghana, though remaining within the British commonwealth, became a republic and Nkrumah its president.

Under British administration, the Gold Coast and Nigeria had both included areas of former German territory under United Nations trusteeship. As these countries began to approach independence, the United Nations decided that the inhabitants of British Togo and the British Cameroons should decide their future by referendum. In 1956, British Togo voted to join with the new Ghana, but the position in the British Cameroons proved more difficult to evaluate. Eventually, however, the more northerly parts opted for incorporation in Northern Nigeria, while the more southerly parts chose to federate with the new Cameroun Republic (the former French trusteeship territory). The independence of the Togolese on the Ghana side of the frontier that divided them determined the French to proceed towards self-government for the Togolese still in their care. Eventually, in 1960, Sylvanus Olympio was able to lead his little country to complete independence.

The approach to self-government in French West Africa, 1946–60

The rapid advance of the British territories to self-government undoubtedly had its influence on the course of events in other parts of French West Africa besides Togo. Indeed, the independence gained by Ghana between 1948 and 1957 was the beginning of a revolution throughout Negro Africa which, by the end of 1961, had brought independence or the promise of it to almost all the African colonies except those in Portuguese or Spanish hands. But the legal position of the French West African colonies differed from that of the British territories in two important respects. Their colonial administrations were subordinate to a federal government, that at Dakar, which possessed considerable powers; and they were part of the French Union with their own representatives in the French legislature. It was generally assumed, by Africans as well as by Frenchmen, that the political advancement of the colonies would be secured by working from the top downwards. To this end, the African nationalists developed close associations with one or other of the political parties in France herself. Most of them were at first disappointed by the fact that the constitution finally adopted for France and the Union in 1946 turned out to be less favourable to the colonies than they had originally expected. Accordingly they joined together in a single federation-wide party, the Rassemblement Démocratique Africain[1] (R.D.A.), led by Félix Houphouët-Boigny of the Ivory Coast, which became closely linked with the French Communists, then the party most favourable to colonial aspirations. The only colony in which the R.D.A. did not dominate was Senegal. Here the Africans of the *communes* had long experience of representation in French parliaments, and Lamine Gueye was in the camp of the French Socialists. Gueye and a new younger leader, Léopold Senghor, representative of the Africans born outside the *communes* who had hitherto had no political rights, came to think that association with the Communists would be dangerous. Eventually Senghor took the lead with a new independent party, the Bloc Démocratique Sénégalais[2] (B.D.S.).

The Senegalese proved right. The Communists steadily lost ground in French politics, and the extremist agitations of the R.D.A. soon brought it into conflict with the French colonial administrations and led to the virtual suppression of the party (1948–50). As a result a number of other independent nationalist parties began to appear in the individual colonies. These Senghor tried to influence towards federalism, with the goal of establishing one, or at most two, strong federal republics within the French Union. But during 1954–6, the R.D.A., which had now severed its connection with the French Communists, began to regain ground. By

[1] African Democratic Convention. [2] Senegalese Democratic Bloc.

1956 its influence in French West Africa was such that its leader, Houphouët-Boigny, was appointed a minister in the French government in Paris. Here he had much to do with a vital shift in French colonial policy, helping to draft the *loi-cadre* ('outline law') of 1956. Under this it became possible for each separate French colony to have a constitution which, like that of the Gold Coast in 1951, permitted some executive power to pass to African ministers who were responsible to territorial assemblies, which were to be elected on a much wider franchise than before. Each territory was to have its own direct links with France, thus limiting the authority of the governor-general at Dakar.

The policy of the *loi-cadre* was hotly criticised, not only by Senghor and his supporters, but also within the R.D.A., and notably by Sékou Touré, a Guinean descendant of Samori and the organiser of a strong inter-territorial trades union movement. Like Nkrumah in Ghana, these critics felt that the ultimate goal of complete independence for Africa could not be properly achieved or maintained unless the African territories came together in units strong enough to withstand pressures from Europe. They thought that many of the individual French colonies were too small and poor compared to France for them to have any real autonomy within the French Union as separate states.

Then in 1958 de Gaulle was returned to power in France as a consequence of the failure of all previous French governments to cope satisfactorily with the problem of an Algeria which was fighting for its freedom from France. De Gaulle appreciated that the clock was rapidly running against colonialism, and he offered to all French colonies the choice, at a referendum, between immediate independence and full internal self-government, within a French 'Community'. This was to be much less dominated by France, and a much looser association than the Union, the member states having little more in common than a single policy for defence and external affairs. The majority of the R.D.A. came out in favour of the Community. With one exception, all the colonies voted for it, though a number chose it as a first step to complete independence. The exception was Guinea, where Houphouët-Boigny was presented as a French stooge, and where Sékou Touré asked for and got an all but unanimous vote in favour of independence. All French aid to Guinea was immediately stopped, and French administrators and technicians quickly withdrawn.

Guinea's decision not to take part in the Community led to the progressive weakening of the whole scheme as far as French Africa was concerned. In 1959, Senegal and the French Sudan decided to come together in the Federation of Mali, and asked for complete independence *within* the Community. When this was granted, the territories still within Houphouët-Boigny's influence—his own Ivory Coast, Dahomey, Niger, and Upper Volta—decided that they should seek complete independence of France before they would negotiate the terms of their association with her. When this also was conceded (1960), the French Community as de Gaulle had originally conceived it had largely disappeared.

Independent West Africa

By the end of 1961, almost all West African territories were legally free from European control, and were independent member states of the United Nations. The exceptions were the Gambia, whose independence, as has been seen, was delayed until 1965, and the Portuguese and Spanish territories.

The Spanish territories, collectively known as Spanish Guinea, were the Gulf of Guinea islands of Fernando Po and Annobon, and the 10,000 square miles of Rio Muni, on the mainland just south of the Cameroons. The latter is outside the geographical limits of this book, and little more need be said about Spanish Guinea here than that, in 1968, the Spaniards, following the general European trend, granted independence to their West African colonies.

Portuguese Guinea, however, remained as a total anachronism. Portugal had totally refused to countenance the claim of her colonial peoples to self-determination. She maintained the idea that Guinea and her other overseas possessions were not colonies at all, but provinces of Portugal overseas. Therefore, it was argued, the people of Portuguese Guinea were as independent as those of Portugal herself. But in fact there was little political freedom in Portugal, and for the Africans in Guinea the result was that they continued to be dominated and exploited by white Portuguese. Their only way out seemed to be to fight for their independence. When they were faced with the example of independent African states all around them, and could receive support from these states, such a fight eventually developed in Portuguese Guinea (as it did elsewhere in Portuguese Africa, in Angola and Moçambique). By the later 1960s, despite a considerable military effort by the Portuguese, it seemed that their effective control over mainland Guinea was limited to the larger towns.

Elsewhere in West Africa, of course, the winning of independence did not mean that there were no further problems to solve. Each country had to work out how it wished to be governed, to consider if, or to what extent, the political and administrative legacies of its former colonial rulers could be adapted to give efficient and honest government, by its own men, suitable to its own needs. The political and constitutional problems facing each country were often, indeed, formidable ones. Some of those facing the new rulers of Ghana and Nigeria (which in 1963 also became a republic) have already been touched upon. Indeed, all the new states were liable to experience major political and constitutional changes in their early years.

One dramatic crisis quickly occurred in the new Mali, where in 1960 the political leader of the former French Sudan, Modibo Keita, parted company with Senghor and the Senegal. The issue was partly one of political philosophy, Keita believing that a much more radical approach to the solution of economic and social problems was needed in African conditions than that favoured by Senghor. But this political difference was to a considerable extent due to the differing situations of their two territories. The inland territory of the former Sudan, which now kept the name of Mali for itself alone, was poorer and less developed than the Senegal. Keita and his government were therefore concerned at its dependence for its links with the outside world on the Senegal, especially since the latter's economy was still closely tied to that of France.

Another dramatic event was the union between Ghana and Guinea that was proclaimed after the latter's break with France in 1958, and which in 1960 was extended to include Mali also. The union never had much practical reality, except that Ghana provided Guinea with a timely loan to help see her through the immediate difficulties following upon the break with France, and it soon ceased to exist even on paper. The union, together with the Mali–Senegal quarrel and, indeed, many of the internal crises in the West African states during the 1960s (though not, perhaps, the most spectacular and tragic of these, Eastern Nigeria's secession from the Nigerian Federation in 1967 and the subsequent civil war in Nigeria), was really a political manifestation of West Africans' need to grapple with basic economic and social problems which were fundamentally far less easy to solve than the political and constitutional issues.

The period of colonial rule had brought to West Africa greater and more rapid changes than any other period in its history. The land and its peoples were brought into much closer touch with the rest of the world than ever before. They became, indeed, parts of a virtually universal civilisation. As such, they became aware of how much less well off they were materially than the pacemakers of this civilisation in Europe and North America, and they also became desperately anxious to try to catch up as fast as they could. Indeed, one of the dominant ideas lying behind their rejection of colonial status and colonial rule was the thought that colonial subjection and colonial policies, by their very nature, impeded their own advancement.

Political independence by itself could not make West Africa richer. Its peoples were still faced with the same problems of poorer soils, less—or less developed—natural resources of minerals and of energy, and poorer facilities to improve their standards of health and education and their general living standards than were possessed by more favoured nations in Europe and North America. Independence made them better off in that they now had freedom to concentrate on programmes of economic and social betterment, and freedom to choose what policies seemed best adapted towards this end, but they now had to work out for themselves how best to secure from the richer nations the aid—the capital and the skills—needed to get such programmes going.

Some of the new states had very little choice in the matter. Dahomey, Niger, the Volta Republic and the Gambia, for example, were hard put to it to cover the day-to-day costs of their independent governments, let alone to embark on any programmes of development. A number of the former French colonies, even the Senegal, depended to a greater or lesser extent on direct or indirect subsidies from France. Radical West African leaders like Sékou Touré, Keita and Nkrumah, noticing also the dependence of the West African states' economies on European or American markets, and the dominance of their trade by foreign trading companies (often, indeed, British and French companies), doubted whether many West African countries were in any real sense independent at all, and spoke of the threat of 'neo-colonialism'. Such men insisted on the need to trade with as many countries as possible, and to seek capital and technical aid from as many sources as possible, from the communists of eastern Europe and China, from the international agencies like the World Bank, from America, as well as from western European countries.

Such policies, however, though sound in principle, could not provide a quick or easy road to salvation, and they created problems of their own. Communist countries were as keen to extend their influence and interests in Africa as the old colonial powers were to retain theirs. Neither they nor the businessmen of the World Bank or of the United States were altruists inherently willing to give or to lend finance or technical assistance without requiring interest or imposing conditions. It was even possible that the former colonial powers might possess larger funds of basic goodwill towards their one-time colonies; it could certainly be argued that they had more practical experience of African conditions and needs. In the later 1960s, both Guinea and Mali were moving back into closer relations with France, while Ghana had provided an awful warning of what could happen if ambition were allowed to get out of touch with reality. Nkrumah's reckless financial administration had turned the richest nation in West Africa into its greatest debtor, and it had been a major factor in bringing about his rejection by the people he had led to independence.

Many of the economic problems facing West Africa might have been more easily dealt with had there been greater cooperation between its independent states. Few of these, for example, had enough consumers with enough purchasing power to afford adequate markets to support the development of local industries, especially heavy industries. Consequently they were apt either to saddle themselves with new industries which were to a greater or lesser degree uneconomic (as happened, for example, in Ghana under Nkrumah), or they had to remain dependent on foreigners for many of the manufactured goods, especially the capital goods—steel, machinery, etc.—which they needed.

But economic cooperation was not easy. The West African countries tended not to have complementary economies, but to compete with each other in the world markets with a few primary agricultural or mineral exports—for example, oil seeds or cocoa, or iron ore. Then their systems of communication were virtually all independent of each other, designed by the colonial rulers not to join the various territories together, but to get the produce of each quickly down to the coast for export to their own countries. Furthermore, the nationalist movements which had brought about independence for each colony had often brought about the dismantling of such organs of cooperation as had been introduced by the colonial powers.

The outstanding example was the federal machinery erected by the French for their colonies in West Africa. This had been destroyed at independence in part because the nationalist leaders in the various colonies had viewed it as one of the means by which they had been subjected to control from France. It had also, however, been a means by which the poorer French colonies could be aided from the surplus funds of the richer ones. But this too provided an argument why the federation should be dismantled, for the leaders and peoples of the richer colonies wanted to keep their surpluses for their own development plans. But the destruction of the Federation of French West Africa was not the only example. For the same sorts of reasons, the new leaders of the former British colonies opted out of such common agencies as they had had, establishing, for example, their own competing airlines and their own national currencies (each bringing its own problems of convertibility and of fluctuating exchanges).

However, by the later 1960s, it was becoming clearer to the West African peoples that the freedom of choice which they had gained through political independence encompassed more possibilities than were involved either in competing national states, or in essentially politically inspired unions—like the Ghana–Guinea–Mali union—to combat the threat of neo-colonialism. The political problems often remained intense, and the internal difficulties of the Federation of Nigeria were hardly a happy augury for programmes of closer cooperation to deal with the underlying economic and social problems perplexing all West Africa. Nevertheless there did seem to be a tendency to discard the single-minded nationalisms which had brought independence, and, with the support of truly international African organisations like the Economic Commission for Africa (E.C.A.) and the Organisation of African Unity (O.A.U.), to adopt broader approaches towards achieving the universal goal of a better life for all the people of West Africa.

A note on further reading

1. Introduction

The historical literature of West Africa is developing very rapidly, with many new books appearing every year. Some of these fill in important gaps, others replace older books. In order to keep in touch with these changes, and to keep abreast of the constant advances of research, it is essential to look regularly at the articles and book reviews in the journals mentioned at the end of the General Works section. All that is attempted in this note is to give a selection of the more important books which were available in 1969. Although it must be remembered that French is one of the principal languages of scholarship in West Africa, books in French are mentioned only when there is no satisfactory equivalent in English. Articles in periodicals are mentioned only when their subjects are not fully covered in book form. The full title of any book is given only once, subsequent references to it being by the author's name and a number: e.g. 3.11, which is book no. 11 in section 3, namely Bovill's *Golden Trade of the Moors*. Paperback editions are marked P.

2. General Works

An excellent general guide is (1) J. F. Ade Ajayi and Ian Espie, *A thousand years of West African history* (1965), with contributions by many authors, covering virtually every aspect of West African history, which are often by far the most useful short surveys of their subjects, and also giving useful short bibliographies. (2) Roland Oliver and J. D. Fage, *A short history of Africa* (3rd ed. 1969, P), will help to place West African history in relation to that of Africa as a whole. (3) J. D. Fage, *An atlas of African history* (1959), is useful for reference. (4) Basil Davidson, *Old Africa Rediscovered* (1959) is a brilliant, if somewhat enthusiastic, interpretation of the development of human society in Africa from the beginning to about the seventeenth century; the same author has also produced a very useful companion volume of documents, (5) *The African Past* (1964 P). For the geographical background so vital for an understanding of historical problems, see (6) W. B. Morgan and J. C. Pugh, *West Africa* (1969). There is really no good one-volume survey in English of the African peoples. (7) C. G. Seligman, *Races of Africa* (1966, P), though recently reissued in paperback, is in essentials still a book conceived forty years ago, and is now dangerously out of date; if used at all, it must be read together with (8) Joseph H. Greenberg, *The Languages of Africa* (1963). (9) G. P. Murdock, *Africa, its peoples and their culture history* (1959), is sometimes stimulating, but contentious and not always accurate. However the West African parts of (10) Daryll Forde (ed.) *The Ethnographic Survey of Africa* (various dates), are extremely valuable for reference.

There are now good one-volume histories of most of the English-speaking West African countries. For Nigeria, (11) Michael Crowder, *The story of Nigeria* (1962, P) and (12) Thomas Hodgkin, *Nigerian Perspectives* (1960), can both be strongly recommended; the latter is an excellent selection of documents with an introduction which is, in effect, a short but percipient history of Nigeria. For Ghana, the standard history, (13) W. E. F. Ward, *A history of Ghana* (1958 ed.), is a revision of a pioneer work of 1948 which is now being overtaken by recent research; the much shorter book by (14) J. D. Fage, *Ghana: a historical interpretation* (1959, P), may therefore be found useful. (15) J. E. Flint, *Ghana and Nigeria* (1967, P), is a very useful short history of both countries. (16) Christopher Fyfe, *A short history of Sierra Leone* (1962, P), will be found much more useful than his enormous (17) *A history of Sierra Leone* (1962), which only covers the period 1787–*c.* 1900. The most useful book on the Gambia is probably (18) Harry A. Gailey, *A history of the Gambia* (1964). Most histories of the French-speaking territories are naturally in French, but (19) John D. Hargreaves, *West Africa; the former French states* (1967, P), is a masterly short history in English, which also contains an excellent list of books for further reading in both languages. For histories of Liberia, the Portuguese colonies and the former German colonies, see sections 8, 12 and 11 respectively.

The importance of journals has already been stressed: (20) The *Journal of African History* (Cambridge University Press) is the prime vehicle for original articles based on new research, while the purpose of (21) *Tarikh* (Longmans) is to present recent developments in historical work in a form suited to non-specialists. The (22) *Transactions of the Historical Society of Ghana* and the (23) *Journal of the Historical Society of Nigeria*, together with some other of their publications, are of fundamental value. There are no exclusively historical journals for Sierra Leone and the French-speaking territories, but, for the former, (24) *Sierra Leone Studies*, and, for the latter, (25) the *Bulletin* (Series B) and (26) *Notes Africaines* of the Institut Fondamental d'Afrique Noire at Dakar, publish historical articles, as do the various (27) *Etudes* in some other French-speaking territories. The weekly (28) *West Africa* occasionally publishes historical articles, and is invaluable for recent developments.

3. Beginnings (chapter 1)

The books by Seligman and by Greenberg mentioned in the text have been given at 2.7 and 2.8. The only concise interpretation of West African prehistory is (1) Oliver Davies, *West Africa before the Europeans* (1967). However (2) Raymond Mauny's *Tableau géographique de l'Ouest africain au moyen age* (1961) is an absolutely indispensable assembly and critique of the written, traditional and archaeological sources for the West African past during *c.* A.D. 600–1400. The following books by archaeologists on significant adjacent areas will help to illuminate some of the arguments in chapter 1: (3) V. Gordon Childe, *New Light on the Most Ancient East* (4th ed. 1954) and (4) *What happened in history* (rev. ed. 1957, P); for Carthage, (5) Donald Harden, *The Phoenicians* (1962); for Nubia, (6) P. L. Shinnie, *Meroe* (1967). For the development of agriculture in West Africa, the views expressed by Murdock (2.9) must be read in conjunction with the series of articles collected in (7) *Journal of African History*, III, 2 (1962). For the Nok culture, see the article by (8) W. E. B. Fagg in *West African Review* (1956). For the Saharan peoples, see (9) L. Cabot Briggs, *Tribes of the Sahara* (1960); for early trans-Saharan trade, the article by (10) R. C. C. Law, 'The Garamantes and trans-Saharan enterprise in classical times', *J. Afr. Hist.*

VIII, 2 (1967) is vital. There is much on this latter subject also in (11) E. W. Bovill (with Robin Hallett), *The Golden Trade of the Moors* (2nd ed. 1968), which is the best general history of the western and central Sudan in English; it is important to use the second edition, which is extensively revised. This may usefully be supplemented by (12) J. S. Trimingham, *A history of Islam in West Africa* (1962), which is basically a history of the western and central Sudan written from Arabic and Islamic sources. For ancient Ghana, there are two useful articles: (13) Raymond Mauny, 'The question of Ghana', *Africa*, XXIV, and (14) J. D. Fage, 'Ancient Ghana, a review of the evidence', *Trans. Hist. Soc. Ghana*, III, 2 (1957); the latter gives extensive quotations from the contemporary sources. A useful statement of the Kisra legend may be found in an article by (15) A. B. Mathews in *African Studies*, IX (1950).

4. The states and empires of the western and central Sudan (chapter 2)

The foundation for historical studies of the western Sudan is (1) M. Delafosse, *Haut-Sénégal-Niger* (1912); the gist of this is given in English in the same author's (2) *The Negroes of Africa* (1931). These books now need to be read in the light of the modern works by Mauny (3.2), Bovill (3.11) and Trimingham (3.12) which have already been mentioned. For linguistic questions generally, and 'Nilo-Saharan' in particular, see Greenberg (2.8). The best studies of ancient Mali and of the Songhai empire of Gao are in French; the following are important: (3) V. Monteil, 'Les empires du Mali', a 150-page article in *Bulletin du Comité d'Etudes historiques et scientifiques de l'A.O.F.* (1929) now reprinted in book form (1968), (4) D. T. Niane, *Soundiata ou l'épopée Mandingue* (1960), and (5) Jean Rouch, *Contribution à l'histoire des Songhay* (1961). However, see also (6) N. Levtzion, 'The thirteenth and fourteenth century kings of Mali', *J. Afr. Hist.* IV, 3 (1963). For Bornu, the best account is (7) Y. Urvoy, *Histoire de l'empire du Bornou* (1949), and the same author's (8) *Histoire des populations du Soudan central* (1936) is also important, especially for Hausaland, though this is better covered in English; see especially (9) S. J. Hogben and A. H. M. Kirk-Greene, *The emirates of Northern Nigeria* (1966); M. G. Smith, 'The beginnings of Hausa society' in (10) *The historian in tropical Africa* (1964), J. Vansina, R. Mauny and L. V. Thomas (eds.), and (11) W. K. R. Hallam, 'The Bayajida legend in Hausa folklore', in *J. Afr. Hist.* VII, 1 (1966).

5. Influences from the Sudan (chapter 3)

Books already mentioned by Mauny (3.2), Fage (2.14), Hodgkin (2.12) and Crowder (2.11) are relevant for this chapter. On the Fulani dispersion see the introduction by (1) H. Labouret to his *La langue des Peuls* (1955). On the Mane, see (2) Walter Rodney 'A reconsideration of the Mane invasions of Sierra Leone', *J. Afr. Hist.* VIII, 2 (1967). (3) Ivor Wilks, *The northern factor in Ashanti history* (1961), (4) Jack Goody, 'The Mande and the Akan hinterland' in 4.10 and (5) E. L. R. Meyerowitz, *Akan traditions of origin* (1952) are all relevant to the expansion of Mande influence to the south-east; this and the spread of influences from the Hausaland–Lake Chad area to the south-west are also discussed in (6) J. D. Fage, 'Some thoughts on migration and urban settlement' in *Urbanisation and Migration in West Africa*, ed. Hilda Kuper (1965). There is important information about the Guinea coastlands *c.* 1500 in (7) Pacheco Pereira, *Esmeraldo de Situ Orbis*, English ed. by G. H. T. Kimble (1937), and a better edition in French by R. Mauny (1956). On Mossi, Dagomba etc., see (8) J. D. Fage, 'Reflections on the early history of the Mossi–Dagomba group of states' in 4.10. A valuable modern treatment of Yoruba history is (9) Robert Smith, *Kingdoms of the Yoruba* (1969), but for traditional history see also the pioneer work by (10) Samuel Johnson, *History of the Yorubas* (1921); (11) William Fagg, *Nigerian Images* (1963) and (12) Frank Willett, *Ife in the history of West African art* (1967) are beautifully illustrated books which are essential to an understanding of the historical culture of the Yorubaland–Benin area. (13) P. C. Lloyd, 'Sacred kingship and government among the Yoruba', *Africa*, XXX (1960), is an important article, so are (14) R. E. Bradbury, 'Chronological problems in the study of Benin history', *J. Hist. Soc. Nig.* I, 4 (1959), and the same author's (15) 'The historical uses of comparative ethnography with reference to Benin and the Yoruba', in 4.10.

6. European activities before the nineteenth century (chapters 4 and 5)

The background to the European arrival on the West African coasts is treated in Bovill, 3.11, but the really essential book on the beginnings of European expansion overseas is (1) J. H. Parry, *The Age of Reconnaissance* (1963). The West African aspects of this are more fully covered in two books by J. W. Blake, (2) *European beginnings in West Africa, 1451–1578* (1937) and (3) *Europeans in West Africa, 1450–1560* (1942), the latter being two volumes of contemporary documents with excellent editorial matter. Other important early sources are (4) G. E. Azurara, *The conquests and discoveries of Henry the Navigator*, an abridged version in English ed. V. de Castro e Almeida (1936), and a much better version in French, G. E. de Zurara, *Chronique de Guinée*, ed. L. Bourdon and R. Picard (1960); (5) G. R. Crone (ed.), *The voyages of Cadamosto and other documents*, (1937); and the editions of Pacheco Pereira mentioned at 5.7. For the seventeenth and eighteenth centuries, the most important contemporary sources are (6) P. de Marees, *Description of Guinea* (1601; abridged English translation in vol. VI of *Purchas His Pilgrimes*, 1905; new full translation by K. Y. Daaku awaited); (7) O. Dapper, *Description of Africa* (1668 in Dutch; no modern edition; but French version published in 1686); and (8) W. Bosman, *A new and accurate description of the coast of Guinea* (1701), ed. J. R. Willis, J. D. Fage and R. E. Bradbury (1967)—this contains Nyendael's account of Benin. On Benin, see (9) R. E. Bradbury, *The Kingdom of Benin* (1957), and the same author's articles mentioned at 5.13 and 5.14; the traditional history of Benin is set out in (10) Jacob U. Egharevba, *A short history of Benin* (3rd ed. 1960).

The background to the European competition for trade and empire in the Atlantic may be gathered from (11) C. R. Boxer, *The Dutch seaborne empire, 1600–1800* (1965), (12) G. S. Graham, *Empire of the North Atlantic* (1950), and from two chapters in the *New Cambridge Modern History*, (13) ch. XXIV. 1, in vol. VII, by J. Gallagher, and (14) ch. VIII. 2, in vol. VIII, by J. D. Hargreaves. For the effects of this in West Africa, (15) Elizabeth Donnan, *Documents illustrative of the slave trade to America* (1930–5) is invaluable, and (16) H. A. Wyndham, *The Atlantic and Slavery* (1935) is also useful. (17) A. W. Lawrence, *Trade castles and forts of West Africa* (1963) is the standard work on its subject, and is excellently illustrated. (18) K. G. Davies, *The Royal African Company*

(1957), and (19) Evelyn C. Martin, *The British West African Settlements, 1750–1821*, are essential for British activities, while French activities are excellently summarised in the book by Hargreaves, 2.19.

7. West Africa and the Atlantic slave trade (chapters 6 and 7)

Any consideration of the Atlantic slave trade and its effects must start with (1) Philip D. Curtin, *Dimensions of the Atlantic Slave Trade* (1969); his tables of statistics supersede all earlier estimates, and his comments on them are invaluable. Population data for Africa in the twentieth century are briefly set out in the United Nations survey (2) *World Population Prospects* (1966). For the operations of the trade in West Africa, see the books already mentioned by Donnan (6.15) and Wyndham (6.16); on the business side of the trade, and on prices, an important article is (3) Marion Johnson's 'The ounce in eighteenth century West African trade', *J. Afr. Hist.* VII, 2 (1966). The general effects of the trade on the economies and societies of West Africa have been relatively little studied, though an outstanding exception is (4) Basil Davidson, *Black Mother* (1961). There has also been relatively little historical study of slavery in West African society, though there is an important article (5) by Walter Rodney, 'African slavery and other forms of social oppression on the Upper Guinea coast in the context of the Atlantic slave trade' in *J. Afr. Hist.* VII, 3 (1966), and types of servitude in Ashanti are set out in chapter VI of (6) R. S. Rattray, *Ashanti Law and Constitution* (1929).

For the individual states of lower Guinea in the slave-trade period, there is important material in contemporary works already cited by Dapper (6.7) and Bosman (6.8); the reported attitudes towards the slave trade of Kings Kpengla of Dahomey and Osei Bonsu of Ashanti will be found respectively in (7) Archibald Dalzel, *The History of Dahomy* (1793; 1967 reprint with introduction by J. D. Fage) and (8) Joseph Dupuis, *Journal of a residence in Ashantee* (1824); the latter and (9) T. E. Bowdich, *A mission from Cape Coast to Ashantee* (1819), were reprinted in 1966 with introductions by W. E. F. Ward. Bowdich and Dupuis were the first to record traditional Ashanti history (their work is critically examined by Wilks in 5.3); a later and fuller version is given by (10) Sir Francis Fuller, *A vanished dynasty: Ashanti* (1921). Important modern studies are (11) Margaret Priestley and Ivor Wilks, 'The Ashanti kings in the nineteenth century', *J. Afr. Hist.* I, 1 (1960); (12) Wilks, 'Aspects of bureaucratization in Ashanti in the nineteenth century', *J. Afr. Hist.* VII, 2 (1966); and Wilks, 'Ashanti government' in (13) Daryll Forde and P. M. Kaberry (eds.), *West African kingdoms in the nineteenth century* (1967). For the states of the Gold Coast generally at this time, (14) K. Y. Daaku, *Gold, Guns and the Gold Coast* (1969), is essential; for Akwamu, see (15) Ivor Wilks, 'The rise of the Akwamu empire, 1650–1710', *Trans. Hist. Soc. Ghana* III, 2 (1957).

There is a stimulating study by (16) I. A. Akinjogbin, *Dahomey and its neighbours, 1708–1818* (1967), which, incidentally, is very critical of Dalzel (7.7). For Oyo, in addition to works already cited by Smith (5.9), Johnson (5.10) and Lloyd (5.13), there is important material in (17) R. S. S. Smith, 'The *Alafin* in exile', *J. Afr. Hist.*, VI, 1 (1965), and in (18) Peter Morton-Williams, 'The Yoruba kingdom of Oyo', in 7.13. The essential references for Benin have already been given at 5.14, 5.15, 6.9 and 6.10.

8. The anti-slave-trade movement and the early British colonies (chapters 8 and 9)

The standard study of (1) *The British anti-slavery movement* is still the 1933 book with this title by Sir Reginald Coupland (reprinted in 1964 with introduction by J. D. Fage); it should be considered in the light of the views expressed in (2) Eric Williams, *Capitalism and Slavery* (1944), and (3) G. R. Mellor, *British Imperial Trusteeship, 1783–1850* (1951). On the naval campaign against the slave trade, see (4) Christopher Lloyd, *The Navy and the Slave Trade* (1949). On the early European exploration, two books by Robin Hallett are valuable, (5) his edition of *The Records of the African Association* (1964), and (6) his *The Penetration of Africa up to 1815* (1965); these should be considered together with the important work by (7) A. Adu Boahen, *Britain, the Sahara and the western Sudan, 1788–1861* (1964), while the early commercial penetration of the Niger is one of the themes of (8) K. Onwuka Dike, *Trade and Politics in the Niger Delta, 1830–85* (1956). Extracts from the explorers' own accounts are given in (9) C. Howard and J. H. Plumb, *West African Explorers* (1951). (10) Philip D. Curtin's *The Image of Africa* (1964) is an important study of British ideas concerning, and actions in, West Africa between 1780 and 1850.

For the early history of the settlement of Sierra Leone, see the two books by Christopher Fyfe mentioned at 2.16 and 2.17. There are a number of histories of Liberia, none of which is wholly satisfactory; however (11) R. L. Buell, *Liberia; a century of survival, 1848–1947* (1948), and (12) Sir Harry Johnston, *Liberia* (1906) may be found useful, while (13) P. J. Staudenraus, *The American Colonization Movement* (1961) is standard for Liberia's foundation. On the Christian missions, (14) C. P. Groves, *The Planting of Christianity in Africa* (1948–58) is the standard general account, while (15) J. F. Ade Ajayi, *Christian Missions in Nigeria, 1841–91* is an important special study. (16) F. H. Hilliard, *A short history of education in British West Africa* (1957) provides a useful outline of its subject. The study by (17) Hollis R. Lynch, *Edward W. Blyden, Pan-Negro Patriot* (1967), throws important lights on Liberia, Sierra Leone and the early educated elite.

The history of the British colonies individually during 1808–74 can be studied in the books by Fyfe (2.16, 2.17), Ward (2.13), Crowder (2.11) and Gailey (2.18). (18) C. W. Newbury, *British policy towards West Africa, 1786–1874* (1965), is an invaluable collection of the essential documents. The study of the Gold Coast (i.e. modern Ghana) during this period has been greatly advanced by G. E. Metcalfe; (19) his *Great Britain and Ghana* (1964) collects together documents for the period 1807–1957, and has pithy introductions for each period; his (20) *Maclean of the Gold Coast* (1962) is essential reading, and mention should also be made of his article (21) 'After Maclean', in *Trans. Hist. Soc. Ghana*, 1, 5 (1955). (22) David Kimble's *A political history of Ghana, 1850–1928* (1963) is an important book, and (23) Douglas Coombs, *The Gold Coast, Britain and the Netherlands, 1850–1874* (1963) is of considerable interest. Nigeria, of course, was less 'colonised' at this stage. In addition to the books by Dike (8.8) and Ajayi (8.15) already mentioned, there is a very useful study by (24) C. W. Newbury of *The Western Slave Coast and its rulers* (1961) during the nineteenth century, and mention should also be made of (25) K. Onwuka Dike's article 'John Beecroft, 1849–54', in *J. Hist. Soc. Nig.* 1, 1 (1956).

9. The Islamic revolution and West African kingdoms in the nineteenth century (chapter 10)

(1) *Islam in tropical Africa*, ed. by I. M. Lewis (1966), is a collection of essays by many hands, some of which are very relevant. The section on (2) 'The nineteenth century *jihads*' by J. O. Hunwick in 2.1 is a perceptive summary; other useful articles are (3) H. F. C. Smith, 'A neglected theme of West African history: the Islamic revolution of the nineteenth century', in *J. Hist. Soc. Nig.* II, 2 (1961); (4) M. Hiskett, 'Material relating to the state of learning among the Fulani before their *jihad*', *Bulletin of S.O.A.S.* XIX, 3 (1957); (5) Marilyn Waldman, 'The Fulani *jihad*; a reassessment', *J. Afr. Hist.* VI, 3 (1965); and (6) John R. Willis, '*Jihad Fi Sabil Allah:* its doctrinal basis in Islam, and some aspects of its evolution in nineteenth century West Africa', *J. Afr. Hist.* VII, 3 (1966). There is also good material in Hodgkin's anthology (2.12), and a somewhat pedestrian general treatment of the subject in Trimingham (3.12).

On (7) *West African kingdoms in the nineteenth century*, the collection of essays with this title edited by Daryll Forde and P. M. Kaberry (1967) is extremely useful, especially for Benin (R. E. Bradbury), Oyo (P. Morton-Williams), Hausa (M. G. Smith), Gonja (J. R. Goody), and Ashanti (Ivor Wilks). To this should be added for Hausaland: (8) M. G. Smith, *Government in Zazzau* (1960); for Yorubaland: the books by Smith (5.9) and Newbury (8.24) already mentioned, (9) S. O. Biobaku, *The Egba and their neighbours* (1957), and (10) J. F. Ade Ajayi and Robert Smith, *Yoruba warfare in the nineteenth century* (1964); and for the Oil Rivers, in addition to Dike (8.8), (11) G. I. Jones, *The trading states of the Oil Rivers* (1963). Hargreaves (2.19) provides excellent short accounts of Macina, El-Hajj 'Umar and Samori, and refers to the relevant literature in French.

10. French activities and the scramble for colonies (chapter 11)

John Hargreaves's book (2.19) provides by far the best treatment in English of early nineteenth century French colonisation, and (1) his *Prelude to the partition of West Africa* (1963) is absolutely indispensable. The accepted full-scale study of the partition as a whole is (2) R. E. Robinson and John Gallagher, *Africa and the Victorians* (1961); their interpretation is, however, controversial, especially perhaps with regard to West Africa, and their book should be read together with such critiques of it as (3) Jean Stengers, 'L'impérialisme colonial de la fin du XIXe siècle: mythe ou réalité?' and (4) C. W. Newbury, 'Victorians, Republicans, and the partition of West Africa', both in *J. Afr. Hist.* III, 3 (1962), and also with (5) Henri Brunschwig, *Mythes et réalités de l'impérialisme colonial français, 1870–1914* (1960). The contemporary account by (6) J. Scott Keltie, *The partition of Africa* (2nd ed. 1895), is useful, as is the selection of readings edited by (7) Raymond F. Betts, *The 'Scramble' for Africa* (1966, P). (8) Mary E. Townsend, *The rise and fall of the German colonial empire, 1884–1914* (1930) is perhaps the most useful of a number of books dealing with the argument on Germany's irruption into the colonial field (but see 11.17 below). Specific West African aspects of the scramble are covered in books by Dike (8.8) and Newbury (8.24) already mentioned, and in the following biographies: (9) John E. Flint, *Sir George Goldie and the making of Nigeria* (1960); (10) Margery Perham,

Lugard (1956–60); and (11) Roland Oliver, *Sir Harry Johnston and the scramble for Africa* (1957). (12) Sybil E. Crowe, *The Berlin West African Conference* (1942), is a standard study of its subject.

11. The colonial period (chapter 12)

There are encyclopaedic surveys of colonial policy in Africa in two classics, (1) Lord Hailey, *An African Survey* (2nd ed. 1957), and (2) R. L. Buell, *The native problem in Africa* (1928), while (3) S. H. Frankel, *Capital investment in Africa* (1938) is the prime source of Hailey's economic information. For the French side, in addition to Hargreaves (2.19), there are (4) S. H. Roberts, *The history of French colonial policy, 1870–1925* (1929); and (5) the important V. Thompson and R. Adloff, *French West Africa* (1958); a useful little book by (6) Michael Crowder, *Senegal: a study in French assimilation policy* (1962, P); and (7) Raymond F. Betts, *Assimilation and Association in French colonial theory, 1890–1914.* (8) Robert Delavignette, *Freedom and authority in French West Africa* (1950) is by a former colonial official.

On the British side, the legislative councils have been studied by Martin Wight, (9) *The Legislative Council, 1606–1945* (1946), and (10) *The Gold Coast Legislative Council* (1947), and by (11) Joan Wheare, *The Nigerian Legislative Council* (1950). For indirect rule, the starting point is (12) Lord Lugard's *The Dual Mandate* (1922), recently reprinted with an introduction by Dame Margery Perham, to which may be added the latter's life of Lugard (10.10), and her (13) *Native administration in Nigeria* (1962 ed.). For the Gold Coast, in addition to Kimble's monumental work (8.22), (14) R. E. Wraith's biography of *Guggisberg* (1967) is important, and both (15) F. M. Bourret, *Ghana; the road to independence, 1919–1957* (1960), and (16) William Tordoff, *Ashanti under the Prempehs, 1888–1935* (1965), are very useful.

For the German colonies, there is (17) Harry R. Rudin, *Germans in the Cameroons* (1938), and much useful material in (18) Prosser Gifford and Wm. Roger Louis (eds.), *Britain and Germany in Africa* (1967). On the economic side, in addition to Frankel (11.3), (19) W. K. Hancock, *A Survey of British Commonwealth affairs*, vol. II (1942) is essential. To this may be added (20) Polly Hill, *The Gold Coast cocoa farmer* (1956, P), (21) P. T. Bauer, *West African Trade* (1954), and (22) N. A. Cox-George, *Finance and development in West Africa; the Sierra Leone experience* (1961). See also the book by Kamarck (12.1).

12. The regaining of independence (chapter 13)

The economic background to independence is very usefully set out in (1) Andrew M. Kamarck, *The economics of African development* (1967, P), which covers the period since *c.* 1945, and which contains invaluable bibliographies. On the social side, (2) P. C. Lloyd, *Africa in social change* (1967, P), will be found very useful. For the politics of West African independence generally, the following are essential reading: Thomas Hodgkin's (3) *Nationalism in colonial Africa* (1956) and (4) *African political parties* (1961, P), and (5) Ken Post's *The new states of West Africa* (1964, P). (6) John Hatch, *A History of post-war Africa* (1965), (7) Ronald Segal, *Political Africa* (1961, with abridged paperback edition, *African Profiles*, 1962, P), and (8) Colin Legum (ed.), *Africa; a hand-*

book to the continent (1962) are all informative, and the latter's (9) *Pan-Africanism; a short political guide* (1962) may also be found useful.

There are a number of important books on Ghana and Nigeria, of which the following may perhaps be singled out for Ghana: (10) Dennis Austin, *Politics in Ghana, 1946–1960* (1964) which is essential reading, (11) *The report of the (Watson) Commission of Enquiry into disturbances in the Gold Coast* (1948—a vital document), (12) J. G. Amamoo, *The new Ghana* (1958, P), and, of course, the writings of Kwame Nkrumah, but especially (13) his autobiography, *Ghana* (1957, P); for Nigeria: (14) James S. Coleman, *Nigeria; background to nationalism* (1958), which is essential, (15) the Royal Institute of International Affairs, *Nigeria; the political and economic background* (1960, P), and books by the three principal political leaders, (16) Awolowo's autobiography *Awo* (1960), (17) Azikiwe's collection of speeches in *Zik* (1960), and (18) Sir Ahmadu Bello's *My Life* (1962). For Sierra Leone, the important modern study is (19) Martin Kilson, *Political change in a West African state; a study of the modernization process in Sierra Leone* (1966).

For the former French territories, in addition to Thompson and Adloff's book (11.5), the following are outstanding works in English: (20) Ruth Schachter Morgenthau, *Political parties in French-speaking Africa* (1964); (21) Aristide R. Zolberg, *One-party government in the Ivory Coast* (1964); (22) Gwendolen Carter (ed.), *African one-party states* (1962), which includes chapters on Senegal by Ernest Milcent, Guinea by L. Gray Cowan, and the Ivory Coast by Virginia Thompson (and also a useful chapter on Liberia by J. Gus Liebenow). There is an important book by (23) Sékou Touré, *Expérience guinéene et unité africaine* (n.d.), and a work by (24) Léopold Senghor, *On African Socialism* (1964), is available in English. Useful comparative studies are Immanuel Wallersteins's (25) *The road to independence: Ghana and the Ivory Coast* (1965) and (26) *Africa; the politics of independence* (1961, P), and the symposium edited by James S. Coleman and Carl G. Rosberg, (27) *Political parties and national integration in tropical Africa* (1964), which includes contributions on Cameroun, Ghana, Guinea, Ivory Coast, Liberia, Mali, Nigeria, Senegal and Sierra Leone.

For the Portuguese colonies, there are two good books by James Duffy, (28) *Portuguese Africa* (1959) and (29) *Portugal in Africa* (1962, P); (30) Ronald H. Chilcote, *Portuguese Africa* (1967, P) is useful for very recent history. On the Spanish territories, see (31) René Pelissier, *Les territoires espagnoles d'Afrique*, a pamphlet of La Documentation Française (1963).

Index

Gregg Revivals

Contents

Forthcoming series

Modern Revivals in Music Studies

Authors wishing to submit titles for inclusion in any of the listed series should send them to the Editor, Gregg Revivals, White Swan House, Godstone, Surrey RH9 8LW.

Orders to:
Ashgate Distribution Services
Unit 3, Lower Farnham Road, Aldershot, Hants, GU12 4DY

Books are available in hardback only.
All books are in metric Demy 8vo format, 216 × 138 approx, unless otherwise stated.

MODERN REVIVALS IN HISTORY
Series Editor: Michael Collinge

Michael Prestwich
War, Politics and Finance under Edward I (0 7512 0000 X)
William Lamont
Puritanism and the English Revolution
Vol I: Marginal Prynne, 1600–1669 (0 7512 0001 8)
Vol II: Godly Rule: Politics and Religion, 1603–1660 (0 7512 0002 6)
Vol III: Richard Baxter and the Millennium (0 7512 0003 4)
Set (0 7512 0004 2)
Henry Cohn
The Government of the Rhine Palatinate in the Fifteenth Century (0 7512 0005 0)
Robin Law
The Oyo Empire c. 1600–c. 1836: A West African imperialism in the era of the Atlantic Slave Trade (0 7512 0006 9)
Jeremy Black
The English Press in the Eighteenth Century (0 7512 0007 7)
Patrick Joyce
Work, Society and Politics: the culture of the factory in later Victorian England (0 7512 0008 5)
Keith Middlemas
Diplomacy of Illusion: The British Government and Germany, 1937–1939 (0 7512 0009 3)
Charles Brand
Byzantium confronts the West, 1180–1204 (0 7512 0053 0)
John Kenyon
Robert Spencer Earl of Sunderland 1641–1702 (0 7512 0055 7)
Peter Thomas
The House of Commons in the Eighteenth Century (0752 0054 9)

Doreen Rosman
Evangelicals and Culture (0 7512 0056 5)
Avner Offer
Property and Politics 1870–1914: Landownership, Law, Ideology and Urban Development in England (0 7512 0066 2)
Robert McKenzie
British Political Parties: The Distribution of Power within the Conservative and Labour Parties (0 7512 0067 0)
Michael Hunter
Science and Society in Restoration England (0 7512 0075 1)
Jonathan Steinberg
Yesterday's Deterrent: Tirpitz and the Birth of the German Battle Fleet (0 7512 0076 X)

Forthcoming

Peter Dickson
The Financial Revolution in England: a study of the development of public credit, 1688–1756 (0 7512 0010 7)
Roger Anstey
The Atlantic Slave Trade and British Abolition, 1760–1810 (0 7512 0112 X)
F B Smith
The Making of the Second Reform Bill (0 7512 0113 8)

MODERN REVIVALS IN PHILOSOPHY

Series Editor: Dr David Lamb

David Archard
Marxism and Existentialism: The Political Philosophy of Sartre and Merleau-Ponty (0 7512 0051 4)
L Jonathan Cohen
The Probable and the Provable (0 7512 0011 5)
David E Cooper
Authenticity and Learning: Nietzche's Educational Philosophy (0 7512 0012 3)
Jorge A Larrain
Marxism and Ideology (0 7512 0013 1)
Jorge A Larrain
A Reconstruction of Historical Materialism (0 7512 0048 4)
Jorge A Larrain
The Concept of Ideology (0 7512 0049 2)
D G C Macnabb
David Hume: His Theory of Knowledge and Morality (0 7512 0014 X)
Richard J Norman
Hegel's Phenomenology: A Philosophical Introduction (0 7512 0015 8)
Anthony O'Hear
Experience Explanation and Faith (new introduction) (0 7512 0052 2)
John O'Neill
Sociology as a Skin Trade: essays towards a reflexive sociology (0 7512 0016 6)
John O'Neill (ed)
Modes of Individualism and Collectivism (0 7512 0050 6)
Stephen Priest (ed)
Hegel's Critique of Kant (0 7512 0064 6)
R A Sharpe
Contemporary Aesthetics (0 7512 0017 4)
George J Stack
Kierkegaard's Existential Ethics (0 7512 0018 2)

George J Stack
Sartre's Philosophy of Social Existence (0 7512 0058 1)
W H Walsh
Metaphysics (0 7512 0019 0)
W H Walsh
Reason and Experience (0 7512 0020 4)
Deirdre Wilson
Presuppositions and Non-Truth–Conditional Semantics (0 7512 0021 2)

MODERN REVIVALS IN ECONOMICS
Series Editor: Professor Mark Blaug

Mark Blaug
An Introduction to the Economics of Education (0 7512 0022 0)
Mark Casson
The Entrepreneur: An Economic Theory (0 7512 0023 9)
Mark Casson
Multinationals and World Trade: Vertical Integration and the Division of Labour in World Industries (0 7512 0024 7)
A J Culyer
The Political Economy of Social Policy (0 7512 0025 5)
John Cullis and Peter West
The Economics of Health: An Introduction (0 7512 0026 3)
G C Harcourt
Some Cambridge controversies in the theory of capital (0 7512 0027 1)
Ian Steedman
Fundamental Issues in Trade Theory (0 7512 0028 X)
Carl Shoup
Ricardo on Taxation (0 7512 0060 3)
Melvin L Greenhut
A Theory of the Firm in Economic Space (0 7512 0074 3)
T W Hutchison
The Politics and Philosophy of Economics: Marxians, Keynesians and Austrains (0 7512 0089 1)
T W Hutchison
'Positive' Economics and Policy Objectives (0 7512 0090 5)
T W Hutchison
Economics and Economic Policy in Britain 1946 – 1966: some aspects of their inter-relations (0 7512 0091 3)
T W Hutchison
On revolutions and progress in economic knowledge (0 7512 0093 X)
J Creedy and D P O'Brien (eds)
Economic Analysis in Historical Perspective (0 7512 0088 3)
D P O'Brien
J R McCulloch: A Study in Classical Economics (0 7512 0096 4)
D M Nuti (ed)
V K Dmitriev: Economic Essays on Value, Competition and Utility (0 7512 0095 6)
J C Dodds and J L Ford
Expectations, Uncertainty and the Term Structure of Interest Rates (0 7512 0097 2)
J L Ford and S Sen
Protectionism, Exchange Rates and the Macroeconomy (0 7512 0098 0)
Mark Blaug (ed)
The Economics of the Arts (0 7512 0099 9)

MODERN REVIVALS IN MILITARY HISTORY

Series Editor: Professor Brian Bond

Brian Bond
Liddell Hart: a study of his Military Thought (new preface) (0 7512 0029 8)
Michael Howard
Studies in War and Peace (0 7512 0030 1)
Charles Carrington
Soldier from the Wars Returning (new preface) (0 7512 0031 X)
Sir Ian Hamilton
The Soul and Body of an Army (new preface) (0 7512 0032 8)
Sir William Robertson
Soldiers and Statesmen, (new preface) (2 vols)
Vol I (0 7512 0033 6)
Vol II (0 7512 0034 4)
Set (0 7512 0035 2)
Charles à Court Repington
The First World War, (new preface) (2 vols)
Vol I (0 7512 0036 0)
Vol II (0 7512 0037 9)
Set (0 7512 0038 7)
Spenser Wilkinson
The Rise of General Bonaparte (new preface) (0 7512 0039 5)
Spenser Wilkinson
Moltke's Military Correspondence, 1870–1871 (new preface) (0 7512 0040 9)
Spenser Wilkinson
The French Army Before Napoleon (new preface) (0 7512 0043 3)
Spenser Wilkinson
The Brain of an Army
The Command of the Sea
The Brain of the Navy (new preface) (0 7512 0081 6)
I S Bloch
Is War Now Impossible? Being an Abridgement of the War of the Future in its Technical, Economic and Political Relations (0 7512 0041 7)
R J Minney
The Private Papers of Hore-Belisha (0 7512 0042 5)
Sir Archibald Wavell
Allenby: A Study in Greatness (new preface) (0 7512 0061 1)
Allenby in Egypt (new preface) (0 7512 0062 X)
Set: (0 7512 0063 8)

MODERN REVIVALS IN SOCIOLOGY

Series Editor: Professor Chris Bryant

Chris Jenks (ed)
The Sociology of Childhood: Essential Readings (0 7512 0044 1)
Zygmunt Bauman
Hermeneutics and Social Science: Approaches to Understanding (0 7512 0045 X)
Howard Parker
View From The Boys: A Sociology of Down-Town Adolescents (new preface) (0 7512 0046 8)
Nicholas Spykman
The Social Theory of Georg Simmel (0 7512 0047 6)

Daniel Lawrence
Black Migrants: White Natives. A Study of Race Relations in Nottingham (0 7512 0057 3)

Peter Halfpenny
Positivism and Sociology: Explaining Social Life (0 7512 0059 X)

William Outhwaite & Michael Mulkay (eds)
Social Theory and Social Criticism: Essays for Tom Bottomore (0 7512 0073 5)

J D Y Peel
Herbert Spencer: The Evolution of a Sociologist (0 7512 0094 8)

Michael Mulkay
Functionalism, exchange and theoretical strategy (0 7512 0103 0)

Michael Mulkay
Science and the sociology of knowledge (0 7512 0104 9)

Michael Banton
Racial and Ethnic Competition (0 7512 0110 3)

MODERN REVIVALS IN AFRICAN STUDIES

Series Editor: Anthony Kirk-Greene

Geoffrey Kay (ed)
The Political Economy of Colonialism in Ghana: A Collection of Documents and Statistics, 1900 – 1960 (new introduction)
(0 7512 0079 4)

E A Brett
Colonialism and Underdevelopment in East Africa: The Politics of Economic Change, 1919 – 1939 (0 7512 0080 8)

Colin Newbury
British Policy Towards West Africa: Select Documents
Vol I: 1786 – 1874
Vol II: 1875 – 1914 (with Statistical Appendices 1800 – 1914)
Set (0 7512 0084 0)

Christopher Fyfe
A History of Sierra Leone (new introduction) (0 7512 0086 7)

Christopher Fyfe
Africanus Horton: West African Scientist and Patriot (new introduction)
(0 7512 0085 9)

Martin S Kisch
Letters and Sketches from Northern Nigeria (new introduction) (0 7512 0087 5)

J D Fage
A History of West Africa: An Introductory Survey (0 7512 0102 2)

MODERN REVIVALS IN ECONOMIC AND SOCIAL HISTORY

Series Editor: Professor Chris Wrigley

Chris Wrigley
David Lloyd George and the British Labour Movement (0 7512 0072 7)

Stanley Chapman
The Rise of Merchant Banking (0 7512 0077 8)

Stanley Chapman
The Early Factory Masters: The Transition of the Factory in the Midlands Textile Industry (new introduction) (0 7512 0078 6)

D E Moggridge
British Monetary Policy 1924 – 1931: The Norman Conquest of $4.86 (0 7512 0092 1)

John Benson
The Penny Capitalists: A Study of Nineteenth Century Working-Class Entrepreneurs
(0 7512 0100 6)

Forthcoming

H W Arndt
The Economic Lessons of the Nineteen-Thirties (0 7512 0065 4)

Sir Alec Cairncross
Home and Foreign Investment, 1870–1913: Studies in Capital Accumulation (new preface) (0 7512 0111 1)